W9-AXJ-560

Linking Home and School

Linking Home and School

Edited by

MAURICE CRAFT

JOHN RAYNOR

LOUIS COHEN

SECOND EDITION

LONGMAN

LONGMAN GROUP LIMITED
LONDON

Associated companies, branches and representatives throughout the world

First published 1967
Seventh impression 1970
Second edition 1972

ISBN Paper edition 0 582 32470.X
ISBN Cased edition 0 582 32472.6

Printed in Great Britain by
J. W. Arrowsmith Ltd., Bristol

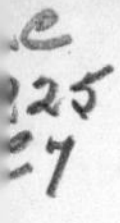

Contents

Part Three: Linking devices and experiment

Acknowledgments

We are grateful to the following for permission to reproduce copyright material:

Authors for 'Social class differences in the relevance of language to socialisation' by Bernstein and Henderson; Basil Blackwell for 'Lawrence Weston School'—an adaptation of 'The Head and the Community School' by C. Poster from *Headship in the 1970's*; The Howard League for Penal Reform for an article adapted from 'School Social Work and Crime Prevention' by Paul Avery and Robert Adamson from *The Howard Journal of Penology* Vol. 12 No. 4 1969; National Foundation of Educational Research for an adaptation from *Counselling in Schools*—Some considerations, by John Raynor and Tony Atcherley published in *Educational Research* Vol. 9 No. 2 1967 and an article entitled 'Relations between Home and School' published in *Educational Research* Vol. 10 No. 3 1968; Routledge and Kegan Paul Limited for extracts from *Samples from English Cultures* by Dr. Josephine Klein and *Education and the Working Class* by Brian Jackson and Dennis Marsden, and the author for a letter by Margaret Wright.

Preface to the Second Edition

Since the publication of the first edition of *Linking Home and School* in 1967, and particularly since the Plowden Report with which it coincided, there has been a burgeoning of interest in home–school relations and a steady growth of research and experiment. This second edition has been reshaped to take account of these developments, and includes several revised and additional chapters in Parts Two and Three.

The research studies in Part Two now include new papers by Professor Bernstein and one of his research associates, Dorothy Henderson, and by Louis Cohen, Patrick McGeeney, and Anne Sharrock. This latter chapter attempts a survey of significant British researches in this field.

Part Three reviews practical experiment, mostly at local authority level, and now includes new papers by Derek Birley, Pauline Avery and Robert Adamson, John Raynor and Tony Atcherley, and Maurice Craft. This latter paper seeks to review trends in practical provision in the several areas of home–school relations.

As in the first edition, *Linking Home and School* has tried to blend relevant aspects of theory with a sampling of current practice; and while tending to focus upon the problems of the disadvantaged, offers a good deal of comment upon less 'therapeutic' relationships between homes and schools.

MAURICE CRAFT
JOHN RAYNOR
LOUIS COHEN

November 1970

Foreword to the First Edition

This book has arisen out of the Main Course in Social Work initiated in September 1964 by Mr Maurice Craft and his former colleagues in this College's Department of Sociology, Mr Raynor and Mr Cohen. The new Course was designed to equip student teachers to undertake an extended role, with emphasis on closer parent–teacher and social worker–teacher contacts.

At the National Conference held here in the following June, which took 'Linking Home and School' as its theme, various theoretical and practical aspects were explored and the papers delivered there form the nucleus of this book. The Editors have sought additional contributions in order to develop the theme, and wish me to express their warm appreciation to all who have participated in its production for their advice and ready cooperation.

In assembling this sample of relevant research studies, informed comment, and practical experiment, the Editors' aims have been threefold. First, to reach a wider audience amongst local education authorities, universities, colleges of education, schools, and social services. Second, to stress what is common to both education and social work. And third, to underline the great benefits to be derived from cooperation between schools and homes, particularly in the underprivileged or the newer communities in our society.

To these I would add a fourth. This is a period of rapid expansion, but also of stimulating change in teacher training. Colleges of education are helping to redefine and to widen the traditional role both of the teacher and of the teacher-trainer. They are pioneering, or are willing to pioneer, new imaginative courses in both initial and in-service training. The development of welfare studies is one piece of tangible evidence of such intent.

If this volume makes some small contribution in these four directions it will have been worth while.

Edge Hill College of Education P. K. C. Millins
November 1966

Part One

The Administrative, Social, and Political Context

1

Some Relationships between Homes and Schools

W. A. L. Blyth

In this opening paper Professor Blyth sketches the theoretical context in which home–school links are to be discussed. Subsequent papers (in Part Two) develop particular aspects of this theoretical background.

Teachers have always recognised that close links between home and school are important. So have parents. So have administrators and Education Welfare Officers and child care workers. Recently the Department of Education and Science has itself developed an increasing interest in home–school relationships, particularly in circumstances of social handicap,[1] whilst official attention has been called to the importance of specific preparation for the educational consequences of imperfect home–school relationships in the Newsom Report[2] and elsewhere. It is therefore not surprising that professional educationists have turned their attention to the same problems.

In fact, this, one of the basic questions in the sociology of education, is now for the first time being approached with an adequate apparatus of criticism and research. As long as it has been primarily the concern of the various professions responsible for the prevention and cure of breakdowns between school and home, there has inevitably been something piecemeal, however well-intentioned, in the way in which we have thought about the whole matter. To caricature the position slightly: teachers have tended to regret that children chose their parents in so unwise and inconsiderate a fashion; parents have been inclined simultaneously to resent the demands made by schools and also their inability to work miracles without making demands; whilst social workers have perhaps been prone to sigh over the naïvety of teachers and parents alike, and to look on large classes as aggregates of individual cases, each with crying needs, rather than as sizeable and sometimes formidable aggregates of vigorous childhood or adolescence. Undoubtedly, in recent years, mutual comprehension has been growing. A sociological perspective can help here by widening the horizons, and also the sympathies, of the various actors in the drama. It is tempting to add that no education should be described as comprehensive unless it implies mutual comprehension of this kind.

The contribution which can be made to the problem through a study of the sociology of education depends on two aspects—perhaps I should say, on *the* two aspects—of scholarship in the subject. The first is the empirical aspect, the outcome of research designed to extend and refine our knowledge of actual relationships between school and home. The second is the theoretical aspect, which helps to direct and to interpret the empirical investigations. I should like to indicate something about both these, and to follow this with a few comments preparatory to our consideration of those practical activities which should be rendered more effective through our academic studies. I shall start, therefore, with some observations about the study of relevant aspects of the sociology of education, and of these I should like to mention the theoretical aspect first. For, although empirical studies have been in progress longer, it is the theoretical aspect which, once it has emerged, can claim to be logically prior.

The sociologist, together with the anthropologist, has added a new dimension to educational thought. To him, education is a social process, a preparation for the assumption of adult roles and values in a particular social and cultural context. He considers systematically the nature and functioning of the institutions which are entrusted with formal education, and their relation with other institutions in a society. In company with the social psychologist, he is particularly interested in the processes of 'socialisation', by which the accepted roles and values are absorbed and internalised. He acknowledges that there are others with an interest in studying the same processes from other standpoints: the individual psychologist, for example, who is concerned more immediately with the cerebral processes involved in learning, or the philosopher whose function is rather with the clarification and criticism of the roles and values themselves, but he makes his own specific claim too.

Viewed in this way, the home and the school figure as two agencies of socialisation, the former being essentially small-scale and domestic in character, and the latter, larger and more overtly 'educational'. The differentiation between domestic and educational institutions is probably at its least marked in situations such as rural villages, or private schools with an upper-middle-class clientele, where for different reasons the school is deliberately conceived as an extension of certain aspects of the home, rather than as a contrast to it. In the majority of cases, however, that contrast is nowadays clear enough.

It was not always so. A consideration of home–school relationships today and formerly can lead a sociologist of education to appreciate what Max Weber meant when he stressed that industrialisation in any society is bound to lead to the differentiation and fragmentation of social institutions. It can therefore also lead him to appreciate what John Dewey implied when he emphasised the need for an educational policy, in the broadest sense, which would effect some new interaction between home and school and the rest of society in a way that would be appropriate to a new age which could contemplate neither a return to a pre-industrial past, whether in Dewey's New England or in our own Romantics' Old England, nor on the other hand a resigned acceptance of a total absence of constructive home–school relationships. Against a backcloth of thought influenced by such considerations, the sociologist of education can view the specific problems of his own culture and his own decade, now that his subject is coming of age, and he can and must assert increasingly his demand that thought of this quality and nature must enter into any discussion of particular problems, and into any research in particular situations.

Moreover, in dealing with issues related to social institutions such as home and school as agents of socialisation, he can draw upon a growing repertoire of studies of other social organisations, as Hoyle[3] has recently shown, and also on their theoretical bases. The number of prototypes for a study of the theoretical relations between two different institutions in a society is much smaller, and here probably there is more guidance from social anthropology, as is perhaps suggested by Professor Musgrove in his *Youth and the Social Order*.[4]

After these few comments on the theoretical background, I should now like to make some observations about the existing state of empirical knowledge in this field. It seems to me that, not surprisingly, most of the actual research that has hitherto been carried out relates to the more measurable aspects of the subject. Chief amongst these has been the relationship between 'home background', as it is rather imprecisely called, and educational progress as measured by standardised tests of intelligence and attainment, or by the results of public examinations. The individual investigations in this category already constitute an honourable series. They include, amongst others, the sections of the work of Floud, Halsey, and Martin[5] which refer to home–school relations, an even larger part of the study by Jackson and Marsden,[6] and the whole of Elizabeth Fraser's classic *Home Environment and the School*,[7] and of J. W. B. Douglas's primary school survey *The Home and the School*.[8] If we consider also the equally tangible and measurable data about school leaving, then the 1954 Report on *Early Leaving*[9] and its many counterparts also merit inclusion under the same heading. One of the weightiest contributions is the study of *Education and Environment*[10] by Professor Wiseman and his colleagues at Manchester. From all of these there emerges a composite but fairly definite picture of the advantages conferred in the educational race by certain types of home, not quite identified with the socio-economic middle class, but characterised by the pattern of motivation for which, as Mrs Floud insists,[11] the French have a particularly apt expression—*la famille éducogène*. It has in fact been customary to extend the interpretation of these studies slightly beyond the purely cognitive sphere and to infer some socio-emotional consequences too; indeed, that may be necessary, as Elizabeth Fraser showed, in order to interpret the study of educational progress itself. But in most cases this goes beyond what is strictly measurable.

Now, this relationship between home environment and educational progress is obviously important. If we are concerned, as we must be, both with individual development and with the optimum use of the nation's resources of talent, then the means of its stimulation or retardation must matter. But it is not necessarily the only aspect which matters and, as already suggested, it is bound to be incomplete unless some explanation of the relationship is advanced. This is more difficult to do, and the authors who have attempted it have been obliged to use observational and descriptive methods, and consequently to depend on a rather more subjective type of interpretation. In the process, however, they can touch more sensitively on the quality of home–school interaction than is possible in the more 'measurable' type of study. It is the merit of Jackson and Marsden's *Education and the Working Class*[12] that the authors attempted to plumb some of these subtleties.

Their study suggests that some teachers—not only in 'Marburton'—have tended to consider the working of home background too exclusively in the light of a certain range of middle-class values according to which a home could be labelled 'good' or 'bad'. (It is of course quite possible to react to the opposite extreme and to praise, in quasi-Marxist terms, the virility of the home which rejects the conventional values.) Personally I consider that the principal service rendered by Jackson and Marsden is that they exposed the widespread and rather horrifying blockage that exists in the channels of communication between schools and homes, though I suspect that this blockage is only relatively less marked in the case of middle-class families. We need many more studies of this sort of problem, preferably carried out by practising teachers who would be in a position to improve their own practice as a result of what they found.

Professor Mays, who contributes to this volume (Chapter 5), has through his ecological studies of Liverpool districts[13] thrown further light on the relationship between teachers' values and procedures and the needs of particular districts. He emphasises the disproportionate impediment caused in downtown schools by a few parents who reject school values and consume a great deal of time and effort through their divergence from legal and educational authority and from the average *mores* of the district.

In a sense this type of study in depth is an extension of the more measurable type and belongs in the same category. To anyone whose contact with home–school relationships is primarily concerned with behaviour problems rather than with academic attainment, as probation officers and others are, the basic home–school link may appear to be quite a different one. If it issues in behavioural manifestations such as truancy and delinquency, it arises primarily from the psycho-social structure of the family itself. Of course there is an overlap with the other type of problem, since emotional difficulties almost always lead also to a deterioration in academic performance, though just occasionally a disturbed child will seek status in high achievement, and succeed. But to a worker trained in a discipline grounded in depth psychology this is a minor issue. The primacy of importance of the emotional situation is to him self-evident, and so it often is to his 'client', and to everyone else intimately involved in the situation, perhaps including the school and certainly the home. The attempt to consider the sociological factors such as socio-economic status appears in these circumstances to be of secondary, though not negligible, importance.

When we look for evidence about the importance of this type of home–school linkage we shall be unlikely to come upon the sort of data presented by Mrs Floud or Dr Wiseman, or Professor Fraser, or even Jackson and Marsden. It is the clinical record and the field case study that becomes our staple diet, and its validity is asserted through the long-term experience of daily contact between worker and case, and through the assimilated experience of the case conference, rather than through the apparatus of statistical proof. However, the evidence is extensive and often startlingly convincing, and in these sociological days it is important to realise that no study of home–school relations can be complete without some consideration of this basic emotional climate.

Recently, the work of Bernstein and his associates has emphasised yet another aspect of our subject, namely the importance of the use of language in the home and its effect on children's equipment to undertake the types of verbal learning and verbal activity expected in primary and secondary schools.[14] Though the full implications of this work have still to be tested in practice, it has obviously opened up a very promising avenue of investigation and has also added an important dimension to the emerging body of theory which will guide future studies. It can have both a sociological and a mental health significance, for the language of word and gesture varies from one social group to another, but the content and emotional tone of the particular communication is more specific to particular family situations. Indeed, Bernstein's work on language in childhood constitutes a bridge between sociological and psychological considerations, though of course it is only one bridge amongst many.

Beyond all of these particular issues there is a whole range of problems leading outwards from sociology into ethics. They include questions of parental responsibility under the Education Acts and otherwise. Truancy is only one of the issues here. When parents and administrators differ in their definition of the education suitable for particular children, quite poignant clashes of values may be involved; but little research has been carried out in this particular area. One meets *ex parte* statements in the Press and elsewhere; otherwise the details are buried in the Law Reports. If I may leave the role of commentator on research for a moment, it seems to me that an important principle is involved when a Local Education Authority requires parents to send their children not just to one type of school but to one particular school; for there can be a score of reasons why that school and that home are incompatible, and there is no point in attempting to conceal this incompatibility beneath official euphemisms.

Some parents resolve this problem by opting to pay fees in independent schools. This raises yet another issue, one on which there are the elements of a genuine clash of principle. It is indeed possible to claim that any parent who does not pay fees to obtain what he regards as the best education, when he can, for his own children, is guilty of failing in his parental duties; whilst it is simultaneously possible also to maintain that if he does pay fees, and thereby purchase advantages that are denied to others, he is guilty of failing in his duty to the community. This, too, has not been made the subject of research, and it is not difficult to see why, but it seems to me that it must be borne in mind when we consider the question of home–school relations in the broadest sense. It is, of course, true that the introduction of the fee-paying or contractual relationship between home and school carries with it the implication of a different type of interaction between the two socialising agencies; but it is one that exists.

May I turn in conclusion to the practical aspect of our subject —what can we do about it? Some practical links between home and school are already commonplace—parents' visits to schools, open days and speech days, and parent–teacher associations. From the sociological point of view these are to be welcomed, and, to draw for a moment upon the findings of comparative education, we must humbly admit that our transatlantic friends do a great deal more of this sort of thing than we do. But a sociologist must also reserve the right to be sceptical about their efficacy. We all have a spiritual ancestor in Matthew Arnold when he warned us against putting our trust blindly in 'machinery'. We have all met the Head who tells us that his parent–teacher association is useless because the parents he really wants to get at do not come, but who seems unaware that it is exactly the suspicion that he wants to get at them that keeps them away. It is necessary to be more subtle, and also more persistent, than that; and I do not want to give the impression that all the failures of communication are on the school's side. However, we have to remember that in this situation it is the teachers who are the professionals, and it is legitimate to expect them to take the major initiative.

A sociologist must retain his scepticism in another respect too. The more we learn about families, the more we have to realise that they cannot be equal in their 'educogenic' qualities, not at least until we become as educated as the Scandinavians, or more so. The professional home which is held up to us as the model of educational stimulus simply cannot, and I think should not, keep in step with the unskilled worker's home. The only viable policy involves a frank recognition of this, together with an intensive attempt to compensate for it in some measure by providing enriching experiences for the less fortunate children, at every stage from the nursery school upwards. In this way, quite a lot can be achieved in one generation; and even Raymond Williams acknowledges that the Long Revolution will take longer than that.[15] If it is unduly hurried, we shall only be in danger of increasing what sociologists call the 'anomic stress' between generations, when children lose cultural contact with their own parents.[16]

As children grow older, it is no longer adequate to speak just of the home–school link. As I came to realise with particular force during my own researches, an intermediate term begins to intrude between the two. This is the peer group. In some cases the succession of groups to which children belong, at school or in the neighbourhood or both, may exercise more influence than either school or home, in which case it may constitute a new reason for the earlier socialising agencies to make common cause. Teenage groups nowadays enjoy (literally) a great deal of publicity, but it should be remembered that adolescent peer associations are much more widespread and influential than is indicated by the incidence of their more spectacular prototypes.

The relationships of home and school are not easily unravelled. The various chapters in this volume indicate some of the ways in which recent research and experience have helped to elucidate those relationships. It is necessary that research and experimentation in this field shall continue, for the link between school and home, between the first and the second major child-rearing agencies within our society, is a matter which concerns us all as parents, as teachers, and as citizens. It is also necessary that this research and experimentation should be built increasingly on the firmer foundations which now exist in social theory and research methods related to it. If this is conducted with scholarships it can increase our insight into the impact of home–school relationships on children. If it is also conducted with sympathy and understanding, it can do something to render those relationships more humane.

REFERENCES

1. See, for example, *Education under Social Handicap* (Parts 1 and 2). *Reports on Education* Nos. 17, 20 and 22, December 1964 and

March and June 1965. London, H.M.S.O., for the Department of Education and Science.
2. *Half our Future* (Newsom Report), Central Advisory Council for Education (England), London, H.M.S.O., 1963, p. 70, etc.
3. E. Hoyle, 'Organisational Analysis in the Field of Education', *Educational Research* VII, 2 February 1965, pp. 97–114.
4. F. Musgrove, *Youth and the Social Order*, Routledge and Kegan Paul, 1964, ch. 7.
5. J. E. Floud, A. H. Halsey, and F. M. Martin, *Social Class and Educational Opportunity*, Heinemann, 1956, esp. Part III.
6. B. Jackson and D. Marsden, *Education and the Working Class*, Routledge and Kegan Paul, 1962.
7. E. Fraser, *Home Environment and the School*, Scottish Council for Research in Education, No. XLIII, University of London Press, 1959.
8. J. W. B. Douglas, *The Home and the School*, MacGibbon and Kee, 1964.
9. *Early Leaving*, Central Advisory Council for Education (England), H.M.S.O., 1954.
10. S. Wiseman, ed., *Education and Environment*, Manchester University Press, 1964.
11. J. E. Floud, 'Social Class Factors in Educational Achievement' ch. 4 in *Ability and Educational Opportunity*, Paris, O.E.C.D., 1961, esp. p. 102.
12. See note 6.
13. J. B. Mays, *Education and the Urban Child*, University Press of Liverpool, 1962.
14. See e.g. B. Bernstein, 'Social Class and Linguistic Development: A Theory of Social Learning', ch. 24 in A. H. Halsey, J. E. Floud, and C. A. Anderson eds., *Education Economy and Society*, Glencoe, III, Free Press, 1961. (Part IV of this volume, which includes this chapter, is particularly relevant to home–school relationships.) See also chapter 6, below.
15. R. Williams, *The Long Revolution*, Chatto & Windus, 1961.
16. The problems involved in this situation are indicated by 'A Flintshire Contributor' on the final page of the second Report on *Education under Social Handicap*, see note 1, above.

It may be regrettably necessary, during the interim, to choose between a sacrifice of potential talent and a sacrifice of familial and social harmony. The problem is similar to that of Hoggart's 'Scholarship Boy': see R. Hoggart, *The Uses of Literacy*, Chatto & Windus, 1957, ch. x.

NOTE: Since the first edition of the present volume was published in 1967, interest in home–school relationships has developed rapidly. A number of important recent studies are listed in the references to Chapter 10 below. W.A.L.B.

2

The Administrative and Political Background

Sir Ronald Gould

This second introductory paper presents a fundamental aspect of our theme, the relationship of home and school in the context of educational administration and organisation.

Those concerned with the state of British home–school integration often allow their fancy to travel westward. They see a land apparently preoccupied with education weeks, school demonstrations, public education rallies, parents' evenings, school exhibitions, parent–teacher associations. To them, every American school day is open day.

A vigorous community interest in schooling was indeed part and parcel of the Founding Fathers' vision of democracy. Many of the notions contained in the American Constitution had been developed in the preparation of school laws, such as those Jefferson designed for Virginia. So germane was local education to freedom that the first task of the Continental Congress was not the Constitution but the approval of a system of school government for the Trans-Appalachian frontierlands. And when they turned from this to delineating the powers of the Federal Government by drafting the United States Constitution, so firm was their conviction in educational localism that neither the word 'education' nor the word 'school' is mentioned once. Community control was an article of faith. It needed no expression in words. And so today in many townships those who enter the polling booth to vote between Johnson and Goldwater for President are required simultaneously to choose a board of managers for the local 'high'.

Those in Britain attracted to this model for community involvement should appreciate its disadvantages along with its advantages. Just before the last war there were over 127,000 separate local education authorities for a population scarcely three times the size of ours. Only in 1965 has Congress empowered Washington to intervene to even up educational opportunity between district and district. Parents in Britain are rightly annoyed that one local education authority admits two per cent less children to grammar schools than its neighbour. That two per cent, seemingly so small, has enormous effects, for it prejudges the future of thousands of young people. But our inequalities are minimal when set against America's. New York spends four times as much per school child as Mississippi. Professor Swift of California, in his *Twenty Five Years of American Education*, writes:

> Generations of local support and local domination of public schools finds the richest nation of earth denying multitudes of her children any educational opportunity whatsoever, and herding thousands of them in dismal and unsanitary hovels, under the tutelage of wretchedly underpaid and proportionately ignorant, untrained and negative teachers.

Even the good teacher is not secure. Excluding retirements, a teacher's average tenure of one post before dismissal or moving in search of better opportunity is only eight years.

At the other extreme, those who acknowledge the havoc of ultra-devolution of authority look across the English Channel to France, where all effective power lies in the hands of the Minister of Education, and all decisions on education are thus political decisions. Professor Brian Chapman states his opinion in his recent *British Government Observed—Some European Reflections*:

> How does one justify the proposition that although the Minister of Education has general responsibility for educational services he does not directly employ a single teacher, he has no control over the educational policies of the 'public school' sector and is not even consulted about the creation of a new

university? What in fact has been created is not the pluralist society dreamt of in more innocent days, but a special form of corporate state in which public institutions become private property.

To put the record straight, one of those charges is no longer valid since the Department of Education and Science had assumed powers from the Treasury for the universities.

But that apart, Professor Chapman's attack is based on a misconception of the British approach to education. We have adopted a system of administration that seeks to steer between Scylla and Charybdis. We try to avoid both formless over-devolution and rigid centralisation.

Such a solution could not work at all unless everybody concerned was steeped in a very old but constantly evolving democratic tradition, which assumes that means can be found of reconciling conflicting local and national claims sufficiently to enable decisions to be taken which lead to action.

The keynote of this approach is partnership. The system stemming from the 1944 Education Act defines separate prerogatives of authority for parent, school, L.E.A., and Secretary of State. The need of the nation, the local community's wishes, the expert opinion of the teacher, somehow or other are to be synthesised into mutually acceptable progressive policies.

This separation of spheres of influence explains why the Secretary of State today cannot strictly 'enforce' comprehensive schooling. It explains why teachers' salaries are paid not nationally but locally, even though the greater part is found by the Government; why they are determined by teacher–L.E.A. *cum* Government negotiations through the Burnham Committee; why, if Burnham fails, recourse is to an arbitration body appointed not by the Department of Education and Science but by the Minister of Labour. A measure of administrative complexity is frequently the price that must be paid for liberty.

From this system flow many benefits to the parent and the child. The devolution of authority encourages the imaginative L.E.A. to blaze new trails. Many of the great leaps forward in our education service have been pioneered in one locality. Margaret Macmillan developed her nursery schools in Bradford. In Leicestershire Sir William Brockington decided to separate the education of under elevens from over elevens and paved the way for national acceptance of the division of primary from secondary education. Henry Morris in Cambridgeshire, in a personal search for home–school integration, started his village colleges, which were to combine the duties of school and community centre. Later Stewart Mason, along with other Directors of Education such as A. B. Clegg in the West Riding, challenged the notions of eleven-plus selection and pointed the way to secondary reorganisation.

Partnership gives free rein not only to the go-ahead authority but also to the pioneering school or teacher. The use of language laboratories to teach French and German, the great advances in teaching infants to read—from learning by rote to look-and-say, the Initial Teaching Alphabet and words in colour—have developed from the original enthusiasm of individuals or small groups of teachers. Over-centralisation demands that such new departures require the original approval of the Civil Servants in the Ministry of Education. As Vernon Mallinson writes in his *Comparative Education*:

> The real vigour of the English system has lain in the wide diversity and variety of aims and purposes that have only been made possible through a policy of decentralisation. The stagnation that has been repeatedly complained of in experimentation in aims and methods in French schools was the inevitable outcome of a strongly centralised system.

But if decentralisation is taken to the extreme, a new menace presents itself to the teacher's freedom over content and methods of instruction. The parish pump can be very tyrannical. A Commission appointed by the American Historical Association gave examples of the assault on the teacher's freedom:

> Evolution can usually be taught in the North but not in the rural South, not because the North believes more in freedom but because the North is generally indifferent to fundamentalist religion, which the evolutionary hypothesis endangers, whereas the South still devoutly believes in fundamentalist tenets.

Northern critics of Tennessean 'intolerance' suppress the teaching of socialism in their own schools because the economic system that such theories endanger seems vitally important to Northern communities.

The real losers under both systems are the children. Proscription of Darwinism in the deep South is the most dramatic instance of hampering the child's quest for knowledge to satisfy community prejudice. But there are more and subtler freedoms of learning curtailed than outright monkey business!

Education systems, however, are not all black or all white, and the U.S.A. and French systems do have some advantages over the British. We lack the close community interest of the U.S.A. and the uniformity of educational provision of the French. But our system does allow maximum experimentation without serious risk either of lay veto or of committing a whole nation irrevocably to what might not in practice match up to expectation.

The British educational system is a cooperative enterprise in which parents, teachers, managers, and governors, education authorities, the inspectorate, and central government are all accorded rights, and yet all must work together if progress is to be made. In simple language, here more than anywhere else in the world progress depends upon partnership. The search for closer home–school integration must go on within this framework, and not by trying to import facets of systems whose whole *modus vivendi* is at loggerheads with our own. Indeed, educational systems cannot be exported or imported *in toto*. They are shaped by the traditions and development of their own countries, and would not work in other contexts.

The 1944 Education Act recognises that the parent has rights. Father and mother have educational prerogatives no less important than those of the L.E.A. or school. Not only can the parent, if he wishes and can afford it, opt out of the publicly provided schools altogether, but if he does not wish to opt out or cannot afford to do so, he has still certain rights. Section 76 lays down:

> In the exercise and performance of all powers and duties conferred and imposed on them by this act the Ministry and local authorities shall have regard to the principle that, so far

as is compatible with the provision of efficient instruction and training and the avoidance of unreasonable public expenditure, pupils are to be educated in accordance with the wishes of their parents.

This is somewhat ambiguous. 'Efficient instruction' is not clearly defined, nor is 'unreasonable public expenditure'. Nor is it clear how education 'in accordance with the wishes of their parents' can always be reconciled with another part of the Act which declares that a child shall be educated according to his age, aptitude, and ability. So not surprisingly there have been varying interpretations. One L.E.A. may help to finance children taking supported places at 'public schools'; another will not. One will allow a parent to choose a grammar school type of education for a child irrespective of aptitude and ability; another will not. One will allow a free choice between a comprehensive and a tripartite system; others will have only one or the other.

There is another right given to parents in the Act, for every child must be given religious instruction, unless the parent decides otherwise. But the teacher is given rights, too, for he is allowed to refuse to give religious instruction, without penalty. These two rights might easily, in some circumstances, conflict with each other. So far, however, there have been sufficient teachers willing to give religious instruction to ensure the parents' rights.

Nevertheless, the intention of the Act is plain enough. The parent is to be closely involved in certain areas of decision. In practice, as well as in theory, it recognises the legitimate concern of the parent in religion, language, medical facilities, coeducation, the availability of certain courses, even 'old boy and old girl' feelings for a particular school. The parent is thus given administrative involvement.

This is one way in which home is integrated into education. But there are others. First, there is legal involvement. In the British system the schools are not immune from the normal law of the land. Both pupil and teacher are legally protected and a parent can always have recourse to the courts on the handling of his or her offspring. Secondly, there is political involvement. L.E.A. prerogatives are ultimately community rights. Although the parent lacks administrative comeback on issues such as access to a grammar school, he or she can exert political pressure and does enjoy ultimate political control. Hence the development in recent years of bodies such as the Confederation for the Advancement of State Education, aimed at the local and national involvement of parents in educational politics. And in the ultimate there is no deadlier sanction than the ballot box.

Lastly comes institutional involvement—the participation of the parent in the affairs of a particular school. The administrative, legal and political rights of the parent, however, stop short of detailed control of the organisation of a school, its curriculum and methods. Because of this division in areas of parental involvement, home–school linkage takes on a special form in Britain. On the institutional level integration is largely for purposes of information. The balance of educational power in Britain would be altered if linkage were to circumscribe the authority of either parent or teacher. The aim of association should be to see that each party uses its prerogatives in concert for the child's benefit, and to eradicate unnecessary conflict between the influence of home and school.

Teachers as much as parents seek for a growth of this form of cooperation. We can only ensure a child's progress if we understand each other. Education is a dialectic between classroom and livingroom. What is taught must develop out of a child's everyday experience. Mathematics, for example, can be grasped only via familiar analogies. You cannot teach a Russian long division by showing him a cricketer's bowling analysis. Above all, educational development depends largely on the grasp of ideas, on the ability to understand them when expressed in speech or writing, and to communicate them to others. Thus children from homes where ideas are discussed and where papers and books are available find school work much more congenial and make more rapid progress than those from homes where little interest is shown in the changing world and where the exchange of ideas in speech or writing is but limited.

Britain is a relatively homogeneous society. We do not fight daily battles with wide differences of cultural experience or language barriers. Bilingual Wales is about the extreme of our dilemma. But to help each individual there are subtler distinctions that the discerning teacher must note. Two developments are vital to this end. First, teachers must be trained in the colleges of education to appreciate the social structure of the country. Sociology is as important as psychology. Secondly, there must be more face-to-face contact between parent and teacher. Some have proposed the appointment of special welfare officers to bridge the home–school gap. I am not convinced there is a place for a third party in this task of communication. Rather we need, on the public side, more official encouragement of parents to involve themselves in school affairs; and, on the school side, much lower staff–pupil ratios and closer contact with the home and social environment of the children. Only smaller classes will allow the teacher to seek out in school and home the real possibilities of each child.

Within the British educational system, the home–school integrationist often puts too much faith in this institutional linkage. The parent also needs to appreciate the vital role of local authority and central government in education. Many of the parents' grievances can only be sorted out in the Town Hall. Low polls at local elections illustrate no overwhelming parental concern in educational decisions. Yet historically the Town Hall has played a vital part in linking the affairs of home and school, as, for example, in the provision of school meals, free milk, school medical and dental services. The education service is closely coordinated with other local government child welfare activities, such as child care and libraries, and juvenile courts require an Education Committee representative before they can function. Yet it is clear that administration of welfare services for the young is diffuse, and in too many hands. It is difficult, even for the persistent parent, to discover who is responsible for the various services. A move towards administrative consolidation might well be a positive encouragement to closer home–school and home–education-service linkage.

The good public relations work of some Education Committees should not be overlooked. In Nottinghamshire, for example, the inspired leadership of the late Edward Mason kept parents in touch with the affairs of County Hall in a way few others have achieved. Tastefully printed pamphlets directed to the parents,

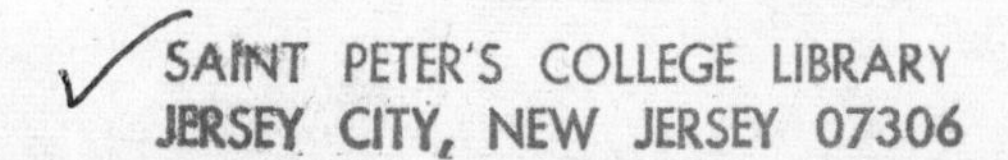

the use of the local Press to disseminate information and to remove misunderstandings, and personal visits to a variety of local meetings, all helped to persuade parents that their understanding and cooperation were vital. Local authorities generally need to do far more on these lines, and particularly when large-scale changes such as secondary reorganisation are contemplated. Only by involving parents and by helping them to understand and accept the purpose of what is proposed will an easy transition to the new systems be effected.

Power in British education is diffused. Home–school linkage on the institutional level is vital, but none of us should lose sight of the role of parents as citizens, as members of the local community, and as voters in general elections. The fusion of the demands of the parent, teacher, and administrator into acceptable policies requires in the British context more than contact at the school level. With such a delicate balance of authority, there is always the danger that British education will lack a clearly defined policy, and will end up like the ass of the philosopher, equidistant from two carrots, unable to make up its mind which move to make. If so, a jab with the pointed stick of united parental opinion might well prove salutary.

Part Two

Recent Studies

3

*The Parents of Schoolchildren**

Josephine Klein

Part Two aims to present in more detail salient aspects of the theoretical background to home–school relations. This first paper has been specially edited by the author from her Samples from English Cultures† *and presents an analysis of social class attitudes, including attitudes towards education.*

Teachers do not always come from the same social background as the parents of the children they teach. The following extracts show something of the great variety of attitudes and relationships which may be encountered, and should help to prevent over-simple generalisations about 'working class' and 'middle class'. The passages have been selected to throw light on aspects of parental behaviour which may especially vex or puzzle the good teacher who wants to cooperate with parents in P.T.A.s, to consult with them about a child's difficulties, or to help in deciding future careers.

TRADITIONAL 'ROUGHS' AND 'RESPECTABLES'

What distinguishes respectable traditional working-class people from the rough is the effort to maintain standards and not to let things slide. In the past poverty may have made it impossible to keep up to the mark, and this would be a grief to the respectable, a glib excuse to the rough. But now standards can be maintained and the effect of the difference in attitude is clear. In Radby

* Extracted from *Samples from English Cultures*, Routledge, 1965, by kind permission of the publishers.

† The page numbers refer the reader back to the book from which the extracts were taken.

(Nottingham), for example, the housekeeping in the rough (Grade II) households is described as showing 'intermittent effort, but no real interest in keeping the house clean and tidy'.[1] In contrast, the respectable (Grade III) households gave evidence of 'effort made to ensure that the appearance of the house does not fall below certain standards'. (p.199)

EDUCATIONAL CHANCES AND THEIR CONSEQUENCES AMONGST THE TRADITIONAL

Some of the remarks heard in St Ebbe's (in central Oxford area) sound quite outrageous to the ambitious ear: 'I'm not worried about what's going to happen to her. The employment officer will take care of that', and 'Oh, they've got to grow up; there'll probably be another war anyway. They'll have to look out for themselves.'[2]

Such parental ambitions as were mentioned in St Ebbe's were vague and unrelated to specific course of action; parents wanted their sons 'to do well', 'to get on well'. Similarly the traditional Newbolts had a vague dream about a 'nice school', but Mr Newbolt 'was not keen on educational advancement'.[3] The Radby Grade III households are reported to be particular about children attending school. They see that they go. 'It's the proper thing to do and there might be trouble otherwise.' But they have no intellectual pretensions.

> Mary Marks, who has just left school apparently never reads anything whatever, while the Bonnington's is the only one of the homes that has any books in evidence, and those belong to the children. Nor are the parents particularly keen on their children getting into grammar school. The Freemans certainly would not bother about it. Mrs Bonnington was disappointed that one of her girls who passed the scholarship could not take it up, but the family really needed her wage. The Waters would quite like young Johnnie to go to a Grammar School 'if he's good enough', but they are really more interested in whether they can get him into the new Secondary Modern School instead of the old Church one and where 'there's too much religion and not good enough teaching'.

In other words, educational ambitions are strictly within the familiar range—these are status assenters (a term discussed in greater detail below on page 37). There may nevertheless be social mobility in the next generation. With greater affluence and a welfare state it comes about without the parents' design, because these parents do the best they can for their children and the children are ready for it. The Radby Grade III children wanted to pass the eleven-plus and told the interviewers that they hoped to do so. They gave the impression of profiting from their education, showing off their lesson books when they talked to the interviewers. Grade III parents could hardly help take advantage of some of the new opportunities offered. When the Bonningtons heard that a playroom was being started in the area, they decided the children should be encouraged to go: 'Here's a chance for Michael to get on.'

Such acquiescence in change may bring painful consequences for status-assenting parents. The children may grow away from them. If the children pass the eleven-plus examination, this may present acute problems for both generations. 'When they get education and a good job, they get ideas. Whenever I speak they try to correct me. They must have it right. I feel that low.'[4]

The children, too, experience a conflict over values.

> After a year or two at the Grammar School the children's natural respect for their parents lay uneasily alongside their own clearer mastery of the new skills, and alongside many other doubts that school and early education promoted. There was the beginning of a split, or at least a growing sense that the child was out on its own, moving into worlds to which the parents had no access.[5] (pp. 592–4)

CONTACT WITH OFFICIALDOM (TRADITIONAL WORKING CLASS)

The avoidance of intrusion and the preservation of privacy is a major problem in these areas: it applies to neighbours in the street, it applies even more forcibly to the avoidance of unregulated interaction with people who are not part of the local network of family or community—'them'.

> The world of 'Them' is the world of the bosses. 'They' may be, as occasion requires, anyone from the classes outside (other than the few individuals from those classes whom working people know as individuals). 'They' are the people at the top, the higher-ups, the people who give you your dole, call you up, tell you to go to war, fine you, 'get yer in the end', 'are all twisters really', 'never tell yer owt', 'will do y' down if they can', 'treat y' like muck'.[6]

The problem of the respectable traditional working man is to preserve his self-respect *vis-à-vis* 'them', and, in particular, to make 'them' appreciate his respectability. The relationship between 'us' and 'them' is part of the total set of external relations of these groups and cannot be fully appreciated without reference to those others which this group considers beneath them—the 'roughs'. 'They' take no account of the difference between respectable and rough working people, between those with standards and those without. If we are to understand anything of ingroup/outgroup relations here, we have to keep in mind at least three levels: 'us', 'them', and 'the roughs'. Interaction with both these outgroups has to be regulated if self-respect is to be preserved.

'Respectability' and 'self-respect' are concepts concerned with people's opinions of themselves and of one another. At another social level the word would be 'dignity', at another 'integrity'. Each of these terms connotes an undamaged self-image, undamaged at least in the sense that other people do not challenge it. This image is easily bruised in interaction with those outside the community.

The respectable take pains to achieve standards of domestic behaviour and social interaction which distinguish them from the roughs amongst whom they live. They are different from them in style of life, but not in economic circumstances. A period of illness or unemployment, or some other misfortune, could push a whole family below the poverty line. Then help from others might be needed. When this happens, it is very bitter to be misclassified by an outer world which does not appreciate that one is managing as best one can, handicapped only by misfortune, not by a failure in character.

The patronising, contemptuous or bullying attitudes of 'them' are felt by the respectable and self-respecting working man to be more appropriately directed to a lower stratum than his own. The traditional 'rough' is more likely to react to 'their' exercise of authority with violence, subterfuge, exploitation, or indifference. In a respectable man, the resentment created when he finds himself misclassified evokes rather a stoic independence, a determination to steer clear of 'them' as long as possible. Associated with this will be a mistrust of 'their' motives; a firm definition of what everyone in the situation is, or is not, 'supposed to do'; often a silence which 'they' interpret as indifference or sulkiness.

> We may understand why working people often seem not 'oncoming' to social workers, seem evasive and prepared to give answers designed to put off rather than to clarify. At the back of the announcement that 'Ah keep meself to meself' there can be a hurt pride. It is difficult to believe that a visitor from another class could ever realize all the ins-and-outs of one's difficulties—there is an anxiety not to 'show y'self up', to defend oneself against patronage.[6]

Independence from external agencies is made possible to the extent that kin or neighbours are able and willing to help. Because this requires both good communications and the proximity of people willing to help, such independence is more likely to be found in the close-knit traditional community. Where there has been more mobility, there is not this feeling against the welfare agencies. On the other hand, it may be noted that everywhere younger people do not feel so strongly against the use of welfare services, perhaps because their need is less, perhaps because 'their' behaviour has improved, perhaps because their own self-respect takes different forms. (pp. 203–5)

PARTICIPATION IN FORMAL ORGANISATIONS (TRADITIONAL WORKING CLASS)

A good deal of the energy that might go into formal associational life is absorbed by interaction within the family in a traditional community. But there are forms of organisation in contexts where there is no admixture of middle-class people to arouse 'us'/'them' difficulties.

There are traditional attitudes which prevent a man from being in a leadership position for any length of time. First and foremost there is the social and psychological pressure not to stand out or 'put yourself forward', and to suspect the motives of those who do so. Secondly, leaders of groups are more likely to associate, by virtue of their role, with leaders of other groups, and are therefore more likely to be in contact with middle-class groups or people.[7] In this way they are open to the accusation of 'giving themselves airs' and thereby calling down upon themselves the sanctions of ridicule. Since, in the traditional working-class community, solidarity is the great value, greater than leadership, association with others elsewhere is correctly perceived as weakening that solidarity, and disliked.

Some of those who might be 'joiners' are therefore deterred because they fear, with reason, that they will grow away from their primary groups if they interact too freely with those who do belong to the community by birth and are often of a higher social class. Formally organised groups create especial difficulties because, if a man is given an organising role—'leadership', 'responsibility'—the stress is by so much increased; whereas, if he is not, this can be an alternative source of resentment.

These considerations may explain the 'widespread lack of desire to be identified with a particular group, sometimes amounting to an inability to enter into any obligation which looks like a contract', which Mogey noted in his Oxford study.[2] Formal associations, and the demands they make, go against the preference for 'effortless sociability'. The reluctance to join is therefore partly social: a dislike of being 'pushed around', and partly it is more intellectual: a doubt as to what one may be 'letting oneself in for', what one is 'supposed to do'.

There is often a clash of norms when two cultures interact, and this clash is likely to be accompanied by ill-feeling, particularly when one culture imposes norms of behaviour on the other in the self-confident assurance that where the two differ, the other is wrong. This difficulty crops up in the most unexpected places.

An American study discovered that not only did the (lower) working-class neurotics not get on with their psychiatrists, but the psychiatrists admitted to a dislike of these patients! The norms of the two sub-cultures were too different.[8]

Americans are more aware in these matters, partly because a continually renewed immigrant element tends to make people more sophisticated about the barriers created by language. Another American study confirms and refines the point here under discussion. Bell, Vogel, and Trieschman made a 'socio-cultural analysis of resistance of working-class fathers of children treated in a child-psychiatric clinic'.[9] These fathers, asked to attend for one afternoon, appeared genuinely puzzled at being thought to be concerned with their child's difficulties. They would point out that they worked hard and saw little of the child, that the mother could be more useful to the psychologists. They minimised the seriousness of the child's emotional disturbance and expressed the belief that it would soon be outgrown. Often they saw the symptoms as wilful misbehaviour.

In considering the reasons for these attitudes, the authors arrive at some important general conclusions. They are struck, *inter alia*, by the difficulty working-class people have in believing that 'just talking will change anything'. Bernstein (some of whose observations on language differences may be found in Chapter 6 of this volume) has analysed this problem in more detail.[10]

> The patient is placed in a situation where treatment depends essentially on the extent to which he can verbalize or be brought to verbalize his particular relationships with the environment, and eventually to understand and accept emotionally the implications of the pattern they form . . . This involves for the patient a mode of communication and orientation which not only he has never learned, but which has been positively discouraged by his previous learning.[10]

Bernstein makes it clear that he is referring here not to the difficulty a patient may have in talking about such personal matter as his sex life, but in talking explicitly about anything at all that he feels or wants. This experience is alien to him. 'To the patient the situation is one of perplexity and bewilderment—

he is under pressure to give a response he has never learned to make.'

The higher social class is verbally the more agile and articulate, more capable of putting ideas easily into words and of arguing convincingly. Since both cultures share an allegiance to the value of rationality, there is a danger that the working man feels he has been 'talked into something', and hence he is likely to feel resentful at having been verbally bullied or beguiled. This is one reason why he will tend to satisfy his need for an associational life as far as possible in associations whose membership is drawn from his own class. It is as indicative of the communication difficulties between the two classes as any argument can be, that the middle-class investigator tends not to consider darts teams and garden clubs convincing evidence of the existence of associational life in the working classes.

What distinguishes these types of formal association from the more middle-class type is that they are more compatible with 'effortless sociability'. A member is likely to hear of the next meeting in the course of everyday contacts within his close-knit network, at home or at work. The notification is casual, the planning short-term, he may turn up or not as he pleases, there are always others available if he is absent.

The more middle-class type of formal association presupposes a more loose-knit network and requires more formal commitment. Then problems arise because future activities need to be planned further ahead and notification has to be organised.

In practical ways this makes formal associational life more difficult. To book a date in a diary for an appointment six weeks ahead is a middle-class act. To call a meeting for some future date then becomes an unreliable method of keeping an association in being, except if people know each other well enough, and see each other often enough to pass reminders nearer the date in casual street encounters.

The status assenter is inclined to take life as it comes, whereas middle-class culture tends to see problems as challenges. Middle-class people are much more apt to use formal organisations for the solution of particular problems. Because of this they cannot avoid planning a programme well in advance, to consider what the association should be doing this time next year and so on. Seeing life as an orderly progression toward goals, they find it natural to plan toward them.

Planning common activities for the future involves making decision now, arguing about alternatives, taking possibilities into account which are not yet present. In a traditional community there is little opportunity for learning these skills, which are all connected with the exercise of choice. As the standard of living goes up there is money to spare and an increased awareness of opportunities. As people become accustomed to using the opportunities to choose for themselves they begin to chafe at inconveniences which were in the past stoically considered part of life itself. (p. 209–19)

CHANGES IN WORKING-CLASS LIFE

The newer way of life can be listed schematically thus:

from a close-knit family network to a more loose-knit one;
from a community-centred life to greater individuation;
from a community-centred life to a more home-centred one;
from a community-centred life to greater participation in formal associations;
from rigidly-defined segregated conjugal duties to partnership in marriage;
from traditional occupational choices to social aspirations and mobility;
from status assent to status dissent;
from ascriptive values to achievement values;
from financial stringency to greater affluence;
from emphasis on the breadwinner to emphasis on the child. (p. 221)

EASIER CIRCUMSTANCES AFFECT FAMILY LIFE

It is a common finding in small-group studies that, when the group's task is considered supremely important by the members, or when the environment of the group makes survival difficult, the relations of group members toward one another tend to take on a characteristic form. Interaction tends to be restricted to matters arising from the task itself, and less time is devoted to the maintenance of happy social and emotional relationships. Members tend to like each other less, and they also tend to begin to resent the task they are engaged in. A more authoritarian structure tends to evolve, with one strong leader whose followers are submissive to him.[11] We may call these characteristics the 'stress syndrome'.

In traditional communities, when financial stress intensifies, the rift between husband and wife must deepen. The man will work more overtime, and so be in the house less than before. The woman will rely more on her kin, and hence be less involved with her spouse than before. The poorer the family is, the more restricted their lives will become, and the less man and wife will have to share emotionally and socially.

Conversely, in groups under less stress, or where the stress is lifting, one tends to find more affectionate relations between members, or at least more interaction which expresses and demonstrates such affection, more consultation between the members and a less authoritarian structure. These conclusions seem to apply to families which have, in their own lifetime, risen above subsistence level or markedly improved their standard of living.

> 'I think we're more interested in the children. I remember them singing to us after our baths, but we never had interesting conversations with our parents, the way I do with my children.'
>
> Children these days, it is said, are able to 'talk to' their parents in a way which, for a considerable number, seems to have been quite impossible before. Partly this reflects a new feeling of equality between parent and child, which allows the parents to accept correction from the child and even to take pride in it; partly, it seems also a matter of frankness: a willingness on the parents' part to answer the child truthfully, without continually taking refuge on the parental pedestal.
>
> 'I never had what you'd call—any love—from my mother. Now with ours I think that's the main thing, because even with our Patricia [five]—I'll put her on my knee and nurse her and love her, and she comes and asks me for it; well, I can

never remember having any of that. I could never hold a conversation with my mother, well even now I can't—seems as though we're distant somehow, funny isn't it? Yet I think a lot of her, but I just couldn't talk to her like I'm doing you. We can't get near each other . . . I don't know if it's because of me being a bit timid of my mam, but my little girl has her say; I have to listen to her say, you see, and then I'm not right you see, the little one knows it all, I don't know nothing.'[12] (pp. 288–92)

With the general though gradual and incomplete easing of stress, there is a greater hope for the future. And the future, in family terms, means the children. It is not easy for a man to change his social class in his own lifetime and, for a manual worker, not easy to increase his income after his twenties, when he is at his strongest and most energetic. But a more liberal educational system makes it possible to achieve such ambitions in the second generation. In a status-dissenting family the focus of attention shifts therefore from the father as breadwinner to the child as a potential credit to the family.

Zweig bears witness to the same effect. The men he talked to rarely had ambitions for themselves, but they had a deal of ambition for their children. One of his standard questions to family men concerned their interest in the upbringing and education of their children. The overwhelming majority took an intense interest. The standard phrases which came up again and again were: 'We want to give them a better chance than we had', or 'That's the finest thing—to give them every opportunity', or 'They come first'.

Because both parents are interested in this kind of improvement, this gives them an interest in common which, as partners, they can discuss and act upon together. In this way the segregation of men's interest from women's interest is further broken down. Indeed, the new focus of interest in the family circle affects the very nature of conjugal interaction, as a Radby Grade IV informant explained to the interviewer: 'The parents must set a good example to the children. Me and my husband never disagree before Peter.' And with more time available for interaction, there is more opportunity for the husband to interact with wife and children than was previously possible. An informant of Young and Willmott's lends this generalisation a historical perspective.[13]

> One good thing is that we have much shorter working hours now than before the war. I'm all for the five-day week—the forty-hour week. I remember my father used to work 72 hours one week and 60 the next. He was on shifts. The week he did the longer hours was on the day. We didn't see anything of him. I was in bed when he got back at night. People get more time with their families now.'

Now, therefore, as another informant in Bethnal Green put it, 'it's all for the kiddies'.

> 'Dad used to be very strict with us. We're different with our boy, we make more of a mate of him. When I was a kid, Dad always had the best of everything. Now it's the children who get the best of it. If there's one pork chop left, the kiddy gets it.'

Shaw[14] gives an indication of what this means in practice. The younger families in the group she studied gave the children noticeably more freedom to play, making fewer demands on them to help in the house and imposing fewer restrictions on their play. When the children played indoors, the whole family had to put up with quite a bit of mess, for they then cluttered up the general living and kitchen space. The father's changed position is exemplified by one young man who could not stand the noise his children made in the house when he came back from work. He solved his problem not by going out again, as the old-fashioned father might have done, but by playing with the children to keep them quiet. Thus the father is drawn into the family circle.

> The spread of the five-day week has created the week-end, a new term and a new experience for the working man. With it has come the sight of young fathers wheeling prams up Bethnal Green Road on a Saturday morning, taking their little daughters for a row on the lake or playing with their sons on the putting green in front of the windows of the Institute of Community Studies.

And Zweig, in almost the same terms:

> Fathers of babies often push the pram, give them baths, see them to bed; fathers of toddlers often read them stories, play with them, take them for a walk at week-ends; fathers of school children often go to the school for progress reports and supervise their homework; fathers of adolescents try to apprentice them or find them suitable jobs. . . .
>
> His hobbies and pastimes also centre round the house. So he is becoming more of a home-maker all round, much more than his father was. (pp. 300–2)

STATUS ASSENT AND STATUS DISSENT

Mogey's summary description of working-class status assenters has a familiar ring: they are traditional.

> They are less vocal; they accept the habits, standards, word usages and values typical of their areas and their street; they talk little about problems of class conflict, about trade unions, work or any other general topic. They are interested in specific people, in the details of daily living, and they make no general observations other than clichés or headlines from recent papers. They are not worried about the future, they make few plans for their children.

Their strength lies in kin-solidarity. Status assenters tend to live in a close-knit somewhat isolated community, beyond which they have no real understanding or interest and within which they are reasonably content. They put up with things. For instance, though most of the stock of condemned houses in Oxford at the time of Mogey's enquiry was located in the St Ebbe's area, three-quarters of the sample there found something to praise about their house, while only a quarter was consistently critical.

Although there are status dissenters in the old areas, the chances are that there will be more on the new estates. Many on the margin between the two approaches to life will be pushed into a dissenting pattern after they move.

> The house is a starting point for many new acquisitions, it whets the appetite for more. Once the barrier of non-possessing

has been crossed a new wave sets in . . . He [the man on the crest of the new wave] knows that money can bring something more lasting than a few hours enjoyment.[4]

Having to some extent broken free from custom, the way is open for further changes to follow. The status dissenter is not a negative character. He assents: and what he assents to is a materially richer, socially more ambitious, more open, freer way of life. Status dissenters are open to many sophisticating influences. They become less accepting, more demanding, more questioning, more aware of the forces which shape and modify the society in which they live. To take a simple example, the residents on the new Barton housing estate took Mogey's right to interview them less for granted than did the inhabitants of St Ebbe's: they asked the interviewers for their credentials, tested their sincerity, wondered visibly how they could make use of them. In spite of this, the social intercourse between interviewer and informant was eventually less gingerly at Barton than at St Ebbe's. Once the interviewers had established themselves, they were treated more nearly as equals, less as 'them'. (pp. 240–2)

Status dissenters are less resigned, or perhaps more free from the tendency to perceive the social world as divisible into an 'us' and 'them'. The greater tendency for dissenters to join formal organisations is connected with a greater freedom from that form of self-consciousness which is basically a consciousness of class-membership. Consequently they feel freer to associate in groupings where they will meet 'them'. Thus for instance in the Radby Grade IV and V stricter and more self-respecting working-class households, the parents cooperated with the school authorities in a parent-teacher association. The men in these grades applauded the idea of a training scheme for lads interested in mining. Some felt that they could not accurately be just called 'working class', they qualified the term in some way. Zweig also found that when he asked manual workers about their class, some made a distinction between their status in the works and their status outside. If they made this distinction they more often belonged to clubs with a socially mixed membership: in the employer–employee context they were aware of differences; outside the factory these were of less significance. (pp. 278–9)

In Radby, the Grade IV and V families had very definite ideas of achievement for their children, and very definite ambitions, based on knowledge of different types of schooling, with the qualifications these would lead to. One or two of the parents displayed a sound knowledge of their children's school careers—what subjects they were studying, what examinations they would go in for. Most were anxious that the children should 'get on'. One mother was overheard pointing out to her daughter that if she worked hard now, she would appreciate it later in life, when she went to apply for a job. General approval is given to a grammar school education, not only because 'it stays with you all your life' (a future-oriented, developmental view of the child, with a long time-perspective) but more particularly from the practical point of view: it was a means of rising socially. It is clearly understood that if the child is to have a better job than his father, he must go to school to learn.

> Those who had children in grammar schools were proud of mentioning the achievements of their children . . . and those whose children had failed the eleven-plus examination could not hide their disappointment, saying, 'We wanted it, but unfortunately he failed', or, 'I am not worried, he will try again', or, 'I sent him to a private school', or, 'It was because of her nerves that she failed'.[4]
>
> The achievement of having a child at a Grammar School is some cause for pride among the parents in Grades IV and V. It is also regarded as a means to an end. These grades are very ambitious for their children—they want their sons to be doctors, architects, and their daughters to be school teachers, dress designers, or at any rate to 'grow into ladies'.[1]

In these families there is definite and consistent training. The child is set standards and taught to live up to them. It is unheard-of for children not to go to school—for the child's sake it is obviously a good thing. With greater drive goes greater strictness and a longer time-perspective. One of Shaw's young fathers (the same who solved the problem of his noisy children by staying home to play with them instead of going out again) asked the interviewer whether he should have his boy coached because at the age of six he was not yet able to read. There is ambition here.

Status dissenters are more aware of the future-oriented aspects of their children's development. We see that in the Radby Grades IV and V the parents' discipline is often consciously aimed at improving the child and is not simply a way for the parent to express his own anger or disapproval.

> The Grade IV and V parents are obviously interested in their children and concerned for their welfare. The emphasis is on training the child 'properly'. . . . A child should be punished for doing something wrong, but punished in a reasonable and consistent way. . . . Punishment is prescribed for corrective purposes, but it is 'no good shouting at a boy' for he will take no notice if he becomes used to being shouted at . . .

The parents' attitude to pocket money is similarly deliberate and non-impulsive.

> They should be taught to save some. The children must learn how to spend money . . . They argue that it is to the child's advantage in later life if he is taught how to spend money properly.
>
> Most of the households with children of the appropriate age encourage them to attend Sunday School. But there is less encouragement for them to attend Youth Organizations , . . Parents in these grades tend to favour Cubs, Scouts and Guides rather than Youth Clubs. For it is felt that these organizations have capable leaders, and also that they attract the 'well-behaved boy' and 'children from good homes'. These views are unconnected with social snobbery but reflect a conception of desirable standards to maintain and to be instilled into the children.

This last paragraph touches upon a worrying aspect. A possibly similar group in the United States was found to have difficulties in social living.[15] They aspired to socially superior friends by whom, however, they were not fully accepted, whilst their former friends rejected them. And it may be noted that the mothers were unaware of the social isolation in which the children lived. This was indeed difficult to perceive. They were active in extra-curricular school affairs and belonged to organisations, but 'they could not enjoy their leisure-time activities as they became part of the mobility process'. They had few intimate friends. Similarly Jackson and Marsden quote a girl who said that, at the top of the class 'we didn't have friends, we had only rivals'. This is bad, but worse may follow: personal relations may become increasingly unimportant in the life of such a child.

> When the new manners, new friends, new accents, new knowledge heightened the adolescent tensions of home life, security and sense of purpose shifted from any wide emotional life and located itself narrowly in school work, in certificates, in *markability*.[5]
>
> Almost every working-class boy who goes through the process of further education by scholarships finds himself chafing against his environment during adolescence. He is at the friction-point of two cultures; the test of his real education lies in his ability, by about the age of twenty-five, to smile at his father with his whole face and to respect his flighty young sister and his slower brother.[6] (pp. 598–601)

THE BLACK-COATED WORKER

In the course of his discussion of the black-coated worker's marginal position, Lockwood[16] argues that the frequent accusations of 'snobbishness' levelled at the clerk were founded on an exaggerated assertion of his middle-classness. Because he was insecure socially, he sought to maximise the social distance between himself and the class immediately below him.

> The black-coated worker's impulse was to orient himself to the middle classes, and this very act of identification produced reactions from the working-class that reinforced his attachment to the former and his alienation from the latter.

This is in line with the idea that class antagonisms are at their most acute where consumption patterns most closely resemble one another. Willmott and Young[17] had occasion to quote many disapproving remarks made by middle-class Woodford people about the spending habits of the working-class. Yet many of these middle-class people were distinguishable from manual workers not by family origin but only by present occupation. They were reacting against a life they had left behind.

In other areas of life, also, this background may lead to contemptuous attitudes. In the course of an investigation not primarily concerned with the social class of the teacher, Himmelweit[18] and her associates found that in some ways the teachers were prejudiced against some boys. Having asked the teachers who were the five most popular boys in the class, and having found that significantly greater numbers of middle-class boys were mentioned by the teachers, they also gave a sociometric test to the boys themselves. They thereupon found that the boys were not affected by class considerations in the same way as the teachers: the five boys who were in fact most popular with other boys were no more likely to come from the middle classes than could be accounted for by chance.

They looked further at the teachers' attitudes and found that those who had come from working-class families had a distinct tendency to opine that the wrong kind of boy was being allowed into grammar schools nowadays; this in spite of the fact that they themselves had been 'the wrong kind of boy' in earlier days. These teachers tended also to be in general more authoritarian in outlook.

> Grammar schools can exert a great—if well-meant or even unconscious—pressure to remove their working-class pupils from attachment to their homes and neighbourhoods; they tend to seek to attach them to middle-class values. . . . A substantial proportion [of the sample] not only reject their working-class background but reject it with scorn, and adhere grimly to their new middle-class attitudes.[19]

Some of these pupils, we are told by Jackson and Marsden,[5] 'are rigidly orthodox . . . [and] . . . wish to preserve a hierarchical society. They sometimes explain their rejection of working-class life by an unpleasant meritocratic rationalization, arguing that those who remain in the working class nowadays deserve to do so, that they are "those who lack abilities" and have been left behind because they were not good enough to get on.' About half the sample have become teachers themselves, and so the process continues.

The love of discipline, or rules, of doing 'what you are supposed to do' was thought by Gorer[20] to reside particularly in the section of the population which might be described as lower middle class.

> The most marked characteristic of the lower middle-class is the extent to which they welcome and approve the authority of the contemporary state. They are the most enthusiastic admirers of the police . . . the most resolute opponents of 'fiddling', the most eager in their belief that laws should be obeyed under any circumstances, that it is always unfair to try to get more than others.
>
> Quite a number of the fathers in this stratum, particularly the middle-aged and elderly, would grant chief authority to the teacher.

Gorer also found that the children tend to be subjected to discipline within a typically authoritarian setting: the father was thought to be entitled to punish the child *because he was the boss*; child discipline was connected with the nature of authority rather than, say, with the development of the child, or the importance of understanding, or with what the offence might have been. The following of Gorer's quotations all come from this stratum of informants.

> The father should be head of his household and therefore settle serious things.
>
> One usually gets punished by the 'boss' and, begging Mum's pardon, Father is the boss of the house.
>
> A child should, for his own sake, have to answer to one authority and by the very nature of that authority, it ought very properly to be the child's father. (p. 404)

THE EDUCATED MIDDLE-CLASS MOTHER

With the growth of large-scale public and business organizations, many young men in this occupational class enjoy higher standards of material luxury and comfort in their working environment (in heating, lighting, air conditioning and quality furnishing, for instance) than they can expect to provide initially for their wives and families at home; furthermore, their wives are often quite well aware of this discrepancy. It may well be difficult for a woman to match her husband's status position at work by contriving a domestic environment which similarly enhances his reputation among friends and neighbours at home; and while she may privately blame this state of affairs on his financial inability to provide her with labour-saving gadgets or domestic help, she may still feel guilty if she fails, within her means, to achieve the kind of home which does him credit.[12]

Connected with this, both as a cause and as effect, is the wife's reluctance to apply her mind whole-heartedly to domestic work as though it were a job to be done well, for the good performance of which she reaps a reward in self-respect and praise from others. There may be a change in this direction when husbands come to appreciate the high degree of skill needed to run a home well—a probability which must increase as conjugal role-segregation declines.

The arrival of young children inevitably restricts her horizons rather drastically to begin with; if she has aspirations to an active intellectual life, this may be a time of frustration and despondency, and at best felt as a temporary phase to be tolerated and lived through . . .

The resulting state of conflict may be shown in a variety of ways. She may live nostalgically in the past, remembering her early adult life, when she was still at work, as a time of unfettered freedom and gay adventure. Alternatively, she may see the humorous side of her present predicament, and put it to social use by telling funny stories against herself: how the elderly visitor, arriving unexpectedly, was guided deftly past the unemptied potty behind the front door, only to come upon the toddler admiring her naked stomach in the hall mirror; or how the cake for a party, collapsed when its baking was interrupted by the baby, was filled up with chocolate icing and passed off as a special new recipe.[3]

There are many reasons which make it hard for the housewife to take pride in the performance of her functions, and make it easy for her to feel rather hard done by. Many of them complained to Bott at one time or another, of their drudgery, their boredom, and their isolation.[3] Especially when the children were young, they felt 'tied to the house'. 'You must forgive me if I sound half-witted,' said one informant, a highly educated woman, to Bott, 'I've been talking to the children all day.' It should be added, as Bott does, that all these mothers achieved nevertheless a good deal of satisfaction from their maternal role. (pp. 339–41)

TRADITIONAL AND NON-TRADITIONAL MIDDLE CLASSES

In Banbury there were some middle-class parents, all non-traditionalist, who sent their children to the state primary schools. They thereby saved the school fees, and they gave a number of additional reasons for their choice: that it was good for the children to 'mix a bit', that their chance of a 'scholarship' would be better, that the neighbouring state school was 'new and [with an implied "therefore"] very good'. But these were exceptions.

None of the 'new professionals', as far as Mrs Stacey could discover, sent their children to state primary schools. They themselves might be state-educated, but they wished to give their children a chance of further social progress and to free them from the limitations with which they themselves had started.

> In Banbury, middle-class parents follow the traditional pattern and send their children to one of the private day-schools in the town. Some make considerable sacrifices to do so. After this their children go to the State Grammar School if they can obtain a place there or to a small public or boarding school. They do not send them to State primary schools because they say they are 'rough' and they do not want their children to 'pick up an accent'. In short, they look to the private schools to teach middle-class manners and they are prepared to trust the grammar school to carry on its tradition of doing the same.[21]

> On the whole [write Jackson and Marsden of secure middle-class parents], they do not think in terms of whether their child's I.Q. is sufficient for a college or university education. This may be the way the teacher looks at things, but here in these households is a much more toughened and optimistic belief in the possibilities of industriousness, of self-help. They do not feel that their sons and daughters have to be brilliant intellectuals in order to carry off high educational prizes. They believe that such things are well within the grasp of any energetic boy or girl providing that they go cannily and wholeheartedly to work. (pp. 602–4)

REFERENCES

1. W. J. H. Sprott, ed., 1952, M. Carter, P. Jephcott *The Social Background of Delinquency.* Mimeograph available from the University of Nottingham.
2. J. Mogey, *Family and Neighbourhood,* Oxford University Press, 1956.
3. E. Bott, *Family and Social Network,* Tavistock Publications, 1957.
4. F. Zweig, *The Worker in an Affluent Society,* Heinemann, 1961.
5. B. Jackson and D. Marsden, *Education and the Working Class,* Routledge & Kegan Paul, 1962.
6. R. Hoggart, *The Uses of Literacy,* Chatto & Windus, 1957; Pelican.
7. G. Homans, *The Human Group,* Harcourt, Brace, 1950.
8. A. B. Hollingshead and F. C. Redlich, *Social Class and Mental Illness,* Wiley; Chapman & Hall, 1958.
9. N. Bell, A. Trieschman, E. Vogel, 'A socio-cultural analysis of the resistances of working-class fathers', *Amer. J. Orthopsychiatry,* 1961.
10. B. Bernstein, 'A public language: some sociological implications of a linguistic form', *Br. J. Sociology,* 1959.
11. J. Klein, *The Study of Groups,* Routledge & Kegan Paul, 1956.
12. J. and E. Newson, *Infant Care in an Urban Community,* Allen & Unwin, 1963.

13. M. Young and P. Willmott, *Family and Kinship in East London*, Routledge & Kegan Paul, 1957.
14. L. A. Shaw, 'Impressions of family life in a London suburb', *Sociol. Rev.*, 1954.
15. J. K. Myers and B. H. Roberts, *Family and Class Dynamics in Mental Illness*, Wiley; Chapman & Hall, 1959.
16. D. Lockwood, *The Black-Coated Worker*, Allen & Unwin, 1958.
17. P. Willmot and M. Young, *Family and Class in a London Suburb*, Routledge & Kegan Paul, 1960.
18. H. Himmelweit, 'Socio-economic background and personality', *Internat. Soc. Sc. Bulletin*, 1955.
19. R. Hoggart reviewing 'Education and the Working Class' (5) in *The Observer*, 11 February 1962.
20. G. Gorer, *Exploring English Character*, Cresset Press, 1955.
21. M. Stacey, *Tradition and Change*, Oxford University Press, 1960.

4
Education and the Working Class*

Dennis Marsden

Following Dr Klein's broader view, Mr Marsden looks in detail at the impact of grammar school education on a selected group of working-class children in this specially edited extract from 'Education and the Working Class'.

In a discussion of linking home and school, the weight of the problem invariably falls at the working-class end of the social spectrum. Many middle-class parents already have close and fruitful partnerships with the schools, as the figures for entry to higher education testify. Because the grammar schools are practically the only route into higher education for the working class, they bear a crucial responsibility for the fairness and efficiency of the education system. But in the book *Education and the Working Class* we suggested that there were serious and even insuperable barriers to a flourishing relationship developing between the grammar schools and a potential new working-class public. Education and the grammar schools are, in some ways, 'owned' by the middle class. This is not inevitably a bad thing. In practice, however—as may be seen in the following extracts from *Education and the Working Class*, describing parents' experiences with teachers and officials—sheer ignorance, and lack of mutual understanding, sympathy, and tolerance, can add up to disastrous failures of communication between schools and parents.

* Extracted from, Brian Jackson and Dennis Marsden, *Education and the Working Class*, Routledge, 1962, by kind permission of the publishers.

The book was about the grammar school careers of eighty-eight young men and women from working-class homes, who had been pupils in the schools of a northern industrial city we named Marburton. These were the successful pupils. They had jumped the major examination hurdles, or—a more apt metaphor—withstood the steady shaking of the sieve and remained in school long enough to take passes at 'A' level. Yet, in some ways, writing the book from the standpoint of examination successes was like presenting *Hamlet* without the Prince. For Crowther had demonstrated, and we suspected, that many of the most gifted working-class pupils did not get through grammar school at all.

A closer look at these families gave a still bleaker picture of the working-class child's chances of success. For, pushing beyond the Registrar General's blanket descriptions, we found not only were there very few children from unskilled and semi-skilled workers' homes, but also this more prosperous section of the working class which had impelled its children through grammar school was unusual in other ways. For example, the parents themselves might be middle-class 'come down in the world', or submerged wings of middle-class families. They were not infrequently first generation grammar school pupils themselves, or they were foremen, W.E.A. educated, or local organisers in that vast mesh of interlocking working-class activities which has yet to be fully documented. Such backgrounds, sometimes of frustrated ambition caught in years of unsatisfying work, sometimes filled with a yearning for a sort of classless millennium which education might bring, could carry even modestly gifted working-class children through school. Yet, somewhere along the way, many other working-class families, perhaps with equally gifted children, had abandoned grammar school. One of our tasks was to search amongst the 'successes' for clues to barriers which these others had failed to surmount. And though the parents of academically successful pupils were eager and *relatively* prosperous materially and in educational resources, they had indeed crossed many difficulties and perplexities.

In *Education and the Working Class* the problem of success was posed in two ways. Why were working-class children not well represented in the higher reaches of grammar school? And why did middle-class children do so well? To suggest answers to the second question we also interviewed pupils and parents in ten middle-class families, and, against the background of their relatively smooth progress through school, working-class difficulties were thrown into sharper relief.

Looking at the middle-class parents first, only two of our ten interviews were with thrusting, newly-established families where vigorous fathers had caught at their scanty educational opportunities and built them into solid financial success. Eight of our interviews were with more established middle-class families. The detail of Mr Peters's family catches the close weave of education, vocational training, and local industry. His grandfather attended Marburton Technical College in its earliest days, and his own father was one of the first members of Leeds University. He then returned to Marburton as head of the Dyeing Department at the Technical College, where Mr Peters took his own diploma directly under his father's tuition. The family became either businessmen, or *science* teachers. One uncle was the first scholarship boy at Rastrick Grammar School, another took his degree in chemistry at the Technical College again. Both these became small business men. Mr Peters's brother teaches science at one local grammar school, and his brother-in-law teaches mathematics at another. The rest of the family are in industry or small concerns of their own—often equipped with technical college degrees or diplomas, or grammar school and university educations. All this lay behind the young Raymond Peters when he was first taken down the road to begin his schooling. A similar account could be given of most of these families.

They display a wide experience and shrewd command of the possibilities of local education. On the whole they do not think in terms of whether their child's I.Q. is sufficient for a college or university education. They believe that such things are well within the grasp of any energetic boy or girl providing that they go cannily and wholeheartedly to work.

Of these ten sons and daughters, nine were placed in what our calculations show to be Marburton's leading primary schools for long-term results. Seven of the children did very well and were somewhere amongst the top six children in their class at school.

And for these children links between family and school were frequently homely and intimate. There was one instance where the teacher came to tea and the little girl would be sat on her knee. There was another where the father invited the girls at a local teachers' training college to get extra practice by trying out their tests on his child at home. But three of the children had real difficulty with their primary school work. Norman Conway was 'not successful' at this stage. Alice Douglas had considerable difficulty with primary school English. Her words came out in a peculiar order, and the teachers definitely forecast that she would not pass the selection examination. The parents arranged for private coaching, and she then passed very high up the list. Raymond Peters had similarly severe difficulties with primary school arithmetic, and again the teachers warned the parents that he would not pass without special help. Despite these weaknesses, all ten children not only passed, but passed well. Their brothers and sisters shared this success, for of twenty brothers and sisters old enough to take the selection examination, nineteen passed.

Later on at grammar school Helen Chapman had got herself into the wrong class.

> 'It got so bad that the headmistress called me to her office and said that I was going to drop maths. So I went home and told my father that I couldn't do maths any more. So he said, "Nonsense! You've got to do maths. Absolutely necessary. You go and tell the headmistress that you're doing it." And so I went back and told her. There was an awful scene. There was my form mistress and her (this was in her room) and she was saying thus and thus and thus about my not doing maths. And all I could say was, "My father says I've *got* to."'

In the end Helen continued with her maths, and in fact took a credit in it with her school certificate.

Of the nine who went on to college or university, six did so supported by the successful cooperation of school and parents. The school advised Mr Denby to let his son try for the law, and family, school, and student persevered together whilst he took his Advanced level three times before he got a sufficiently good one to take him to university. Mr Chapman asked the school to help him choose the best training college for his daughter—a request for both excellence of training and distinction of 'tone'. Helen was sent on a three-year course to the Froebel Institute. Mr Douglas's family believed, through personal connections, that the National Training College of Domestic Science was both professionally good and socially superior. The school cooperated, and Alice took a place there. Norman Conway went to Leeds and took a first. Shirley Firbank finally went to Cambridge, though the headmistress on grounds of age had first of all suggested that she shouldn't take the scholarship papers. Mr and Mrs Firbank immediately saw the Education Officer formally, and communicated with a member of the Education Committee informally; the difficulty was straightened out and all impediments removed. For Dr Peters the school thought university too ambitious and advised hotel management. Father and son regarded the suggestion as insulting and pursued their way. The next year Raymond won an open scholarship at London University, and took a first class degree and did his Ph.D. there. There was a similar difficulty over Allan Broomfield. The school informed the parents that he had no prospect of getting to university. The parents disagreed. Allan was withdrawn at eighteen and sent to the Technical College. There he won a scholarship to Edinburgh and read his degree in brewing.

In a host of small but telling ways these middle-class families had an educational inheritance with which to endow their children. State education had been worked into the very grain of these families since its first major stages in Marburton. In half of these instances there was a shrewd and trusting understanding between school and family, supporting the child. But when things went 'wrong', the family was able to interfere and maintain the child even against the school's opinion—whether it was preparation for the eleven-plus, grammar school streaming, early specialisation, staying on into the sixth form, choosing a university, deciding on a career.

Whereas the middle-class parent was quietly and justifiably confident about handing on an educational inheritance to his children, the parent of the successful working-class child was more often nervous and anxious to break through and snatch grammar school education for his children. When the moment came for schooling to begin many of the parents were unsure of their choice and guidance. This was the point of entry to unfamiliar worlds. Those families with blood relatives in the professional classes, or with middle-class links through church or club, sometimes took advice about the choice of primary school. But apart from those with middle-class connections, parents accepted the local school in a natural 'neighbourhood' spirit. When they seemed equi-distant from two schools, their reasons for preferring one rather than the other were warm and child-centred, but extraordinarily short-term. Mrs Black chose in this way for her little girl:

> 'Yes, there *were* two schools in Broadbank but we didn't know much about them. Well, there were some children passing on the road, and I said, "Which school do you go to?" and they told me the Church School. So I told our Doreen, "Those children go to the Church School. Would you like to go to that school?" And she said, "Yes," so I went along there, and after that she went to school with the children.'

Similarly, in choosing a secondary school, knowledge as to the best and the second best only circulated freely in those families with some history of grammar school education or with middle-class connections. Others tried the neighbours, workmates, even a friendly bus-driver for advice. Some went to the school, but in that atmosphere felt antagonistic or defensive.

> 'That's right, I saw the headmaster, and I said: "We've got this form with all these schools down, and we don't know anything about any of them." "Well," said the headmaster, "What's his father's job?" "He's a lorry driver." "Well, then you'd better be sending him to Mill Cross" (the secondary technical school). "Mill Cross? Why, is that the best school?" "No, it's not, but it's the best school for you." "How do you mean, it's the best school for me? Where would you send your lad?" "Oh, I'd send *my* lad to Marburton College . . . " So what do you think of that story? Fair cheek, isn't it?'

A few visited the City Education Office for the first time and retired defeated and unenlightened by the clerical staff. Mr Pollard was more persistent.

'"Can I have an appointment?" I said. "Oh no," they said, "You can't." "Can't? I wan't an *appointment*, I don't want to see him now." "No, Mr Pike [the Education Officer] can't see you. Mr Pike's too busy." I had all the lot . . . Well, I wouldn't have that. I banged on the counter, but I got nothing, no. They wouldn't make anything. I went back to the foundry, and I said, "Oi," to Councillor Boggis. He was a stonemason and he'd been put on the Council like. I told him the story, and didn't he play pop! He got on the telephone and he said, "Who's there?" And they told him. "I don't want thee," he says, "I want Mr Pike." So he got Mr Pike in the end. "Sithee," he says, "tha's a public officer like everybody else, and tha can make appointments like everybody else . . ."'

The result of this ignorance, embarrassment, and bewilderment was that in many cases a vital decision was taken for quite trivial reasons. A school was chosen because it was near enough for the child to come home at dinner time, or because it meant one bus journey instead of two, or because its situation seemed to offer a greater abundance of 'fresh air'.

Grammar school for their children was a new extension of living for the parents too. This does not hold true in every case, but in almost every interview with the fathers and mothers we recorded some flicker of excitement at knowledge for themselves as well as their children. Here is one voice playing over the experience. Mr Lucas is a bus driver who left school at fourteen; a man in whom large areas of curiosity, delight, and intelligence had lain dormant until his daughter passed the scholarship exam. To hear him speak now is to hear him use words like 'culture' and 'civilization', if not with full confidence at least with a very real sense of what their meanings reside in.

'Now when your child is coming along and going to Grammar school, you begin to get excited, you begin to be interested, and you want to know more things. That's how it was with us.

It was a wonderful thing for us our children learning all these new things. Now when I was at school we learned history and geography and it was all battles and such like. But for our Mary history and geography aren't all like that, they're bigger things. It's as if she can see ten times, a hundred times, as much as we were taught. She doesn't talk about *battles*. Now we went on a coach trip up in the Yorkshire Dales and she goes poking in the fields and she hoicks out of a field this here thing. Come and have a look out in our garden. Dost tha' see it? Now that's a fossilized fern is that, and you know I'd have kicked a dozen of them things over and I wouldn't have known what it was. Aye, she explained all this and how it happened thousands and thousands of years before all these battles were thought on! . . .

'Last summer the wife and I went on a trip to London. We went to the British Museum. Now at one time that's the *last* place we'd have gone to, but I was filled with wonderment in that British Museum. We went into one big room where it was all about the civilization of Babylon, and there were these great big statues that they'd fetched all the way back from Babylon. My! you should go and see them! Great big things they were, made them to last in them days didn't they? Aye, and all that civilization gone—you get to thinking about that. All their civilization has gone but ours is here. How does all that come about? . . . Education brings all kinds of things, doesn't it?—same as the people round here, they just think you go to school and then you go to work, but it's not like that when you've been educated. You can see big things like a civilization, you don't just think about the job you're going to do.'

Not all the parents had been roused in this lasting way, but in the first two years of grammar school there were very few who were not touched by the excitement of knowledge in some way. After a year or two, however, the children's natural respect for their parents lay uneasily alongside their own clearer mastery of the new skills, and alongside many other doubts that school and early education promoted. There was the beginning of a split, or at least of a growing sense that the child was out on his own, moving into worlds to which the parents had no access. Many of the parents sought to reassert control over their children's education by demanding some clear statement about the kind of job this was leading to. And this voice was generally the father's. The central pattern—though it was often broken and sometimes reversed—was one in which the mother protected and pushed the child, whilst the father raised the awkward practical questions as to where it all led. By the third and fourth year questions about future jobs were becoming insistent. And it was perhaps natural that there should be this early anxiety about a job from men and women who knew only too well how much secure work mattered.

> '. . . I'd come home and I'd sit opposite our lad in the chair, and I'd say, "What do you think you'll be when you leave school?" "I don't know, I don't know at all, don't bother me," he'd say and that was it. When the neighbours bothered me, I hadn't got an answer and I felt soft. They'd look at you as much as to say, "Staying on at school all that time and don't know what he's going to be, well!"'

Most children were as unsure of the future as their parents and as uninformed about possibilities. How was it that so many of the parents did not get more advice? Clearly the obvious place to get this was the school. We asked the parents why they did not go to school more, and their answers were so various and sometimes so barely sensible, as to be merely sketchy rationalisations. Yet only very rarely could this failure to take advantage of the teacher–parent relationship be put down to simple neglect. Some said they were always working late or the bus journey was a difficult one—despite the fact that their children had managed it daily since the age of eleven. Others felt their attendance would upset the child, others still reported how uncomfortable they felt in the presence of the teachers and other parents. Some felt that one visit a year was worse than no use at all, and complained of the hurry and the big crowds on that night. Others again spoke of the teachers as not being interested in them or their children.

No doubt many of these charges are unfair. But some of these statements made more sense than others and ran true to the rest of the interview. There was, for instance, no doubt why these parents so seldom belonged to the formal parent–teacher organisations. These groups were run, and often very ably run, by professional-class parents, and it was sheer social discomfort that kept working-class parents at a distance. There was no bad feeling over this, rather it was recognised that in a sense the school 'belonged' more to the professional parents and it was only natural that they should also 'own' the parent–teacher body. Besides, they clearly did the work well, and gave generously of their time and talents. But this feeling of intruding into an alien world 'belonging' to others spread over the whole school, hindering the interested and worried parents and hardening the few careless and idle ones. Some parents, like their children, put on a bilingual act for the school. Mrs Proctor observed this in a neighbour, 'She was talking right posh to all the teachers, but when we got out of school I walked her down and the language she used! "I'll flatten the bugger!" she said.' Or the tension might come out in angry scenes with the staff. It was not so much a case of the school being 'right' and the parents 'wrong', or *vice versa.* It was again these two touching worlds, and the brittle contacts between insensitivity and hypersensitivity. Other parents came away bitterly disappointed with their meeting. For them the grammar school undertaking was such a venture in the dark, and there seemed so many doubts about it and no clear future. What they sought on their visits was above all information and reassurance. 'I don't know why we went. I expect that what we wanted was encouragement,' said Mrs Teasdale. But what they reported and resented was the meagre opportunity of seeing teachers, and the irrelevance of the comment and advice they did receive. The last things they desired were either sharp little pep talks urging their child to work even harder and take more marks, or any sign of lacking interest. Yet (to them) this was how the school could seem: all parents were unimportant, but they were the most unimportant.

> 'Well, we can't tell you much about bloody schooling because they didn't tell *us* so bloody much about the job! They did not! Once a year you went to that bloody college, a great big bloody queue, two or three minutes each. They don't know your lad in it. You talked to Spierpoint, the head, didn't

you, Mavis? And he didn't know who our lad was. No, he had no idea under the sun, he just looked up there into the sky, like he does, and said yes and said no. I don't think it's bloody right. They should either give a lot more time or let you go up more often. You should have it six times a year. But we never knew owt. You'd see this bloody Glen-Smith fellow and he'd look at you and hum and bloody haw and he'd give you no encouragement at all, none whatever, not a bloody bit of encouragement. And me and Mavis, we'd go down the steps of that bloody college and we'd be right depressed, right downhearted. We never thought the lad had a chance, and there in the end he gets a scholarship to university. There it is! . . . aye, don't come talking to me about Marburton bloody education, it's time that the bloody rate-payers went and shook them buggers up. We're good citizens aren't we? We might be poor folk around this way, but we've as much bloody right as any other buggers in this bloody town to get the job done properly.'

A flood of language like this shows well the misunderstanding of needs, the anxieties, the sense of 'us' and 'them', the social unease and the bewilderment that we encountered so often. It is hard to estimate how much this failure of contact between school and parent tells, but clearly it could have been decisive in many of those cases where able children have left at fifteen or sixteen. And especially so when we remember that the parents least likely to attend school were the ones whose children were in B and C streams: and most of the working-class entry went that way. There was a vicious circle here, for when the children found themselves graded as 'C's the parents felt ashamed, felt it was all for 'of no use' and communicated this feeling to sons and daughters. In so far as they understood unfavourable 'streaming', they did not, like middle-class parents, contest it; for them it was an absolute judgment by the experts in the field.

Most of the children who survived were A stream children, but even in these cases the lack of flow between parent and school became critical, and especially so when one of the parents was sceptical, reluctant now about the whole scheme. 'Whenever I used to go and see Miss Woodall,' said Mrs Holdsworth, 'it wasn't comfort for *me* that I wanted, it was a story to keep *him* happy when I got back home.' And so on top of this, one parent's doubts might be directly reinforced by the child's discomfort. He might be painfully reluctant about his parents presenting themselves. 'Oh no, we never went up to the school. We took him on the first day, of course, but we never went after that. He used to bring invitations home, but he'd say, "I don't think you'll be bothered about that," and so we never used to go.'

These touches of detail suggest in what various ways working-class parents felt the grammar school to be peculiarly alien, and how it was that so few of them—though clearly excited and anxious about their children—turned successfully to the school for advice and explanation. Two other effects of this situation need to be noted. First of all, it meant that the working-class child at school carried his own fate in his hands far more than did other children. He was conscious of being on his own, and the habit of taking educational decisions came to him early. Secondly, the parents' failure to come to terms with the school, and the frustration of their anxious questions sometimes became a part of the background of home tension which helped to widen the gap between the parent and child at a remarkably young age. It took its place amongst those many small details (such as Mr Holdsworth giving up smoking in order to pay for the 'extras' of his daughter's schooling), which made some parents over-conscious of their children's obligation, and so quick to resent any sign of 'uppishness'.

Inevitably, this selection of parents' experiences must distort and blunt the original analysis in important ways. It's easy to imagine, for instance, when parents only are being discussed, that the pupil's own reaction to school counts for relatively little; so tightly does the home background predestine the student to this or that course of action or stratum of society. We have to remember that the pupils had their difficulties too, often in larger and more disturbing measure than their parents. Nevertheless it is useful to look simply at the borderline between neighbourhood and school, and see what can be done to ease parent–teacher relationships here.

We suggested several relatively simple improvements: the provision of information early, whether parents ask for it or not, with an understanding of the very simple and non-technical nature of the parents' call for reassurance; easier access to teachers (we suggested that perhaps the right thing might be to have the pupils sent home for a week and let the teachers be available for helping the parents); and Mr Pollard's brush with the Education Office possibly points up the value of an education 'adviser' at the school or council office. Brian Jackson's work at the Advisory Centre for Education in Cambridge has followed a number of lines—a question-answering service, a parent-to-parent service for passing on information about individual schools. To get nearer to the working-class parent, he has tried out the idea of an education 'shop'—a department of a big store where, as he says, along with the bacon parents can get information about schools. This may be the best line of all. Access must be as easy and informal as popping into the grocer's.

There are other ideas, not new, as sections of this book show. Anyone with experience of interviewing parents in their own homes about education must have noticed how eager many of them are to ask questions of the interviewer, and how much more confident they are on their own ground than they have appeared in the extracts quoted above. Why not add an 'education visitor' to the ever-growing list of social workers? The gain might be manifold, for there is another, latent, function of the interview, sometimes difficult for the interviewer, but fruitful for the parents. The interview can have a logic of its own which acts as a catalyst to set going or bring to the surface ideas, topics, and questions which parents had not previously put in the educational context. Parents with a generalised, but unpractical, desire for education, might be brought to a canny use of local educational facilities. But it is worth asking if such a service could not more usefully be performed by the teachers, who must benefit from the insights into working-class life such visits would bring.

For, while the key schools, indeed 'education' itself, belongs in however valuable and useful a way to middle-class parent and teacher, it is all too easy to think merely in terms of easing the flow—of information, 'culture' or whatever—*out* of the schools to the working-class families beyond their walls. It is this sort of thinking which led one of Marburton's head teachers to call *Education and the Working Class* an 'ungrateful' book. And a subsequent probe about the establishment of an education 'shop' in Marburton brought from the Chairman of the Education Committee the reply that there was no need of such a device—the schools and Education Committee were handling the situation quite adequately. Possibly after publication of the book the communication of information from the schools to parents did improve (for instance, the immediate effect in one of Marburton's grammar schools was a staff meeting which resulted in reorganised procedure for contact with parents). But this was the easier lesson to learn. Later on this same school was ever more assiduously erecting barriers against the surrounding working class, by, for example, refusing to countenance any form of joint activity with secondary modern schools. In another of Marburton's grammar schools, working-class pupils who had to take Saturday morning work to earn money to go on the school trip were debarred from going on the trip expressly for that reason! Such innocence of even the economic facts of the working-class child's life at grammar school seems hardly credible in responsible teachers. This, and the behaviour described previously, seem to spring from a fear of 'contamination' by working-class life. Overt class warfare may be dying down in England, but we can see here how freshly, if quietly, our education system is repairing the barriers between the chosen and the excluded.

Linking home and school must imply a flow in both directions; otherwise more knowledge for parents can only lead to increasing manipulation of the system and more bitter competition for a few favoured schools. Teachers evidently have much to learn also, both about and *from* Mr Lucas and Mr Pollard. One would hope that the more they learn, the more they will question the grammar school's continual sifting and rejection of children from working-class families.

5
The Impact of Neighbourhood Values

John Barron Mays

This paper examines in detail the clash of norms between home and school in a lower working-class area in a northern city, and is based by Professor Mays upon the researches published earlier, in his 'Education and the Urban Child'.

Some of the empirical material to be presented in this paper was collected some years ago in relation to the work of a set of schools in one of the older and least favoured parts of residential Liverpool.[1] Since the data were collected and the original report written and published, there will certainly have been some changes in the survey area, although personal observation does not suggest that these changes have yet been substantial enough to modify the generalisations which were made on the basis of the original enquiry. Later figures regarding admissions to selective schools, for instance, which were subsequently supplied by the local education authority indicate that, although the downtown schools gain more selective places than they did seven years ago, they still obtain very many fewer than those being gained by pupils in suburban neighbourhoods. The pattern of disadvantage that I commented on then is still in being, too, in many other ways; only one of the schools I studied has since been rehoused and most of the grosser manifestations of physical inequality are still observable in the locality.

The central theme of my paper is the relationship between the norms upheld by the local residents and the institutionalised values of formal education; the differential attitudes of teachers and educational administrators, on the one hand, and many of the pupils and parents, on the other; and, above all, the ways in which these various social and normative standards interact and modify each other to produce the typical ethos of the downtown school in the underprivileged neighbourhood. As an educational sociologist I am interested in how purely social influences outside the school condition what goes on in the classroom, and, more especially, why in some localities the apparent influence of formal education is so slight in comparison with other and better-off districts. A number of general assumptions underlie my discussion and had better be exposed at the start. These assumptions are by no means novel and, to varying degrees, have been demonstrated in the writings of many educational researchers. The basic position is that children's behaviour (including their response to the experience of schooling) is substantially conditioned by influences emanating from the home, the school and the peer group in the immediate locality. Different writers have emphasised these influences to varying extents, and the American literature at least seems to suggest that the family and the peer group are usually predominant.

Hollingshead in *Elmtown's Youth*[2] discovered a functional relationship between the class position of the adolescents' families and their social behaviour, and, in particular, how they fared at school. He also found that behaviour and behaviour traits tended to develop along lines approved by their clique mates who were themselves invariably members of the same social class and status group. James Coleman[3] in his study of American high school teenagers decided that they were strongly oriented to one another, although not entirely so. American adolescents, for Coleman, comprise a society, or rather a series of societies within a society, with the focus upon inward-looking teenager interests rather than upon the responsibilities and goals approved by the wider community. How far all this is true of young people in Britain is difficult to decide, but one would be surprised if most of the tendencies outlined above were not discovered here to some extent, if only as future potentialities. Dr Douglas[4] has shown that very interested parents can, by their help and support, enable children to overcome the disadvantage of a lower ability level than is normally consonant with grammar school admission. One would imagine that sustained family care could also assist children to overcome the contrary pull of the local peer group. It is when the peer group works against the school and where the family itself fails to supply the necessary support that the work of the schools and the teachers becomes most extraordinarily difficult.

It will be apparent that in a situation in which influences deriving from three separate and powerful institutional sources are operating there will be a possibility of a series of conflicts of values arising, and that such a conflict or ideological dispute will be a continuous process, seldom if ever finally resolved so that one dominant force prevails. The values of the school may conflict with those of the home, and those of the peer group with both. The norms of the latter may on the other hand conflict with the school's but be harmonious with those of the home in many important regards. The situation is complex and many-faceted; so far, to the best of my knowledge, no writer has gone very far in analysing and describing all the possible permutations. A thorough institutional analysis of the school as a school in relation to family life and parental attitudes, and in relation to the norms of the peer group and the local youth culture, still remains to be effected.

This being the case it is clear that we are only at the beginning, in this country at least, of an educational sociology soundly based on firm empirical foundations.

Clearly the way different people perceive their roles is of crucial significance to any understanding of what is really involved in the educational process. People, moreover, have complex roles to play. There is, for example, both an individual and a formal or institutional aspect of their professional role. A teacher perceives himself as a teacher in an educational system; he also must regard himself as a particular teacher in relation to a specific group of pupils and their families in a particular milieu. Thus, one often hears the lament go up from many a harassed teacher to the effect that he is permitted to do everything in the school except teach.

The teacher, then, has a generalised and a specific aspect to his role. He has an idea of what being a teacher in general involves and also, possibly in some ways conflicting with this conception, there is his own assessment of his job in face of a particular group of individual pupils and families, not in the abstract but in the here and now, in relation to whom he must make decisions and exert influence. Parents, too, have complicated ideas of what their duties are, and of how they ought to behave. They may have a general impression of what the school and the local education authority expect of them; they may also have a fairly clear idea of what the neighbours think, or of what grandma did, or again, if they are members of a worshipping community, of what the priest enjoins upon them. Possibilities of confusion, of misunderstanding, of underlapping and overlapping, of conflict and disagreement arise from every side. And doubt and anxiety and uncertainty are often the result for all the parties involved in the bringing up and training of the young.

My own research has been confined to working-class areas and to the children of manual workers. These children, it has been shown in many researches, do less well in the academic sense than the offspring of professional and middle-class parents in general. So gross are the differences of performance that the idea that some kind of basic psychological inferiority is the cause of this must be ruled out. I found in Liverpool, for example, that the children of the inner city wards in what we have come to call the Crown Street district obtained a ridiculously small proportion of selective secondary school places in comparison with pupils at schools in good suburban areas, the range between inner and outer areas being in the region of 8 to 63 per cent for the relevant age group. Dr Crawford's[5] careful psychological study of a small sample of the children of all districts of the city showed that pupils in the Crown Street district were, as far as basic endowment goes, only fractionally inferior to children in better class areas who gained much higher marks in the General Entrance Examination. The only possible explanation for such a disparity of achievement must lie in the social environment itself, in the quality of schooling being offered, in the nature of family life and in the social influences emanating from other children in the neighbourhood. Further substantial support for such a contention comes from

Dr Douglas's work, already mentioned, on over five thousand children born in March 1946 in England, Wales, and Scotland whom he and his collaborators have so far followed systematically from their birth into adolescence. He has shown that children from manual worker backgrounds seem to be most prone to environmental differences in the junior school between the ages of eight and eleven, and that those with parents who take a considerable interest in their school work improve their test performance, whilst those lacking such parental support tend to fall away. Hence a child's capacity to prosper academically depends to a considerable extent on the amount of parental support he receives and the quality of home he is lucky or unlucky enough to inherit. (The academic record of his school is also a strong determinant, but will not be pursued here.)

Furthermore, Elizabeth Fraser's[6] important study of school children in Aberdeen has highlighted the fact that home environment is rather more closely connected with progress at school even than I.Q. She suggests that the factors in the home environment which are most influential in this respect are only partly economic, but that they are also partly emotional and partly motivational.

We therefore arrive at a general presumption, based on a growing crowd of informed witnesses, that type of home and type of neighbourhood are two of the most powerful, if indeed not the two most powerful, conditioning forces, which determine to a large measure a child's school performance and further the general quality of his life and attitudes.

The question now before us, then, is how do these two forces interact? How far do school and home work together, to what extent do they pull in the opposite directions, and how do the values of the neighbourhood operate on both fundamental institutions?

There is a fair amount of evidence to show that many residents in traditional working-class neighbourhoods seriously undervalue education.

A. B. Wilson[7] has shown this very clearly in his study of high school boys in America. He found that educational achievement was comparatively devalued in working-class neighbourhoods, to such an extent, in fact, that even the products of middle-class families in the same area felt the draught of this influence. A process of what might be called anticipatory socialisation in reverse seemed to occur. What influences will predominate in any one case seems to depend to some extent upon whether the working-class pupils have middle-class peers to emulate or not. Where working-class peers' values are more conspicuous in a neighbourhood they tend to draw the others down with them. There is thus in any socially mixed area a potentiality for cultural conflict where the children attend common schools. Where they do not attend the same schools, it seems fair to assume, the influence of the home and the parents should be sufficient to counteract the adverse attractions of the peer group and the local neighbourhood, providing, of course, as has so often been stressed, they are giving adequate support and encouragement in academic matters.

Evidence available in this country substantiates the view that education is often undervalued, and there is no doubt that a great many teachers working in schools in the poorer districts would take it as a self-evident fact. In my own limited enquiry in the Crown Street area of Liverpool I found that few parents seemed to make any positive demands on the schools and that, for the most part, they seemed to leave educational decisions to the teachers and to accept their advice more or less unquestioningly. It was, in a way, a compliment to the teaching profession, which indicated the high social status they enjoyed in the area, but such an attitude is very different from that which characterises the higher-class neighbourhoods where teachers find themselves under constant and often embarrassing parental pressure to concentrate on pupils' academic performance. As Professor Swift[8] has shown, it is the socially aspirant middle-class and lower middle-class parents whose own careers have been unsatifactory and whose personal ambitions have been frustrated who make such a fuss about schooling, and who over-actively cooperate with the more limited aims of schools, in the way, that is to say, of passing examinations rather than in terms of widening children's cultural interests.

As far as the schools in the Crown Street district went, there was little to suggest that either teachers or parents pressurised children to become academic high-achievers or even, at a more humble level, to do well at the General Entrance Examination and obtain a place at either a technical or a grammar school There were a few cases which teachers could cite in which parents had actively worked against the wishes of the school and refused to allow their children to sit the eleven-plus, or, when their children had obtained a grammar school place, had refused to let them take it up. Michael Carter hinted at the same kind of anti-educational attitude on the part of some families in his Sheffield study where parents expressed 'doubts about the worth of examinations . . . and dark pictures were drawn of the amount of studying that would be necessary'.[9] The general attitude of the teachers may be summed up by saying that if a child had obvious ability and came from a supporting home background he should be encouraged to do well academically; otherwise no special influence should be exerted one way or the other. Practices varied from school to school, but in the main seemed to reflect the social aspirations of the locality. In some schools all children were given a limited amount of experience in intelligence tests, but others would not go this far. A little over half the junior departments in the survey area gave prospective candidates a little practice in answering intelligence tests, but in none did this involve anything remotely resembling cramming. Furthermore, some schools set homework for those taking the eleven-plus, but others refrained. A few schools organised special learning groups and gave some coaching. Homework, even in schools where it was set and marked, was usually confined to children about to sit the examination. Of all Crown Street children who were doing some homework at the time of the survey (1957), some 60 per cent were doing it at the request of their parents, which indicates a fair degree of family interest. One cannot help wondering whether the schools themselves might not have done more at a somewhat earlier stage to encourage this interest, and to what extent the reluctance to set work is related to the dislike of the extra marking and correcting entailed.

Headteachers' views on the desirability of homework throughout the junior school, as opposed to homework specially set for those about to take the examination, were conflicting. The majority were against it, and only two of the ten questioned were in favour. Thus it can be seen that the emphasis upon academic performance and measured attainment varied to a considerable extent with headteachers' interpretation of their duties. One head stressed the need to care for the backward pupils—a most laudable attitude surely, provided it does not in turn imply that the more able and advanceable children are allowed to drift. In some schools and departments there were teachers keen to encourage a high academic standard and eager to assist the more gifted pupils to get on via the examination system. I met at least one very keen man who was chafing at the lack of impetus in the schools he was serving, and who felt very keenly that not all was being done that could be done to promote the future prospects of the children. It is perhaps not very surprising that, very soon after, he left the district to work in a new school with better equipment and a higher level of endeavour.

It is clear that inequality and differential treatment exist on every hand, and especially in the downtown schools in poorer-class neighbourhoods. The degree of interest on the part of the parents is one side to this differential process; the other side of the coin is the extent of the teachers' and particularly of the headteachers' zeal and enthusiasm to do more than an average routine job.

Parental apathy is frequently commented on by teachers when questioned about their work in downtown schools and the many problems associated with their work. Many of the teachers are critical of the parents and consider them to be seriously failing in their duties. There is little doubt, also, that an over-censorious attitude on the part of teachers, where it exists, must make relations between school and home more difficult than they might otherwise be.

But some of the criticisms of teachers can be substantiated and they reveal emphatically the divergence between what we may term the standards of the wider community and those of the local subculture. They show also that to some extent the work of the schools must be thought of as being in opposition to the surrounding subculture. It is a nice question to determine how far some of the teachers accept this as a challenge to promote social change or how far they merely accept the adverse influences as excuses for their own dislike of becoming too involved? How many accept that the notion of their standing *in loco parentis* commits them to something much more thoroughgoing than a disciplinary function and the right to administer punishment? How many are willing to reach out imaginatively and creatively into the lives of the local families, as the settlement movement, for example, has been trying to do for well over half a century, and strive to raise the prevailing standards of family care so that their pupils may have a better chance to polish and exploit their talents in their own and in the country's interests?

Evidence against parents rests on the failure of many of them to cooperate actively. Even when it is objectively clear that they ought to come to the school, many stay away for one reason or another. All the Crown Street schools invited parents to attend when the school nurses or doctors were examining their children, but the response varied. In one all-age school it was stated that all the juniors were accompanied by a parent or relative when being medically examined, but few of the seniors received similar support. In another senior department no more than 15 per cent of the parents were said to attend these sessions. The general impression of the area as a whole can best be summed up by saying that only a minority ever attended; for the most part the parents left it to the school to do their share of the job without overt support. This is a serious indictment, but one which is not necessarily confined to the parents who failed to respond. One would like to know to what extent the schools impressed on the parents the fact that not only was it their job to attend such interviews but that they would be warmly welcomed when they came. What steps were taken to overcome parental diffidence or to arrange mutually convenient times for the inspection? How far is the medical review laid on in a routine way without any special build-up and publicity? It is dangerously easy to use a phrase such as 'parental apathy' and leave it at that.

Analogous visits are made to interview school leavers during their last year by officials of the Youth Employment Service. The purpose of this service is much more than job placement and aims at vocational guidance. Vocational guidance involves a tripartite collaboration between school, home, and youth employment officers, and this in turn should mean that all three are enabled to meet to discuss the future careers of leavers in the light of the pupils' abilities, temperaments and aptitudes, and also in relation to the local labour market. Procedures to effect this varied between the various schools I surveyed. In a few schools the parents were invited to attend meetings with the vocational guiders, but it is undeniable that full collaboration was not possible in a majority of cases, nor was it even attempted. For schools to invite parents to attend meetings especially concerned with their own children's welfare and future and to find them not interested enough to come must be a most depressing experience. By the same token, for parents not to be asked to come to such meetings is to suggest that they are not regarded as partners in shaping the destinies of their own offsprings. It is idle to claim that parents are not interested in what the schools are attempting to do if the latter are not themselves doing everything in their power to foster a responsible and collaborative relationship. The relationship must be structured so that all concerned at least have the opportunity to be present and to make their contribution. Anything less may be regarded as a failure on the part of those responsible to meet the minimum needs and rights of the pupils.

Parents will lean on the schools if the teachers encourage leaning. If, in important areas of pupils' lives they fail to elicit parental support and don't every try to get it, then they have less excuse for lamenting that 'the parents leave it all to us around here'. Hard-pressed parents, not unnaturally, seize on whatever voluntary or statutory help is available to them, and no doubt, being weak and human, they tend to leave as much as they can to those who have the skill and training to perform such services. If a child has an accident in school it is assumed that it is the teacher's job to go with him to the outpatient clinic. Cases were reported in Crown Street of pupils receiving injuries during the lunch hour and being sent back to the school by their mothers to obtain first aid whilst they themselves went off to their own work or went out shopping.

From what I have just been saying, it will be clear that there is still disagreement and misunderstanding about the function of the school and the role of its staff in relation to the immediate environment. I have no doubt in my own mind that the role of the teacher in socially deteriorated districts must incorporate aspects of the role of the welfare officer, and that academic achievement will itself improve only when teacher and parent work in close harmony with each other towards the attainment of commonly understood and agreed objectives. Teachers need to spend time out of the classroom getting to know parents. Parents need to be brought more and more into the schools so as to realise that they are vitally connected with the whole educational process and not mere touchline figures. Concomitant with such attidudinal and organisational changes, and indeed an inseparable part of the development of the teacher's function and role, is the pressing urgency for an expansion of extracurricular activities and organisations. Most of our Crown Street schools undertook such out-of-school activities involving a sacrifice of time and energy on the part of members of the staff. Boys were much better catered for in this way than girls; men presumably having fewer additional responsibilities than women in out-of-school hours. Extracurricular events ranged from the organisation of holiday camps to participation in civic music festivals. They included the ever popular football and swimming for boys, and, much more rarely, tennis and netball for girls.

The most important additional activity from the viewpoint of linking school and home is the organisation of 'at home' days, special displays in the schools and parent–teacher associations. In spite of the firm support for the latter expressed by representatives of the local education authority, Crown Street schools, at the time of the enquiry, with one notable exception, were either against the idea or claimed to have tried them and abandoned them as failures. Most of the reasons given for the fact that the schools were not running P.T.A.s seemed to be merely excuses and rationalisations of prejudice. Whilst there was unanimous support from teachers for the need for more support from the home and many complaints about the adverse nature of the environment, only four out of ten heads, when asked the question 'Do you feel the need for a closer link and more cooperation with the parents of your pupils?' said 'Yes'. The prevailing attitude towards P.T.A.s seemed to be extremely confused and illogical. One head said that he wanted to form one but simply could not rely on obtaining the necessary backing from his colleagues. It is true, moreover, that, even if the majority of the staff should want an association, it could be forbidden by fiat from the head, and that would be an end to the matter.

So far I have said very little about family life or about the contents of the subculture as it affects the work of the schools in areas such as Crown Street. Dr Klein refers to many of these matters in Chapter 3 of this volume, but if I may summarise a whole series of data, I think it is still true to say that the inhabitants of these older slum areas have comparatively narrow horizons and humble aspirations. The local and the concrete loom large in their eyes: they are fixated on the home and the neighbourhood. The family is still a fairly tightly-knit group of immediate relatives surrounded by an outer fringe of friends and neighbours who seldom cross each other's thresholds. Neighbours tend to borrow from one another. Standoffishness is acutely disliked, and life is social in the narrow sense that people seem to dislike doing things on their own or being conspicuously individualistic in their behaviour. 'They go through life with their arms linked, holding one another up', commented one headteacher somewhat tartly. But, at the same time, the security and solidarity afforded by the group cannot so lightly be dismissed. Young people are especially gregarious and are invariably seen in small groups and clusters about the streets of the city. At an early age they are apprenticed to the neighbourhood peer group, and they come to dislike being cut off from their associates to such an extent that they have little desire to do well in the General Entrance Examination and so be translated into another kind of setting and obliged to mix with unfamiliar faces. In terms of middle-class norms, the early years tend to lack consistent discipline and active training. Routines are neglected and a happy-go-lucky, sometimes a spendthrift, atmosphere prevails. Male and female roles still tend to be sharply segregated on outmoded Victorian lines. Housework and child care are female spheres of interest: the man's duty is to bring home the money, deal out exemplary justice in the last resort, and, in his off-duty hours enjoy himself relaxing at the 'local' or watching football in the company of similarly placed males. Girls are expected to help at home and assist in looking after the infants. Boys are, by contrast, like their dads, much more fancy free. Family life tends to be segmented, even the meals are seldom shared, and there is no tradition for group discussion or long-term planning. This does not mean that there is any lack of emotional warmth of interpersonal regard. It does mean, however, that since most of these families are comparatively large, children are left very much to their own resources, bringing one another up, and extremely vulnerable to influences emanating from the surrounding milieu. Mothers are especially overburdened, and, where the husbands are away from home for long periods or have abandoned the family, they find the load too much to bear. Small wonder, then, that they turn eagerly towards the school and the social services to get what help they can!

In general, then, we may say that the pattern of life in localities such as Crown Street is in many ways the antithesis of the more carefully organised middle-class existence and, in so far as this is true, is simply not geared to secondary education as it has developed in this country during the past fifty or so years. Admittedly, I am painting the extreme in such a picture. There is a proportion of ambitious small families in such areas who are keen to rise socially, and who see education as a way to achieve their ambitions and a higher social status. But such households are the ones which are most willing to move away into the newer neighbourhoods, for the very reason, as they say, that in suburban localities their children will be healthier and get a better education.

What we are seeing at the present time is, I believe, no less than an elaborate exercise in social segregation, unwittingly promoted by rehousing and redevelopment policies, in which the aspirant families are given a degree of opportunity to get on and get out, whilst the residual group of less ambitious, possibly of less able and more inert families remain behind to perpetuate a tradition of underprivilege and inferiority which will, unless I am very much mistaken, prove most difficult and stubborn to eradicate. We are living, in the central city neighbourhoods, in the long twilight of the Two Nations; the divided groups are no longer the rich and the poor of former times, but the culturally deprived and intellectually divided of today and tomorrow. The final impression is somewhat depressing. Inferior physical provision, plus ineffective home background, plus schools with poor academic traditions, plus peer group indifference or even hostility, add up to a total of disadvantage which is a formidable challenge to any kind of social engineering. Small wonder that the teacher at times feels helpless and inclined to give up the fight.

The problems that confront teachers in these downtown schools are multiple and complex in their mode of presentation and deeply grounded in the psycho-social matrix. They are not in fact purely educational problems. They certainly are not the kind of problems that they have been trained to deal with or hope to meet in their professional careers. As we have already said, faced with a seemingly impermeable barrier of public indifference and private apathy, some teachers cut their losses and get away by seeking transfers to schools in neighbourhoods where at least they will feel that the parents understand what they are trying to do and the authorities are supporting them. Give a school or a locality a bad name and it will increasingly be seen to live up to its reputation.

How can we hope to break into so vicious a circle? Are there any general administrative actions which might usefully be taken to improve the situation? Are any changes in the traditional conception of the teacher's role worth making?

Evidence accruing from Dr Douglas's research, from Elizabeth Fraser's and from the investigations in Manchester and Salford described by Dr Wiseman,[10] seems to indicate that, in spite of adversities and manifold disadvantages, neither parents nor teachers are completely helpless in the face of neighbourhood norms unpropitious to educational objectives. The task resolves itself into ways of making school more intelligible to pupils and more attractive to parents. We have got to try to diminish, in the atmosphere of formal education, what Frank Riessman has called 'the hidden dissuaders'.[11] They are potential in every school, and they are to be found much more extensively than we like to admit. A child's years at school have got to be made more and more a meaningful experience for him. The policy of drift which characterises our general attitude to education has got to be halted and something more positive substituted. The Newsom

Committee wrestled for a long time with some of these basic problems. They have made a number of useful suggestions which we do not seem to be eager to put into practice. One of these, the longer school day for boys in their last two years, with a rich provision of cultural and recreative activities introduced into the formal arrangements, has much to commend it for the children of the back streets. But why not start this at a much earlier age? Say at the entrance to the primary school, or, if that seems too early, at the age of ten-plus? Another allied idea is that of the four-term year, with much shorter holidays. Such a policy would help to reduce the end-of-term fatigue in both scholars and staff, and it might be more acceptable to some families and teachers than a longer working day.

In the actual day-to-day organisation of school life it now seems abundantly clear that streaming should be done away with and methods of dividing sheep from goats avoided. Children have different abilities, different interests. Not all are bookish and theoretical, nor should we regard the cultivation of neuroticism, introspectiveness and personal ambition as the be-all and end-all of the academic process. Frank Riessman, Richard Hoggart,[12] and Raymond Williams[13] have all indicated that traditional working-class culture has its assets as well as its weaknesses. Feelings of solidarity are not always to be dismissed as herd-mindedness; the absence of a restless personal aspiration need not always indicate a social misfit or a clamlike mind. In this regard, I would like to join with Dr Wiseman in cautioning against too hasty a rejection of the intelligence test as a useful scholastic device. Far from handicapping pupils from lower-social-class backgrounds, it can in fact operate as an instrument of social justice *as and when such an instrument may be required.* The grammar school and university have us all very much in thrall. Their spell needs to be unbound and other forms of schooling and higher education encouraged. To this end we should welcome the growth of comprehensive schools, the expansion of colleges of advanced technology into technological universities, and the idea of extending degree-giving power to teacher-training colleges. The impudently vicious circle of privilege must be decisively broken and, if it is in the interest of the community as a whole, some educational institutions which at the moment are exalted should be systematically downgraded. Quite honestly, one of the main reasons why many middle-class and lower middle-class parents feel obliged to use private schools is because the state schools are overcrowded, and hence may give an inferior education. Secondary modern schools are often avoided not because they are secondary and modern but simply because, as schools, they are frequently bad.

But let me return to my main theme, which is the problem of primary and secondary schools in downtown neighbourhoods. Many points have been made incidentally during the expansion of my main material. By way of conclusion let me try to summarise what are, I think, the chief points, and to offer a number of constructive suggestions.

THE HOME

It is widely agreed that the quality of family care and parental interest is one of the crucial influences determining what a child makes of his education. Parents in adverse environments need to be helped financially to enable them to keep their children at school as long as it is clearly in their interests so to do. The tie between school and home should be made more stable by the institution of parent–teacher associations, and where necessary, by the appointment of special teacher-*cum*-social welfare workers to the staffs of schools in difficult areas. Fathers should be brought more openly into school life. Male welfare workers might have a valuable basis of appeal for this purpose, as would, to follow on Frank Reissman's recommendation, the greater masculinisation of education as a whole. Both teaching and social work are far too dominated by women at the present time to allow them to make inroads into the local subculture where, you will recall, a fairly sharp division between masculine and feminine roles is traditional.

SCHOOL

Schools should strive to become the new focal points of the local community, offering hospitality to all manner of institutions such as youth service groups, athletic clubs, play centres, evening classes, youth employment and kindred services. The distinctions between formal and informal education need to be broken down. This implies an enrichment of extracurricular activities and closer liaison with the Youth Service. A development of pupil-counselling along tutorial lines, with teachers maintaining a close personal link with groups of pupils throughout their school life, should be experimented with: for this to be effective as few changes of school as possible needs to be aimed for, together with a minimal turnover of staff.

PEER GROUP

A combination of the techniques outlined above should help to neutralise the less desirable aspects of peer group influences. Furthermore, a more comradely spirit between pupils and teachers, and the incorporation into classroom methods of skills so far confined to so-called 'progressive' schools and to the youth service groups would assist in anchoring peer group loyalties to the educational base, and thus making the very forces which sometimes work against the school today their most positive allies.

Clearly, what I am advocating is a fundamental, though I hope not too agonising, reappraisal of the work of schools in difficult areas. The key to the success of such a venture is, as always, the quality of the teaching profession itself. I have said some hard things about the profession during the course of this paper. This is surely a sincere and indirect compliment to them. So much depends on them and on their attitudes of mind that we, as a community, must evaluate their work afresh and give to it the status and regard that it truly deserves and needs. New equipment and buildings will help teachers not only to be more comfortable and to teach better, but they will also help to convince them and the parents and the pupils themselves that we are really in earnest in our often expressed desire to provide an appropriate education for all, irrespective of background or resources, and so furnish all children with a thoroughly sound educational start in life. But, and here I feel I must end on a note of doubt, if not of utter gloom, at the present time there sleeps behind the educational system of this country the deep inertia of uninformed and morally unenlightened public opinion. What values shall finally prevail? Upon the resolution of this question depends not only the future of our schools, but the very quality of the civilisation we hand on to unborn generations of the future.

REFERENCES

1. J. B. Mays, *Education and the Urban Child*, Liverpool University Press, 1962.
2. A. B. Hollingshead, *Elmtown's Youth*, John Wiley, New York, 1949.
3. James S. Coleman, *The Adolescent Society*, The Free Press, Glencoe, 1961.
4. J. W. B. Douglas, *The Home and the School*, MacGibbon & Kee, 1964.
5. See *Education and the Urban Child*, pp. 133–50.
6. Elizabeth Fraser, *Home Environment and the School*, University of London Press, 1959.
7. A. B. Wilson, 'Residential Segregation of Social Classes and Aspiration of High School Boys', *American Sociological Review*, Vol. 24, 1959.
8. D. F. Swift, 'Who Passes the 11-Plus?', *New Society*, 5 March 1964.
9. M. P. Carter, *Home, School and Work*, Pergamon, 1962, p. 86.
10. S. Wiseman, *Education and Environment*, Manchester University Press, 1964.
11. Frank Riessman, *The Culturally Deprived Child*, Harper and Row, New York, 1962.
12. Richard Hoggart, *The Uses of Literacy*, Chatto & Windus, 1957; Penguin Books, 1958.
13. Raymond Williams, *Culture and Society 1780–1950*, Chatto & Windus, 1958; Penguin Books, 1961.

6

*Explorations in Language and Socialisation**

Basil Bernstein and Dorothy Henderson

In this chapter, adapted from an earlier paper, Professor Bernstein and one of his research associates examine the critical importance of language in the socialisation of the pre-school child.

One of the most important movements in behavioural science since the war is the convergence of interest upon the study of basic processes of communication and their regulative functions. The Sociological Research Unit at the University of London is engaged upon an exploratory study of forms of familial socialisation which affect orientations towards the use of language. We shall present here the results of an investigation designed to reveal the relative emphasis which members of social class groups place upon the use of language in different areas of the socialisation of the preschool child.

HYPOTHESES AND METHODS

The following hypotheses (derived from Bernstein 1961 and 1967) were tested:

1. Both middle class and working class would place greater emphasis on the use of language in interpersonal aspects of

* Adapted from 'Social class differences in the relevance of language to socialisation', *Sociology*, Vol. 3, No. 1 (1969), pp. 1–20, by kind permission of the publishers. This version omits the more detailed treatment of methodology, discussion and results to be found in the original.

socialisation than the emphasis placed upon language in the socialisation into basic skills.

2. The shift in emphasis in the use of language from the skill to the person area would be much greater for the middle-class group.
3. Within the skill area the middle-class group would place a greater emphasis upon language in the transmission of principles.

Fifty mothers randomly selected from a working-class area, and fifty from a middle-class area were presented with a schedule of eleven statements which covered the major aspects of socialisation. The statements are listed below in the order in which they were presented on the schedule:

1. Teaching them everyday tasks like dressing, and using a knife and fork.
   (Motor skill)
2. Helping them to make things
   (Constructional skill)
3. Drawing their attention to different shapes
   (Perceptual skill)
4. Playing games with them
   (Dummy)
5. Showing them what is right and wrong
   (Moral principles)
6. Letting them know what you are feeling
   (Mother-oriented affective)
7. Showing them how things work
   (Cognitive)
8. Helping them to work things out for themselves
   (Independent-cognitive)
9. Disciplining them
   (Control)
10. Showing them how pleased you are with their progress
    (Dummy)
11. Dealing with them when they are unhappy
    (Child-oriented affective)

Nos. 1, 2, 3, and 7 are concerned with the transmission of skills and are labelled the 'skill' area of statements; 5, 6, 9, 10, 11 are concerned with aspects of social control and are referred to as the 'person' area of statements; 4 and 10 were deliberately inserted as dummy statements.

The mothers were presented with the schedule and asked the question 'If parents could not speak, how much *more* difficult do you think it would be for them to do the following things with young children who had not yet started school?' Mothers were able to reply on a six point scale: very much more difficult, much more difficult, more difficult, not too difficult, fairly easy, easy.

It will be remembered that the aim of the schedule was to examine the effect of the social class position of the mothers on their perception of the role of language as a socialising process. In order to obtain such information it was necessary to focus the mother's attention upon the relevance of language across a number of different areas. It was thought that mothers would experience great difficulty if they were simply asked to what extent they relied upon language when dealing with their children. We constructed a general situation such that each mother was faced with a problem of comparison. She also had to assess the difficulty of transmitting skills and dealing with interpersonal processes without language. This focused her attention on the relevance of the linguistic component of the interaction. At the same time it was necessary to ensure, as far as possible, that the mother should not feel that the problem was a challenge to her own extraverbal ingenuity with her child, and so the problem was presented with the general referents *parents* and *young children*. It was equally necessary to preclude the possible use of other linguistic alternatives and therefore we stated the problem in terms of young children who had *not yet started school* and were thus unlikely to be able to read written instructions or explanations.

SUMMARY OF RESULTS

Differences in response were shown to be to (*a*) the statements within each area, (*b*) the social class of the mothers, and (*c*) the interaction between social class and individual statements.

Table 1. Summary Table of Mean Scores: skill statements

	1	2	3	7	Total x̄
x̄ Middle class	0·48	0·12	0·04	0·62	0·30
x̄ Working class	0·48	0·28	0·36	0·36	1·50
Sample x̄	0·01	0·20	0·20	0·49	

We find that middle-class mothers consider language less relevant to the situations described by the *skill* statements than do working class mothers. There is one exception. Middle-class mothers considered that 'Showing them how things work', would be *more* difficult to deal with without language than working class mothers.

Table 2. Summary Table of Mean Scores: person statements

	5	6	8	9	11	Total x̄
x̄ Middle class	1·54	1·36	1·56	1·70	1·28	7·44
x̄ Working class	0·74	0·60	1·18	0·94	0·54	4·00
Sample x̄	1·14	0·98	1·37	1·32	0·91	

Conversely, middle-class mothers place greater emphasis on language in response to the *person* statements than do working-class mothers. However, *all* the mothers considered the *person* situations more difficult to cope with than the *skill* situations.

DISCUSSION

The results show that the middle class, relative to the working class, place a greater emphasis on the use of language in dealing with situations within the person area (Table 2). The working class, relative to the middle class, place a greater emphasis on the use of language in the transmission of various skills (Table 1). However, within the skill area the middle class place a greater emphasis upon the use of language in their response to the statement, 'Showing them how things work', whereas within the same area the working class place a greater emphasis upon the use of language in response to the statement, 'Teaching them every day tasks like dressing, and using a knife and fork'.

Can these differences in emphasis be accounted for in terms of differences in the relevance of these two *areas* for the social classes? In other words, does the move to language simply reflect the relevance of the area? Or is it the case that both areas respectively have equal relevance to the social classes but their verbal realisation is different? It is unlikely that the middle class relative to the working class value basic skills less and yet it is this group which places a reduced emphasis on language in the skill area. It would be just as difficult to maintain that socialisation into relationships between persons is not of *equal* relevance to every subcultural group, although the *form* of that socialisation may well vary. On the other hand, the very marked shift by *both* groups towards language in the person area and away from language in the skill area may well reflect the greater importance of control over persons rather than control over the development of skills in the socialisation of the very young child. It is therefore unlikely that the shifts in emphasis placed on the use of language in each of the two areas respectively, by the two social class groups can be explained in terms of the difference in the relevance of the skill area and the person area. It may be that middle-class mothers can conceive of a variety of ways, other than linguistic, for the acquisition of skills, and for this reason place less emphasis on language; whereas working-class mothers can conceive of fewer alternatives to language for the acquisition of skills. This may seem to be a plausible explanation, but we think that it by no means accounts for the differences between the social classes.

We shall argue that the explanation is to be found in the nature of the social relationship when skills and person relationships are transmitted. If it is the case that in the working class knowledge is transmitted through a social relationship in which the receiver is relatively passive and if, in the middle class, knowledge is transmitted through a social relationship in which the receiver is active, then we might expect the distribution of responses which have been revealed. It may be that motor, perceptual and manipulative skills are acquired by the child in the middle class by his exposure to varied and attractive stimuli which the child explores on his *own* terms. In other words, in the acquisition of motor, perceptual and manipulative skills, the child regulates his own learning in a carefully controlled environment. It is of significance that despite the relatively greater emphasis placed on language in the skill area by the working class group, the middle class place greater emphasis upon language in response to the statement, 'Showing them how things work'. It is likely that this statement, for the middle class, raises questions of the transmission of principles, whereas the other three statements within the same area *do not.* If this is the case, then the situation for the middle-class child is particularly fortunate. For, on the one hand, he is socialised into elementary skill learning through role relationships which emphasise autonomy *and* he has access to principles.

In the working class group, the concept of learning may well be different and, therefore, the form the social relationship takes when skills are acquired would be of a different order. The concept of learning here seems to be less one of self-regulated learning in an arranged environment and more a concept of a didactic theory of learning implying a passive receiver, in which a mother has little alternative but to tell or instruct a child. Although the emphasis in the working-class group, relative to the middle class, is on language, presumably on *telling* or instructing, the child is much less likely to receive explanations of principles. Thus it may be that the working-class child learns skills in terms only of an understanding of the operations they entail, whereas the middle-class child learns both the operations and principles.

Other work of the Sociological Research Unit can be referred to here in support of these hypotheses. Two years before the interview in which the present schedule was administered, a sample of 351 middle-class and working-class mothers (of which the sample used in this paper is a sub-sample) were given a questionnaire in which the mothers were invited to give their views on a range of experiences relevant to their child's behaviour in the infant school. We found that when middle-class mothers were asked to rank in order of importance six possible uses of toys, they ranked more highly than did the working-class mothers 'To find out about things' (Bernstein and Young, 1967). Further, middle-class mothers saw the role of the infant school child as an active role, whereas the working-class mothers tended to see this role as a passive one (Jones, 1966). Middle-class mothers, relative to working-class mothers, indicated that 'play' in the infant school had educational significance (Bernstein, 1967).

It would appear then that the difference in the response of middle-class and working-class mothers to the relevance of language in the acquisition of various skills is more likely to arise out of differences in the concept of learning than out of differences between the social classes in terms of the value placed upon the learning of such skills. The socialisation of the middle-class child into the acquisition of skills is into both operations and principles which are learned in a social context which emphasises *autonomy*. In the case of the working-class child, his socialisation into skills emphasises operations rather than principles learned in a social context where the child is accorded *reduced autonomy*.

We will now turn to discuss the differences between the social classes in their emphasis on the use of language in interpersonal contexts. The results are clear. Where the context is interpersonal, the middle class, relative to the working-class, move markedly towards the use of language. Further, the shift in the emphasis on language from the skill area to the person area is very much greater in the middle class than in the working class. Thus, the verbal realisation of affects, moral principles and their application to behaviour, and independence in cognitive functioning, is much more likely to be linguistically elaborated in the middle class than in the working class. This is *not* to say that these aspects of socialisation do not have the same significance in the working class, only that (according to the mothers' responses) language is of less relevance in the form of the socialisation.

Indeed, *both* classes rank the statements (in the person area) in the same order of difficulty.

It is not possible to infer from the mothers' responses what they would actually say to the child, but again we can refer to evidence obtained from the first interview with mothers two years earlier. This evidence strongly suggests that:

1. The middle-class mothers are more likely than working-class mothers to take up the child's attempts to interact verbally with the mother in a range of contexts.
2. The middle-class mothers are less likely to avoid or evade answering difficult questions put to them by their children.

3. The middle-class mothers are less likely to use coercive methods of control.
4. The middle-class mothers are more likely to explain to the child why they want a change in his behaviour (Bernstein and Brandis, 1970).

Thus we have good reasons for believing that not only is there a difference between the social classes in their emphasis on language in contexts of interpersonal control, but there is also a difference in the meanings which are verbally realised. It would seem that the internalising of the principles of the moral order, the relating of this order to the specifics of the child's behaviour, the communication of feeling, is realised far more through language in the middle class than in the working class. The social is made explicit in one group, whereas the social is rendered less explicit in the other. Where the social is made explicit through language then that which is internalised can itself become an object (Mead, 1934). Perhaps here we can begin to see that the form of control over persons in the middle class induces a reflexive relation to the social order, whereas in the working class the form of control over persons induces a relatively less reflexive relation.

The question of the relatively greater emphasis on the use of language in the interpersonal area raises fundamental questions about the nature of middle-class forms of socialisation which would take us beyond the confines of an empirical research report. In Bernstein (1966 and particularly 1968) there is an extensive discussion of the social antecedents of forms of language use and socialisation. The view taken in these and other papers is that linguistic codes are realisations of social structure, and both shape the contents of social roles and the process by which they are learned. In short, it has been suggested that the use of elaborated codes renders the implicit explicit, whereas the use of restricted codes reduces the possibility of such explicitness. Thus the codes and their variants regulate the cultural meanings which are rendered both explicit and individuated through the use of language. Whilst there is no evidence in this paper that middle-class mothers use forms of an elaborated code and working-class mothers use forms of a restricted code, Robinson and Rackstraw's (1967) analysis of the answering behaviour of mothers in the main sample indicates grounds for believing that these coding orientations are likely to be found. Further, the works of Bernstein and Brandis (1968) and Cook (1968) show that the forms of control used by the middle class and the working class are consonant with the predictions derived from the socio-linguistic theory. We will have further evidence when Miss Cook's analysis of the speech of the mothers is completed.

We have suggested that in the middle class skills are acquired in such a way that the child has access both to operations and principles. He tends to regulate his own learning in an arranged environment which encourages autonomy in skill acquisition. For this reason the middle-class mothers place less emphasis on the use of language in the statements within the skill area. In the case of the working-class child, we have argued that he is socialised more into the acquisition of operations than into principles through a social relationship which encourages passivity in the learner and so reduces autonomy in skill acquisition. Thus the working-class mothers, relative to middle-class mothers, place greater emphasis on the use of language when responding to the statements in the skill area. In the case of control over persons, we have suggested that the forms of such control in the middle class arise out of a social structure which is realised through the use of elaborated codes, whereas the forms of control in the sub-group of the working class under examination arise out of a social structure which is realised through forms of a restricted code. As a result, the form of control in the middle class induces a reflexive relation upon the part of the child towards the social order, whereas in the working class the forms of control induce a much less reflexive relation to the social order.

We should point out that a developed reflexive relation to the social order does not necessarily imply role distancing behaviour. In the same way, reduced reflexiveness to a particularistic social order does not necessarily imply that role distancing behaviour will *not* occur in relation to members of a society holding universalistic status.

We can now develop our discussion in regard to possible discontinuities between implicit theories of learning in the home and explicit theories of learning in the school. It is suggested that there may be, for the working-class child in the primary school, two sources of discontinuity: one in the area of skill acquisition and the other in the area of interpersonal relations. If, for example, the school emphasises autonomy in the acquisition of skills but the implicit concept of learning in the home is didactic in relation to skills, this will be a major source of discontinuity. Similarly, if the school is concerned with the development of reflexive relations in the area of interpersonal relations but the implicit concept of social learning in the home operates to reduce reflexiveness in this area, then this will be another source of discontinuity. It may be unreasonable to expect children exposed to such discontinuities to respond initially to forms of control which presuppose a culture and socialisation very different from their own.

Earlier in this discussion we referred to the fortunate situation of the middle-class child in terms of the results of our analysis. His role relationships emphasise autonomy in the acquisition of skills and reflexiveness in the area of interpersonal relations. He is accorded discretion to *achieve* his social role. On the other hand, the role relationships of the working-class child, in terms of our analysis, reduce his autonomy in the skill area and reduce reflexiveness in the interpersonal area. He has much less discretion—his social role is *assigned*.

In this paper we have shown that maternal definitions of the role of language as a socialising process are dependent on the area of orientation, and that this differential emphasis on the use of language is related to different forms of social relationship within the social structure. Further, we have argued that the differential emphasis on the use of language in relation to certain areas of orientation may reflect different implicit theories of learning which affect the self-concept of the child. We have suggested that these different implicit theories of learning in the home may conflict with the theories of learning in the school, and in this way give rise to major sources of discontinuity between the home and the school.

CONCLUSION

We must emphasise that our data consists of mothers' reports and not of their actual behaviour, and that these reports have been obtained through the use of a closed schedule. The analysis of the degree and type of discrimination on the part of the middle-class and working-class mothers gives us reasonable grounds for believing that the scaling procedures and the statements were appropriate. We also believe that the situation constructed was such that the 'right' or conventional response was not obvious to the mothers. We have shown that both groups ranked the statements in the person area according to the same gradient of difficulty. However, we cannot present at the moment an analysis of possible differences between the social classes in their interpretation of the statements. We may be able to throw some light on social class differences in the interpretation of the statements when the responses of the mothers to the closed schedule is related to their responses to the other schedules within the language section of the second questionnaire *and* to the results of the analysis of the initial questionnaire.

The findings presented here indicate very clear differences between the social class groups in their relative emphasis on language. We hope to be able to utilise the model offered in the conclusion of the discussion to show, when the total sample is analysed, *intra-class* differences in the orientation to the use of language in these two areas of socialisation. Perhaps the most important conclusion of this paper is to stress the need for small-scale naturalistic and experimental studies of the channels, codes and contexts which control the process of socialisation.

In conclusion, it is the case that the three hypotheses given in the introduction have been confirmed. The findings have also revealed that working-class mothers relative to middle-class mothers place a greater emphasis upon language in the acquisition of basic skills. The inferential structure developed in the discussion makes explicit the relationships between macro aspects of social structure and micro aspects of socialisation.

NOTES

1. The work reported in this paper was supported by grants from the Department of Education and Science and the Ford Foundation to whom, gratefully, acknowledgement is made. Thanks are

also given to the Local Education Authorities for their close help and cooperation in the research.

2. The schedule was designed by Marian Bernstein and Basil Bernstein.

3. We are not here elaborating on the more complex issues of subcultural differences in the interpretation of statements within closed schedules.

4. On implicit theories of learning, see J. Klein, *Samples from English Cultures*, Vol. ii, Routledge & Kegan Paul, 1965; G. Trasler, ed., *The Formative Years*, B.B.C. Publication, 1968; R. D. Hess and V. C. Shipman, 'Early Experience and the Socialisation of Cognitive Modes in Children', *Child Development*, 1965, 36, no. 4, pp. 869–86.

5. We are very grateful to Mr Michael Young, Lecturer in the Sociology of Education, University of London, Institute of Education, for his comments on this formulation.

REFERENCES

BERNSTEIN, B. 1961. 'A socio-linguistic approach to social learning', *Social Science Survey*, ed. Julius Gould, Penguin.

— 1967. 'Play and the infant school', *Where*, Supplement ii, Toys, Christmas, 1967.

— 1968. 'A socio-linguistic approach to socialisation', *Directions in Socio-linguistics*, ed. J. Gumperz and D. Hymes, Holt, Rinehart & Winston, (1968); also in *Human Context*, Vol. 1, Dec. 1968 (in press).

BERNSTEIN, B. and BRANDIS, W. 1970. 'Social class differences in communication and control', in *Social Class, Language and Communication* by W. Brandis and D. Henderson (University of London Institute of Education, Sociological Research Unit Monograph Series directed by Basil Bernstein), Routledge & Kegan Paul, (1970).

BERNSTEIN, B. and YOUNG, D. 1967. 'Social class differences in conceptions of the uses of toys', *Sociology*, Vol. 1, no. 2, May 1967.

CICOUREL, V. 1964. *Method and Measurement in Sociology*. Free Press of Glencoe.

COOK, J. 1968. *Familial Processes of Communication and Control.* To be published in the Sociological Research Unit Monograph Series (see above) in preparation.

FISHMAN, J. 1966. *Language Loyalty in the United States*. Mouton & Co.

GARFINKLE, H. 1967. *Studies in Ethnomethodology*. Prentice Hall.

GRIMSHAW, A. D. 1968. 'Socio-linguistics', in *Handbook of Communication,* ed. W. Schramm and others. Rand McNally, (1968).

HYMES, D. 1967. 'On Communicative Competence'. This paper is revised from the one presented at the *Research Planning Conference on Language Development Among Disadvantaged Children,* held under the sponsorship of the Department of Educational Psychology and Guidance, Ferkauf Graduate School, Yeshive University, 1966. It is available from Department of Social Anthropology, University of Pennsylvania, Philadelphia.

JONES, J. 1966. 'Social class and the under-fives', *New Society*, Dec. 1966.

LOEVINGER, J. 1959. 'Patterns of parenthood as theories of learning', *J. Social and Abnormal Psychol.,* pp. 148–50.

MEAD, G. H. 1934. *Mind, Self and Society*. University of Chicago Press.

ROBINSON, W. P. and RACKSTRAW, S. J. 1967. 'Variations in mothers' answers to children's questions, as a function of social class, verbal intelligence test scores and sex', *Sociology*, Vol. 1, no. 3.

WINER, B. J. 1962. *Statistical Principles in Experimental Design*, chs. 4 and 8. McGraw-Hill.

7
*Education and Environment**

Stephen Wiseman

This paper, edited from Dr Wiseman's 'Education and Environment', examines the effects of progressive school organisation and teaching methods and relates them to pupils', parents', and teachers' attitudes. Its focus on the school serves to complement earlier papers with their emphasis on social structure.

EDUCATIONAL GUIDANCE

The study of individual schools in our two surveys brought out not only the large inter-school differences, but also the amount of overlap between selective and non-selective schools. The overlap revealed by a comparison of percentages of 'brightness' is the most interesting, and the most significant. Our results support those of Pidgeon (1960) who found 4 per cent of pupils of fourteen-plus in non-selective schools scoring above the grammar school mean. It must be remembered, however, that these results, and ours, are derived from scores from single tests, whilst selection for grammar and central schools is made on a broader basis. We select, at eleven-plus, the 'all-rounder'; those who are highest on aggregate marks in intelligence, English, and arithmetic. Pupils who are outstanding in only one of these directions, and merely mediocre in the others, are less likely to be selected. Wolfle (1961) points out that the inclusion of such pupils would approximately double the number selected. This makes such results as ours inevitable. Thus, using the arbitrary level of a standard score of 115 as the

* Extracted from *Education and Environment*, Manchester University Press, 1964 (ch. 8), by kind permission of the publishers.

lower boundary of 'brightness', we find that about one-quarter of the brightest children—in each of our tests—are to be found in non-selective schools. The growth of G.C.E. and other advanced courses in secondary modern schools is seen to be a development based on sound logistics, and not merely a trend following educational fashion.

The organisation of such courses may not always be as efficient as it might be. The tendency in some large modern schools—and comprehensive schools—to identify whole forms for G.C.E. work is a mistaken one. With an adequate system of testing and guidance, pupils may be allocated to 'sets' in individual subjects: this will give opportunities to those whose interests and talents lie in one or two fields only, instead of restricting such opportunities to the all-rounders. Indeed, the whole picture of our research results underlines the need for an adequate system of educational guidance in the secondary school. By this is meant an organisation, staffed by teachers trained in educational psychology, charged with the task of measuring and recording not only pupils abilities and aptitudes, their scholastic strengths and weaknesses, but also their environmental assets and handicaps, their interests and ambitions, their outstanding traits of personality and temperament, and their general development through the early years of adolescence.

I do not believe that the American system of 'counselling' is fully importable to our culture, but much can be learned from their experience in this field. An appropriate British system would avoid their tendency to excessive emphasis on 'depth psychology' and the controversy over 'directive' and 'non-directive' counselling, and would give more weight to the identification of talent and aptitudes, and the tailoring of courses to particular patterns and profiles of abilities, leading to a soundly-based system of vocational guidance at the end of the secondary school course.

The chances of such a development on any significant scale appear pretty small. It is far from being a new or novel idea; writers such as Burt, Hamley, and Oliver in the 1920s and 1930s were making the same suggestion. Movement in this direction was slow, but nevertheless fairly steady, up to the outbreak of the last war. Since then the climate appears to have changed for the worse. The social–political controversy over secondary school organisation, tripartite versus comprehensive, with eleven-plus selection as the chief focus of attack, has led to a suspicion of educational psychology and educational measurement among many teachers and administrators. Many of the enthusiastic supporters of comprehensive schools—and some of the staffs of such schools—reject completely the objective tests of attainment and aptitude which, in my view, are essential tools in the efficient organisation of these schools. There is a belief that the judgment of the teacher is always more reliable, more valid (and more humane) than the result of any test. This belief is one which is partially correct, and so is all the more difficult to counter; yet the results of research after research demonstrate the fallibility of many such judgments, when made without the help and guidance of efficient and tested measuring instruments. No doubt some day the pendulum will begin its slow swing back. Meanwhile how many of our pupils will suffer from lack of a liberal and informed system of educational and vocational guidance?

SCHOOL FACTORS: PROGRESSIVENESS

Some of the most interesting results to be found in Dr Warburton's chapter 'Attainment and the School Environment' in the symposium *Education and Environment* are those for progressiveness, showing that the schools adopting progressive methods have fewer backward children and more bright children. This effect is more strongly marked with reading than with arithmetic. This is a useful piece of factual evidence in a field of educational controversy where opinion is more often mediated by attitude and prejudice than by the results of actual investigation. 'Progressiveness' in school organisation and teaching methods is usually contrasted with 'formal' or traditional education. By and large, 'progressive' methods of organisation and teaching are now accepted as normal and desirable in the infant schools of England and Wales. The controversy arises over the question whether such methods are 'right' for children in junior and secondary schools. Antagonists see activity methods as dangerous to standards (and values). 'Letting children do what they like' will inevitably lead to the avoidance of difficult tasks and difficult subjects: literacy and numeracy are bound to fall. But in those primary schools which adopted this approach no catastrophic decline in standards was observed, and the outstanding improvement in the energies and enthusiasms of the children, and their attitude towards school and learning, was clearly demonstrable. There are many teachers in junior schools, and a smaller number in secondary schools, who believe that progressive methods are generally superior—in every way—to more formal methods of education. The number of junior schools organised entirely on these lines is not large, but is growing slowly.

Methods which have proved successful in infant schools with children of five and six cannot be transferred unchanged to junior and secondary schools. Much harm has been done to sound progress by the uncritical and thoughtless adoption of 'progressive methods' by teachers with little grasp of the basic philosophy behind them, or of the essential aims of such methods, motivated merely by the desire to climb on the bandwagon of fashion. Techniques in the secondary school still remain somewhat tentative and experimental, but much can be done by those teachers whose educational philosophy leads them to value the 'child-centred' school, with an active approach to learning as the main ingredient.

The schools in Dr Warburton's survey were graded on a scale 'ranging from the extremely formal, rigid, and orthodox to the most informed, free, and progressive, with a curriculum organised through activities related to the interest of the children'. The fact that such a rating was shown, unequivocally, to be associated with the results of the attainment tests, and particularly with ability in reading comprehension, is one of the most significant findings of all those reported in this book. It may give heart to the progressives in the teaching profession, and remove many of the doubts of those who see the advantage of such methods but fear some of the 'side effects'.

In view of the results of other environmental research, the result for progressiveness should occasion no surprise. The importance of the attitude of parents to education comes out strongly in research. Success in the secondary school depends more on the attitude and motivation of the pupils than on any other school factor, and this is the strength of progressive methods. By linking method and curriculum to the interests of the pupils, and by encouraging active exploration and participation rather than the passive acceptance of formalised instruction, the school becomes a more attractive place. If we can stimulate and feed interests, and provide activities and materials for the felt needs of the children, we are more likely to achieve cooperation and response, and produce an attitude towards school which may defeat the unfavourable attitude of many of the parents. A more formal and rigid approach, on the other hand, too often breeds apathy and lethargy among the captive pupils, progressing to active hostility in the upper school and an intensification of the dichotomy, 'us' and 'them'.

There is no doubt that progressive methods make more demands on teachers than do formal methods; demands not only of time and energy, but also of flexibility, adaptability, and intelligence. For the very weak teachers such methods may be beyond their capacity, and they are perhaps safer with the formal methods which they understand and to which they have been conditioned in their own education. It follows that they are better employed in the 'good' schools in the outer suburbs, where problems of attitude and motivation are less severe. This is also desirable in their own interests: the plight of a weak teacher in a 'tough' school is indeed unenviable—and an unruly and rebellious class may form a focus of unrest that infects the rest of the school.

ATTITUDES TO SCHOOL: PUNISHMENT

It will be clear that this question of progressiveness, linked with the attitude of pupils towards education, is only one facet of a larger problem. The attitude of pupils to a school is largely dependent upon the attitudes of the teachers towards the pupils: the two are inseparable. The effectiveness of what are called 'progressive' methods is produced not so much by the methods themselves but by the philosophy underlying them. One of the clearest indications of the attitude of teachers towards pupils lies in the kind of sanctions and punishments employed in a school. Britain is one of the few remaining countries in Western Europe to retain corporal punishment in schools and, although its use has diminished very greatly over the last few decades, it still remains firmly entrenched as a 'right' and a 'necessity'. The arguments in its favour most often stem from teachers in 'difficult' schools in bad areas. Its connection with environmental factors is so often underlined that we must consider them in this context. It is claimed that corporal punishment must be retained as a final and ultimate sanction, particularly in schools drawing their pupils from areas of poverty, crime, and social disorganisation. It is implied that without it control would become impossible, and that the behaviour of children, both in and out of school, would become worse. What evidence is there for the truth or falsity of such claims?

Our arguments in favour of progressive methods are also arguments against the use of corporal punishment, since this is completely contrary to the view of the teacher–pupil relationship which is central to the underlying philosophy of the 'progressives'. Our evidence so far, then, lies against caning, but it is not direct evidence, and can carry little weight for the convinced believer in this ultimate sanction. Direct evidence is difficult to come by, and most researchers in this field have contented themselves with surveying teacher opinion. A recent enquiry, however, by the West Riding Education Committee (1961) produces some interesting data of a more direct kind. An investigation amongst the secondary schools of the West Riding showed a positive association between corporal punishment and juvenile delinquency. Since this might well be caused by the concentration of 'caning' schools in the poorer areas—where, it is claimed, corporal punishment is necessary—data were obtained on the average rateable value of the district, and on the percentage of homes having an occupancy rate of more than two per room. This showed little connection with either delinquency or corporal punishment and gave no support to the theory that their correlation was a statistical artifact caused by an association with the third variable of quality of neighbourhood. This suggests that, far from caning reducing delinquency, it might well be increasing it. The psychologists and the sociologists would undoubtedly agree that such a result is not only possible, but even likely, the use of corporal punishment leading to an early establishment of the 'us' and 'them' attitude, and the development of hostility to authority in all forms. Taken in conjunction with other evidence, and with our results from the Salford analysis, the balance of judgment lies heavily against corporal punishment as a device for improving behaviour, raising moral standards, and improving children's attitude to authority.

ATTITUDES TO SCHOOL: ATTENDANCE

One of the important variables when considering children's attitudes to school is that of attendance. The view that attainment depends upon attendance is undoubtedly true in the primary school, but in the secondary school it is arguable that attendance depends upon attainment. Few would disagree with the hypothesis that children well motivated towards school will attend more regularly than those less well motivated. Fewer still would disagree if one goes on to suppose that successful pupils (i.e. achieving pupils) are more highly motivated towards school than less successful pupils. *Ergo,* high achievers attend more regularly than low achievers. Now lack of achievement in reading is more pervasive, and involves a much broader band of the school curiculum than does lack of achievement in arithmetic. Poor reading ability is therefore likely to have a more profound effect on attitude to school—and therefore on attendance—than is poor arithmetic ability.

Recently some new evidence has come to hand which tends to support this general argument. The West Riding Education Committee (1962) has recently produced a report on attendance. This shows that in twenty-seven streamed secondary modern schools, attendance figures 'followed the pattern of streaming', with the A streams showing the highest attendance, and the differential tending to increase as the forms progress up the school. A significant finding was 'that where a particular form contradicted the pattern the headmaster often emphasised the exceptional qualities of the form teacher'. A second survey included grammar and comprehensive schools: 'In the mixed grammar schools the attendance percentage differed only slightly between the streams. In the comprehensive schools the higher streams on the whole attended better than the lower, though the difference was not marked.'

Now these effects could well be ascribed to streaming. There are many opponents of this type of organisation who would argue that such a result is not so much a concomitant of intelligence and ability, but of the rigid sociological groupings imposed and the behaviour 'expected' by the teachers. But the West Riding answered this argument by investigating an unstreamed secondary modern school. No significant pattern of attendance differences was found between forms—the expected result—but when children were arranged in 'imaginary streams the "high stream, high attendance" pattern clearly emerged. . . . Bright children attended better than dull children, whether streamed or not.' There seems little doubt that poor achievement produces poor attendance, which in turn produces poorer achievement and yet poorer attendance. The effect is cumulative.

TEACHERS' ATTITUDES

The argument developed here is that factors of attitude and motivation are more important—in the secondary school particularly—than the more obvious physical factors such as quality of building, size of class, etc., and more important than even the quality of teaching, if this is used in the narrow sense of teaching technique and instructional method. The Salford investigation supports the few other researches dealing with class size in finding this factor of little significance. This is a curious result, and one at variance with the strongly-held beliefs of both parents and teachers. It seems that this factor is important only with respect to its interaction with school organisation. If the school age-group lies between thirty and forty, or some multiple of this figure, attainment tends to be higher. With schools falling outside this range, the shifts and groupings of children made necessary by the awkwardness of its entry-size in relation to the capacity of its classrooms and the numbers of teachers permitted, seem to have an adverse effect on attainment not compensated for by the reduction in absolute size of some of its classes.

The motivation of pupils and the attitude of teachers are more important, and are likely always to be more important, than the quality of accommodation or size of class. Technique is only important inasmuch as it is allied to motivation and attitude. But as well as attitude of pupil and attitude of teacher, we have a third factor: attitude of parent. The interactions of these attitudes, of child, parent, and teacher, may be the greatest single force affecting the end-result of education for a particular child. It may even be agreed that all other environmental factors—school and neighbourhood—only affect educational attainment through their mediation of these attitudes. This is stating, in different terms, the theories of the social anthropologists in identifying cultures and sub-cultures within the urban environment. The sociologists, too, recognise the importance of these interactions. Floud (1962) writes:

> The child may come to school ill-equipped for, and hostile to, learning under any educational regime; but for the most part his educability depends *as much* on the assumptions, values and aims personified in the teacher and embodied in the school organization into which he is supposed to assimilate himself, *as on those* he brings with him from his home. (p. 533)

The phrases which I have italicised indicate a judgment of degree of influence which may perhaps be valid for some children in some schools, but is unsupported by direct evidence. Nevertheless the stress on both sets of values, and the importance of the conflict—when there is a conflict—to the educability of the child, is not exaggerated. When we come to analyse more closely the conflicting attitudes, the possible underlying mechanisms, and the ways in which the attitudes might be expressed, differences of interpretation may be more radical. Floud's 'assumptions, value, and aims' may be interpreted in psychological and educational terms as we have tended to do; or in terms of social class, as Jackson and Marsden (1962) have done. The thesis of the latter book is, simply, that schools are run by, and organised by, teachers; that teachers are middle class, with middle-class values; therefore schools and the system tend to discriminate against working-class children and working-class parents. There is no doubt that many teachers are ignorant of the accepted mores of the neighbourhoods from which many of their pupils come; that many teachers are, consciously or unconsciously, uncompromisingly hostile to these more alien 'cultures'; and that either attitude handicaps them in their work as educators (as distinct from instructors).

But such attitudes are much less important in the educative process than those other attitudes we have already described: attitudes towards children as individuals, towards education as an active partnership between teacher and pupil, towards learning as progressive activity involving the child's interests, skills, and aptitudes. The distinction being drawn is, of course, an artificial one in one sense: both sets of attitudes are closely connected and stem from a common social and educational philosophy, whether liberal or reactionary. But the distinction is a real one in terms of operational validity. The 'social class' view of attitude is on a more superficial level than the other, and is less fruitful in its suggestions for therapy and progress. Those of us with experience in teacher-training find little correlation between socio-political attitudes or social class on the one hand and progressive educational methods on the other. What seems far more important is the personality of the teacher, and his ability to initiate warm and friendly relations with other people. A 'liberal' philosophy, in the widest sense, is what matters most, together with a significant degree of 'tender-mindedness'. Eysenck's two dimensions of personality are far more applicable to this problem of teacher attitude than the middle-class/working-class dichotomy.

PARENTAL ATTITUDES

Let us turn now to the attitudes of parents: more important, because of their primacy, than those of either children or teachers. If the parents believe in education, if they support the school in its efforts, if their aim is broadly similar to that of the teachers, then the child already has an enormous advantage over other pupils who come from less conforming homes. To use the expressive French phrase, *la famille éducogène* is one which every teacher would like to see multiplied. One of the sources of unquenchable optimism of the teaching profession is the belief that, no matter how few there seem to be now, one of the major functions of the teacher is to produce more and more in succeeding generations. I would go so far as to claim that such a measure might well form a single criterion of progress and development for any national system of education.

At the other end of the spectrum from *la famille éducogène* is the family not only indifferent to education, but actively hostile to it. Although our own research has been on an area basis and has not concerned itself with individual families, who can doubt that, behind the statistics of the 'black' areas of the conurbation lie very many families of this kind. Many sociological enquiries and case studies have shown the existence of 'problem' families which, among all their other characteristics of crime and delinquency, of social rebellion and contempt for the law, show equal contempt for the schools and all they stand for. These 'active' problem families may be distinguished from the (larger) groups of 'passive' nonconformists. Here the root of the problem is more often sheer inability to cope, often because of low intelligence and an almost complete lack of organising ability. Education is not valued because nothing is valued, but active hostility is absent. Children from such families do not present such an intractable problem to the schools as do those in the 'actively hostile' category, but the large numbers of such children in the schools in the worst urban areas make this group perhaps the most difficult of all to cope with successfully.

These families do not exhaust the list of those whose attitudes to school prove serious handicaps to the educability of their children. There is another group whose effects, in some ways, may be more serious—viewed nationally—since their children are those above average in intelligence and attainment. McMahon (1962) indicates the problem:

> In the industrial north of England where I was brought up I know many able working-class people whose reaction to the suggestion that they should use their talent occupationally was 'It's not for the likes of us', stated explicitly or by implication. It seemed that the motivation to remain with the social group of one's kith and kin was stronger in the working class than in any other social class.

We are familiar with the 'Keeping up with the Joneses' in suburbia: here we have a contrary 'Keeping down with the Smiths', to use McMahon's graphic phrase. It may be that a major part of the variance found between particular occupational groups—skilled and semi-skilled workers, shopkeepers, and clerks—

reported by many investigators (e.g. Fraser and Furneaux) is caused by this mechanism.

PEER ATTITUDES

For the adolescents of secondary school age a powerful force shaping their attitudes and value-systems is the prevalent climate of opinion and pattern of action amongst their friends and their contemporaries. Where this group pressure supports the attitudes found in the home it becomes very powerful indeed. Where the two are in conflict, the peer-group value-system frequently becomes dominant. This may be only temporary, but it comes at a vital educational period in the adolescent's life, and by the time he grows through it some of his educational opportunities may be lost irretrievably.

What can be done for the adolescent during the time he is 'at risk' to this peer-group influence? A more rapid development of the youth service is an obvious line of attack, but youth clubs cannot be expected to solve the problem single-handed. Unless such out-of-school provision is linked closely to the schools themselves—a 'psychological' linking by pursuing common aims and methods, and employing enlightened methods based on a full analysis of the mechanisms underlying the 'teenage revolt'—any success reported is likely to be limited to the less than fully committed. The hard core will remain untouched: and in the blackest of our urban areas this hard core may contain the majority of the age groups.

Attitude towards school is closely linked to attitude towards authority in general. Backwardness and delinquency show high correlations in all researches. This is not surprising, since they are products of a common value system. Wilson (1962) uses the term 'delinquescence' to describe the delinquency potential of the worst urban areas, and comments:

> It is feasible that a concentration of inadequate homes would set behaviour-patterns for the children of the neighbourhood, and that the delinquescence of an area consists of home-produced primary delinquency plus a secondary type of delinquency which, so to speak, has been caught by contagion. (p. 25)

It seems highly probable that this is a basic mechanism, linking family attitude and peer culture. It follows that the role of the school (like that of the youth club) in preventing delinquency and the rejection of authority, is to combat the influence of bad parental attitude. This cannot be done in the secondary school by the use of authoritarian methods and excessively rigid and formal organisation. A more acceptable attitude to authority can only be fostered by making authority acceptable. This brings us back to the basic question of the educational philosophy of the teacher and his own attitude towards children and their education. A gradual spread of more liberal and progressive methods offers the best hope of reducing the number of teenage rebels, and of ensuring that those who resist do so only temporarily.

NEIGHBOURHOOD FACTORS

Any ecological investigation such as ours tends to lead to an overall conclusion which is unhelpful and unenlightening: that there is an entity *educational attainment* which is apparently affected by *neighbourhood factors*, *school factors*, and *home factors*. This vague concept of a plastic haggis-like entity being attacked by forces outside it, some pulling it out, and others pushing it in, is one very easily formed, and carries with it the illusion that it somehow explains what is happening. It leads to the asking of sterile questions (e.g. about the relative strength of these outside forces) or the formulation of useless therapeutic recipes (e.g. the strengthening of the skin of the haggis by intensifying 'discipline'). We can only protect ourselves from such a view of the problem by insisting that *educational attainment* is not a single entity, but a short-hand description of the reactions of *individual pupils* to various forms of educational measurement. And the whole of this chapter up to this point has been pressing the general view that the picture is not one of the pupil being surrounded by a multitude of forces, some favourable, some adverse—a picture that inevitably suggests that progress lies in the provision of adequate insulation from these forces—but rather that the pupil himself produces some of the forces and interacts with others. He is, in fact, one active element in a complex *Weltschmerz*. Before any amelioration becomes possible (except accidentally) it is necessary to investigate this complex

Some factors affecting educational attainment

I PUPIL	II PARENT	III TEACHER	IV SCHOOL	V HOME	VI NEIGHBOURHOOD
1. Intelligence	5. Intelligence	9. Intelligence	15. Atmosphere	19. Atmosphere	23. Level of housing
2. Physical health	6. Temperament	10. Temperament	16. Status in the neighbourhood	20. Cleanliness and order	24. Age of building
3. Temperament	7. Educational experience	11. Educational experience	17. Contacts with local industry	21. Type and severity of discipline	25. Economic level
4. Attitude towards school	8. Occupational experience	12. Training	18. Relations with youth clubs	22. Possession of books and papers	26. Occupational level
		13. Attitude towards children			27. Crime rate
		14. Attitude towards education and authority			28. Cultural provisions
					29. Moral climate

and begin to understand the main interactions. It is, essentially, a *multivariate* problem and one which must be attacked by appropriate multivariate methods. Accepting this approach, let us attempt to list some of the factors which might affect the level of educational attainment of a single adolescent.

This can conveniently be done under six headings, three representing the persons most closely concerned (*pupil, parent,* and *teacher*), and three covering the major environmental agencies (*school, home,* and *neighbourhood*). The following table lists twenty-nine possible factors under these six heads. The table is largely speculative—as any such information must be at the present stage of knowledge—and no attempt has been made to suggest degrees of importance. But it will serve to indicate the extent of the field, and, perhaps, to suggest line of enquiry.

What matters, as has been suggested, is the extent of the interactions or covariances between the various factors. Research has already indicated many of these—for example, among the factors listed under 1—but many others still remain to be explored. It is an interesting and instructive exercise to make a 29 by 29 matrix, and to mark known or suspected covariances by placing a cross in the cell at the intersection of a particular row and column. For example, for 4 *(attitude towards school)* we might suggest major interactions with 1, 7, 8, 10, 13, 14, 15, 19, 21, and 27, and smaller, but possibly significant covariance with 2, 3, 5, 9, 12, 17, 26, 28, and 29. Many of these associations have already been demonstrated by research; others are more speculative. Such a matrix, when completed is likely to show a heavy concentration of crosses along the diagonal, since, for example, the column III variables tend to show associations with each other, as do those in II and those in VI. The value of such a speculative exercise lies in the demonstrations which it affords of the gaps in our knowledge of the areas where research is still needed.

REFERENCES

FLOUD, J. 1962. 'The Sociology of Education'. In Welford, Argyle, Glen, and Morris, *Society*, 521–40.

FRASER, E. D. 1955. *Social Factors in School Progress.* Ph.D. thesis, Aberdeen Univ. Library.

FURNEAUX, W. D. 1961. *The Chosen Few: an examination of some aspects of university selection in Britain.* Oxford University Press.

JACKSON, B. and MARSDEN, D. 1962. *Education and the Working Class.* Routledge & Kegan Paul.

MCMAHON, D. 1962. 'The identification and use of talent', *Advancement of Science*, Vol. 19, pp. 322–9.

PIDGEON, D. A. 1960. 'A national survey of the ability and attainment of children at three age levels', *Brit. J. Educ. Psychol.*, Vol. 28, pp. 271–6.

WEST RIDING C.C. EDUCATION COMMITTEE. 1961. *Caning, Behaviour and Delinquency in Secondary Schools.* Report by the Education Officer to the Education Committee.

— 1962, Report on attendance. *The Times Educ. Supp.*, 14 September 1962.

WILSON, H. 1962. *Delinquency and Child Neglect.* Allen & Unwin.

WOLFLE, D. 1961. 'National resources of ability', *Ability and Educational Opportunity*, ed. by A. H. Halsey. O.E.C.D. pp. 49–68.

8
The Headteacher's Point of View

Louis Cohen

Like the previous paper, this too takes the school situation rather than society as its point of departure in its discussion of home–school relations. Dr Cohen discusses elements of his recent research study which are particularly relevant to our theme.

INTRODUCTION

The success or failure of any programme aimed at effecting closer cooperative links between home and school depends not only on the quality of the relationships established between parents and the staff of the school, but more fundamentally on the purposes which bring these two groups of people together. In Chapter 20 Professor Taylor provides a timely reminder that those purposes are not and *cannot* always be in coincidence. Success in joint social activities and fund-raising events, for example, may be followed by shock and disappointment at the hostility which proposed ventures into parent–teacher curriculum planning may generate.

One may seek to understand such successes and failures in school–parent cooperation in a variety of ways. One fruitful approach is through the use of concepts from role theory. Recent empirical studies which have employed role perspectives have shed light upon some specific problems in connection with home–school links (Cohen, 1965; Glossop, 1966; Musgrove and Taylor, 1969).

This paper focuses on one particular member of the school staff, the headteacher, for it is he who occupies a position which more often than others serves as a point of articulation between the home and the school. Although the term *position* is used in the special sense of a 'collectively recognised category of persons' (Biddle and Thomas, 1966), it has not gone unnoticed that the usual 'position' of the headteacher's room, at the entrance to the school, acts both as the boundary separating the school from the outside world (Collins, 1969) and as the location of the school's most frequent contact with representatives of its external environment.

Of particular interest in the paper are the *role conceptions* of headteachers. Role conceptions refer simply to the beliefs that headteachers hold about what they should or should not do as occupants of the headteacher position. Knowledge of their beliefs is important in understanding the form and the scope of the links that may be instituted between home and school. For a variety of reasons (King, 1968) headteachers possess considerable authority in connection with the internal and external affairs of their schools and, as Taylor (1969) shows, in 'making policy—sometimes with only a minimum of consultation with those likely to be affected'. Teachers and parents, two of the most likely positions to be affected by policy decisions, were selected in a recent study (Cohen, 1970) as important sources of *role expectations* for the headteacher. Despite the suggestion by Taylor of a certain arbitrariness in policy-making on the part of some heads, it is more than likely that to a considerable degree, the headteacher's *role performance* (what he actually does as a head), is related both to his particular beliefs (his *role conception*) and to his *awareness* of what significant others expect of him. The importance of such awareness is emphasised by Burnham (1969): 'What counts is not only what teachers . . . parents and others *really* expect of the head, or what they *say* they expect, but what the head *perceives* them to be expecting.'

Surprisingly, we know very little either about headteachers' role performances or about their role conceptions. A previous study (Cohen, 1965) concerned with the teacher's liaison role between home and school, elicited the expectations that some 183 primary and secondary heads held for this aspect of the teacher's work. A number of items in the teacher role inventory were intended to explore expectations for the extension of the teacher's role to include skills and practices called for in the Newsom conception of the *teacher–social worker*. Generally, headteachers showed significantly less support for the suggested liaison activities than either student-teachers or their college of education tutors. Where, for example, 64 per cent of the future teachers gave support to the proposition that the teacher should visit the homes of problem children to discuss their difficulties with their parents, only 18 per cent of headteachers indicated their approval. The substantial differences between the expectations of headteachers and others for a number of aspects of the teacher's role including the latter's liaison function, suggested the need for knowledge of headteachers' role performances and the ways in which they conceived their role. Studies are now in hand (Taylor, 1969) which will throw light on the jobs heads do, the people with whom they are principally involved, and the amount of time they devote to various aspects of their work. In connection with headteachers' role conceptions, the present paper, part of a larger study (Cohen, 1970), provides some insights into the problems that headteachers believe exist at those points of contact between the school's internal and external system which bring teachers and parents together. The way in which headteachers perceive these situations is important to our understanding of the pattern and scope of current as well as future home–school links.

THE HEADTEACHER STUDY

Three hundred and ninety-five headteachers, randomly selected from infant, junior and secondary schools throughout England and Wales were invited to respond to a 78-item role definition inventory on which they were asked to indicate the direction and the intensity of their role conceptions in connection with headteacher behaviour over a wide range of activities with pupils, teachers and parents. *Direction* refers simply to headteachers' beliefs that they *should* or *should not* engage in a particular activity. *Intensity* refers to the strength of feeling that heads attached to those beliefs.

The initial content and form of the role inventory resulted from discussions with headteachers and ex-headteachers directed towards illustrating aspects of their leadership in school affairs (Stodgill and Coons, 1957).

The final form of the inventory arose out of field trials during which the content and wording of items were carefully scrutinised. A test-retest run with some forty-four headteachers not drawn in the national sample resulted in an acceptable level of reliability ($r = 0{\cdot}804$).

In addition to indicating their role conceptions, the sample of heads also completed an identical 78-item inventory on which they recorded what they *perceived* to be the expectations held for a headteacher's role performance by *teachers in general*. Finally, they again responded to the role inventory as they *perceived* the expectations of *parents in general*. From the three parallel forms, it was possible to construct a 'phenomenological' view of the head-teacher role as held by a representative group of headteachers; 343 (86·8 per cent) completed inventories were eventually returned, of which 340 were usable.

Although we are concerned here with the findings which relate to home–school cooperation, it is relevant to that task to refer in some detail to a major perceptual structure which underpinned headteachers' role conceptions in connection with a wide range of their activities. Irrespective of the type or size of the school for which the head was responsible, or its location, or the sex and age of the incumbent, a consistent feature common to all headteachers was their perception that on certain items on the role inventory, there were differences in direction and intensity between the expectations for a headteacher's role performance that were attributed to teachers and those attributed to parents. It was the case, moreover, that on many of those items headteachers' role conceptions were themselves incongruent with the expectations attributed to both teachers and parents, or with the expectations attributed to one or other of them. Henceforth, to avoid cumbersome language, we refer to those items on which differences between role conceptions and attributed expectations were found to occur simply as *incongruent items*.

The initial task of the analysis was to differentiate between those items which were perceived by headteachers to be marked by role-set congruence and those which heads believed to involve them in role-set incongruence.

HEADTEACHERS' CORE BELIEFS

A common feature of the 'congruent' items was that they specified headteacher behaviour which was directed solely towards the *internal system of the school.* They described such aspects of the headteacher's work as his attention to the welfare of pupils, his supervision of their work and progress, his communication of policies and procedures governing the everyday running of the school, and his professional relationships with his teachers.

These items represented the *core beliefs* of headteachers concerning their role; they specified mandatory role behaviour to which heads themselves subscribed, and, so they believed to which teachers and parents attached the greatest priority.

INCONGRUENT ITEMS AND 'POTENTIAL-FOR-CONFLICT'

A common feature of many of the 'incongruent' items was that they specified headteacher behaviour which articulated the internal system of the school with its external environment. In the case of some items, the form of that articulation was explicitly stated; for example, 'invite parental discussion of new practices before their introduction into the school programme'. In other cases, the likelihood of articulation was implied—'support a teacher's disciplinary decision even when he (the head) believes it to be unfair to the pupil'. Certain incongruent items were held to possess *potential-for-conflict* for headteachers. The potential-for-conflict of any item was inferred by reference to quantitative* measures of direction, intensity and consensus by which the item was described 'statistically' and to qualitative concepts (power, sanctions, perceived legitimacy of attributed expectations, collegiality and frequency of interaction) by which the relationships between headteacher, teachers and parents were specified.

A CLASSIFICATION OF HEADTEACHERS' PERCEPTIONS

A classification scheme was developed in order to categorise the various patterns of perceived relationships reported by head-

* The significance of the differences between headteachers' role conceptions and their attributions to teachers and parents was determined by an adaptation of the McNemar test for the significance of change (McNemar, 1955). The 0·01 level of significance was adopted throughout the analysis.

teachers. A number of the categories by which 'incongruent' items were identified are now described. Their designations provide a shorthand for the later discussion of the role of the headteacher in home–school cooperation.

THE HEADTEACHER AS 'MAN-IN-THE-MIDDLE'

Numerous industrial studies have identified the unenviable positions occupied by middle-range executives and shop-foremen who are caught between, and at times torn between, conflicting demands for their role performance originating from higher and lower placed members of their organisations. Commonly they are referred to as 'men-in-the-middle', and man-in-the-middle conflict has been shown to be associated with psychological discomfort, stress, and anxiety (Kahn *et al.*, 1964). We refer to the headteacher as 'man-in-the-middle' not because his position is in any way analogous to that of the industrial executive (in the hierarchical structure of the school the very opposite is true), but rather to identify a common pattern of relationships which heads themselves perceived in respect of a number of the 'incongruent' items. Diagram 1 illustrates two man-in-the-middle patterns identified in the analysis.

Diagram 1. 'Man-in-the-middle' situations

H = headteachers' role conceptions
T = attributed expectations to teachers
P = attributed expectations to parents

P **H** T ——— (+ to −)   T **H** P ——— (+ to −)

(** = differences significant beyond the 0·01 level).

Headteachers used the following five-interval response scale to give their role conceptions and indicate their attributed expectations to teachers and to parents in respect of each of the 78 items.

AM = absolutely must PS = preferably should MMN = may or may not PSN = preferably should not AMN = absolutely must not

AM	PS	MMN	PSN	AMN

\+   −

For purposes of illustration the scale is simplified in Diagrams 1–3.

THE 'COGNITIVE ALLIANCES' OF THE HEADTEACHER

On a number of items, incongruence arose out of the incompatibility of headteachers' role conceptions with the expectations they attributed to only one member of their role-set. For example, whilst heads perceived that teacher expectations were congruent with their role conceptions as heads, they attributed to parents expectations which were incongruent. We refer to such examples as 'cognitive alliances'. In the example quoted above, headteachers were cognitively allied with teachers. Cognitive alliances with teachers and parents were further differentiated by reference to the direction of the expectation attributed to the 'incogruent' member. Diagram 2 distinguishes four patterns of cognitive alliances identified in the data.

Diagram 2. 'Cognitive alliance' situations

H = headteachers' role conceptions
T = attributed expectations to teachers
P = attributed expectations to parents

H/P ** T			T ** H/P	
+	−		+	−
H/T ** P			P ** H/T	
+	−		+	−

THE HEADTEACHER 'OUT-ON-HIS-OWN'

On certain items on the role inventory, the pattern of perceived relationships showed that headteachers believed themselves to be 'out-on-their-own' in so far as their role conceptions expressed greater or lesser support for the item of role behaviour than they believed either teachers or parents thought appropriate. Diagram 3 illustrates two patterns found in the analysis. We refer to them as 'out-on-his-own' situations.

Diagram 3. 'Out-on-his-own' situations

H = headteachers' role conceptions
T = attributed expectations to teachers
P = attributed expectations to parents

H ** T/P		T/P ** H	
+	−	+	−

RESULTS

The classification of headteachers' perceptions.

Those items of headteacher role behaviour which were commonly-perceived by all 340 headteachers to involve them in situations which have been described as 'man-in-the-middle', 'cognitive alliance', and 'out-on-his-own', are shown in Table 1 below.

Table 1. 'Man-in-the-middle' situations

T ** H ** P

+	−

Item 9 Put the welfare of all pupils above that of an individual child.

Item 32 Support the teacher's disciplinary decision even when he believes it to be unfair to the pupil(s).

Item 61 Apply a general school rules policy when particular parents request special consideration for their child.

Item 69 Exclude parents from expressing opinions about the introduction of new courses or the choice of external examinations.

Item 70 When dealing with a 'difficult' parent speak in a voice not to be questioned.

P ** H ** T

+	−

Item 6 Support the child in a pupil–teacher discipline problem where the teacher, in the head's opinion, has acted unfairly.

Item 29 Forbid teachers to use classroom methods that are, in his opinion, too 'outlandish' and impracticable.

Item 53 Implement suggestions made by H.M.I. for the improvement of some aspect of the school curriculum or teaching method.

Item 54 Invite parental discussion of new practices before their introduction into the school programme.

Item 59 In formulating general school policy, carefully consider the wishes of the majority of parents.

Item 62 Encourage the development of joint parent-teacher social activities.

Item 73 Provide meetings when parents' suggestions and requests can be discussed with the head and the staff concerned.

'Cognitive alliance' with teachers

H
T ** P

\+ —

Item 12 Allow a child to confide in him with problems he does not wish to discuss with his parents.

Item 37 Encourage an equal voice in school matters to young and old teachers alike.

Item 72 Seek information from parents about children's homework habits, bedtime, weekend activities, reading habits.

H
P ** T

\+ —

Item 16 Require children's movement about the school to and from classes and to play to be supervised by teachers or by prefects.

Item 50 Reprimand a teacher about his work in front of other members of staff.

Item 65 Schedule a definite period during which parents may discuss problems with the headteacher.

'Cognitive alliance' with parents

H
P ** T

\+ —

Item 40 Require records or forecasts of every teacher's work.

Item 43 Use veto power when a staff decision is contrary to his firmly held convictions.

Item 52 Expect staff to support in-service professional courses relevant to their subject or age range.

T ** H
    P

\+ —

Item 68 Refuse parents admission to the school building without appointment.

Item 76 Publicly express disappointment at the lack of parental cooperation.

'out-on-his-own' situations

H ** T
     P

\+ —

Item 14 Encourage children to form class councils to make rules for their classroom behaviour.

Item 17 Allow children to act on what he considers to be wrong decisions on their part.

Item 22 Require important incidents concerning pupils in out-of-school hours to be brought to his notice.

Item 75 Publicly thank parents for their cooperation.

T ** H
P

\+ —

Item 3 Stress the teaching of the 3Rs as the school's most important task.

DISCUSSION

The data in Table 1 suggest that three broad areas of incompatibility are perceived by headteachers in connection with teachers' and parents' expectations of a head's role performance. The first is referred to as the incompatibility between particularism and universalism.

1. *Particularism—universalism*

Parsons distinguishes between a universalistic ethic stressing the application of uniform principles or rules and a particularistic ethic emphasising the claim to special consideration on the basis of some specific criteria, for example friendship, collegiality, or minority age. Though limited in its utility to research because of its high level of generality (Dubin, 1960), the distinction between particularism and universalism is useful in the present context in highlighting two dilemmas that headteachers believe they face.

Firstly, heads perceive incompatibility arising out of what Professor Taylor describes in Chapter 20 as the 'essentially ascriptive subjective basis of the parent-child relationship' as contrasted with the 'more objective achievement oriented' teacher–pupil relationship.

Secondly, in connection with disciplinary infractions, heads perceive incompatibility between teacher demands for particularistic support, based no doubt upon strong professional considerations, and parent demands that justice should guide the headteacher's behaviour in such matters.

On items 6, 9, 32, and 61, the man-in-the-middle posture adopted by headteachers in respect of their role conceptions may point to a realisation on their part that any role performance will inevitably involve them in some 'costs' (Thibaut and Kelley, 1959). In the light of these considerations, potential for conflict is inferred in connection with all four items.

2. *Boundary maintenance—boundary permeability*

A second area of incompatibility is suggested in the differing expectations that heads perceive in connection with what we shall term *boundary maintenance* as opposed to *boundary permeability*.

As incumbent of the major boundary position between the internal and external systems of the school, the head is uniquely placed to control the degree of outside influence impinging upon school policies and planning. He is able, as no one else, to speak authoritatively about the school's aims and interests to outside groups (Kelsall and Kelsall, 1969) and to play a protective role towards the outside world on behalf of staff and pupils (Westwood, 1966).

Headteachers perceive incompatibilities between teachers' expectations for professional autonomy in connection with the formulation and planning of school policies and parents' expectations for some voice in those specific school issues which are of direct interest and concern to them.

Headteachers indicate that while they do not support the degree of boundary maintenance which they believe teachers wish to see implemented, neither do they accept the degree of boundary permeability which they believe parents expect (Items 54, 68, 69, 73, 76). Their man-in-the-middle position is held to be potentially conflictful for them on two counts.

Firstly, teachers have at their disposal effective sanctions by which to sabotage any structured parent–teacher relationships which may be *imposed* upon them. Professional leadership on the head's part rests upon authority *earned* from his staff (Burnham, 1969); he must convince teachers of the validity of his policies if he is to gain their genuine cooperation. Heads perceive that teachers in general are less convinced of the wisdom of the closer parent–teacher contact that they (the heads) believe should be encouraged.

Secondly, for the headteacher more than for his staff, parents are powerful latent role-definers. They are important sources of legitimation of the head's authority (King, 1968). Heads need accurate knowledge of parental opinion since policies which are instituted in contravention of parents' wishes direct criticism and hostility primarily towards the headteacher rather than towards his staff. To the extent that the head complies with teacher expectations to restrict contact with parents to infrequent, formal, and ritualised occasions he minimises his ability to perceive the expectations of an important reference group whose support legitimises his authority. To the extent that the head too readily acquiesces to parental influence he runs the risk of alienating his teachers.

3. *Professional leadership*

A third area of perceived incompatibility which holds potential for conflict for headteachers is concerned with the innovative aspects of their professional leadership. Lipham's (1964) useful distinction between *school leadership* and *school administration* serves as a reminder that in addition to his responsibilities for maintaining the school as an efficient and effectively functioning organisation, the headteacher has a key role in moving the school towards the achievement of certain educational objectives.

It is specifically in connection with innovation in educational methods that headteachers perceive that they are 'out-on-their-own'. In comparison with what they themselves believe to be appropriate behaviour, heads attribute both to teachers and to parents *more support* for formality in curriculum content and presentation (item 3), *less support* for the fostering of personal responsibility in children (item 14), and *less support* for the creation of opportunities leading to self-discovery on the part of pupils (item 17).

These perceived incompatibilities, it is held, are potentially conflictful for heads. 'Leadership and innovation', as Burnham (1969) reminds us, 'generate costs . . . and give rise to increased tension and conflict within the organisation'.

Home–school cooperation and the headteacher

Whether or not headteachers' perceptions accurately map the *actual* expectations that teachers and parents hold for a head's role performance is a matter that awaits research. The discovery of variations in the goodness-of-fit between headteachers' perceptions and the actual expectations of teachers and parents would pose interesting questions concerning the purposes served by such 'inaccuracies' among role-set members (Biddle *et al.*, 1966).

From a phenomenological point of view, however, headteachers' perceptions of situations and events are important determinants of their subsequent role behaviour. Studies of educational, commercial, and social control agencies (Gross, Mason and McEachern, 1958, Miller and Schull, 1962, Ehrlich, Rinehart and Howell, 1962) have shown that a person's perception of an expectation as legitimate or illegitimate is an important factor in predicting his subsequent behaviour. So too, the individual's perception of the range of sanctions incurred for non-compliance is a powerful predictor of his later performance.

In the present context, headteachers' perceptions of the expectations of teachers and parents in terms of both legitimacy and sanctions, are held to be influential in delimiting the range and the form of the relationships that headteachers may be willing to initiate between home and school. It seems vital therefore in assessing the feasibility of any proposed venture in home–school cooperation to have some knowledge of the perceptions that are brought to the project by the headteacher and the other principal actors involved.

From the data presented here, heads show that they are frequently required to make decisions and to initiate policies in the knowledge of what they perceive to be opposing claims to their friendship and collegiality on the one hand and their parent-surrogate responsibilities on the other.

Heads' own beliefs about the desirability of effecting closer links between home and school and giving greater opportunities to parents to express their opinions in school affairs are circumscribed by what they see as strong misgivings on the part of teachers and perhaps over-zealousness on the part of parents.

In connection with their innovative role as educational leaders headteachers perceive a challenge from both teachers and parents to the approach to the school curriculum that they would like to encourage within their schools.

One firm conclusion of the study is that the development of fuller and closer links between the home and the school will present most headteachers with the strongest challenges to their professional skills as school leaders.

REFERENCES

BIDDLE, B. J. 1968. *Role Conflicts of Teachers in the English Speaking Community*, Paper presented at 40th Congress of the Australian and New Zealand Association for the Advancement of Science, Christchurch, New Zealand, January 1968 (mimeographed).

BIDDLE, B. J. and THOMAS, E. J. 1966. *Role Theory: Concepts and Research*, Wiley.

BIDDLE, B. J., ROSENCRANZ, H. A., TOMICH, E. and TWYMAN, J. P. 1966. 'Shared inaccuracies in the role of the teacher' in Biddle and Thomas (1966).

BURNHAM, P. S. 1969. 'Role theory and educational administration', in *Educational Administration and the Social Sciences*, ed. G. Baron and W. Taylor, Athlone Press, pp. 72–94.

COHEN, L. 1965. 'An Exploratory Study of the Teacher's Role as perceived by Headteachers, Tutors, and Students in a Training College', M.Ed. dissertation, University of Liverpool.

— 1970. 'Conceptions of Headteachers concerning their Role', Ph.D. dissertation, University of Keele.

COLLINS, M. 1969. *Students into Teachers*. Routledge & Kegan Paul, London.

DUBIN, R. 1960. 'Parsons' actor: continuities in social theory', *Amer. Sociol. Rev.*, Vol. 25, pp. 466–73.

EHRLICH, H. J., RINEHART, J. W. and HOWELL, J. C. 1962. 'The study of role conflict: explorations in methodology', *Sociometry*, Vol. 25, pp. 85–97.

GLOSSOP, J. A. 1966. 'A Study of Certain Aspects of Teaching as a Career', M.A. (Soc.) dissertation, University of London.

GROSS, N., MASON, W. S. and MCEACHERN, A. W. 1958. *Explorations in Role Analysis: Studies of the School Superintendency Role*. Wiley.

KAHN, R. L., WOLFE, D. M., QUINN, R. P., SNOEK, J. D., and ROSENTHAL, R. A. 1964. *Organisational Stress: Studies in Role Conflict and Ambiguity*. Wiley.

KELSALL, R. K. and KELSALL, H. M. 1969. *The School Teacher in England and the United States: The Findings of Empirical Research*. Pergamon.

KING, R. A. 1968. 'The headteacher and his authority' in *Headship in the 1970s*, ed. B. Allen. Blackwell.

LIPHAM, J. M. 1964. 'Leadership and Administration' in *Behavioral Science and Educational Administration*, ed. D. E. Griffiths, University of Chicago Press.

MCNEMAR, Q. 1955. *Psychological Statistics*, 2nd edn. Wiley.

MILLER, D. C. and SCHULL, F. A. 1962. 'The prediction of administrative role conflict resolutions', *Admin. Sci. Quart.*, Vol 43, pp. 143–60.

MUSGROVE, F. and TAYLOR, P. H. 1969. *Society and the Teacher's Role*. Routledge & Kegan Paul.

STODGILL, R. M. and COONS, A. E. 1957. *Leader Behaviour: its description and measurement*. Bureau of Business Research Monograph

No. 88: the Ohio State University.

TAYLOR, W. 1969. 'Issues and Problems in Training the School Administrator' in *Educational Administration and the Social Science*, ed. G. Baron and W. Taylor, Athlone Press, pp. 97–123.

THIBAUT, J. W. and KELLEY, H. H. 1959. *The Social Psychology of Groups*. Wiley.

WESTWOOD, L. J. 1966. 'Re-assessing the role of the head', *Educat. for Teaching*, Vol. 71, pp. 65–75.

9
*The Involvement of Parents**
Patrick McGeeney

This paper is taken from the author's descriptive study of parent-teacher relations, as he found them in visiting schools and talking to teachers and parents in several different parts of the country, in 1968.

> Few other social institutions have changed their attitudes and techniques as quickly and as fundamentally as the primary school. Sometimes there has been little short of a revolution, since the parents were at school themselves. They may hear about these changes in a garbled way from other parents or perhaps from the mass media, before they learn about them from the school. The school should explain them so that parents can take an informed interest in what their children are doing. Parents will not understand unless they are told.[1]

Implicit in this statement from the Plowden Report is the assumption that parents need to understand how their children are taught so that help with school work can be given at home. Resistance to this proposal on the part of some teachers may arise from a fear that their professional status will be undermined if it is conceded that outsiders with no specialised training should assist in the teaching process. The argument is that most parents would object strongly if their children were to be taught at school by untrained teachers and that in effect this is what a parent becomes if he tries to educate his child at home. The weakness of this argument is twofold. First, it is not suggested that parents be asked to usurp the teacher's professional responsibility, but to support it. Help

* Extracted from *Parents Are Welcome*, Longman, 1969, by kind permission of the publisher.

with reading, for instance. Ideally in the early stages of primary schooling, each child should have the opportunity of reading aloud to the teacher day by day, but with a class of forty or more this is not always possible. Many parents already listen to their children reading and, given the right advice, could be encouraged in this respect to support the teachers more effectively. Second, it may well be that where parents do encourage reading, writing and number work at home this can have an appreciable effect upon educational achievement. One study of a junior school[2] suggests that few parents managed to avoid getting involved in their children's efforts to learn. Though some managed to help unobtrusively and enjoyably, others failed to appreciate the need for patience and understanding in handling a child's difficulties. Those who have either a conviction or hunch that parental support can make a difference will not easily be persuaded by directions from the school that tuition should be left entirely to the teachers. Would it not be wiser to accept the parents' desire to help by channelling their enthusiasm in the right direction? This would necessitate telling them what *not* to do as well as what they might do in the way of home encouragement.

INNOVATION IN SCHOOLS

The principle that parents should be well-informed about experimental changes in teaching techniques is already well established in many schools where i.t.a. (initial teaching alphabet) has been introduced—perhaps of necessity because of the publicity given to it through the mass media. The i.t.a. Reading Research Unit at the outset issued a booklet[3] explaining the new alphabet. The preamble unequivocally supports the view that parents should be invited to become partners in the experiment. 'Parents like to know how their children are being taught because they want to help the teachers give their children the best opportunity to learn reading and writing.'

The first section explains simply 'Why i.t.a. has been introduced', followed by 'How i.t.a. works'. In this latter section, the principle that parents need to learn in order that they may teach more effectively is further reinforced (in the i.t.a. script).

Some parents may wish to learn i.t.a. so that they can understand how their children are progressing, or they may want to write words for their children to read. May we introduce the alphabet of i.t.a. to you parents who would like to have a try at it?[4]

The exposition of i.t.a. is simple, clear and brief—a model for the kind of written communication required if parents are to be told how their children are being taught. Following the sound educational principle that theory should be reinforced by practice, the booklet ends with a few exercises for parents to try out themselves. The assumption is that parents more readily identify themselves with their children's learning when confronted with similar problems and difficulties.

If the assumption is valid[5] in the case of experimental teaching techniques which constitute an extremely radical departure from traditional teaching methods, why not in the case of less radical changes? 'Look and Say', for instance. Many of the mothers I have interviewed felt puzzled and helpless in their attempts to assist their children to read, because of the differences in approach compared with the method used when they were at school. 'They don't learn them the alphabet which I thought would have been better. They learn them more by looking at pictures. We had to teach the boy the alphabet ourselves.' The attempts on the part of this parent to teach the child capital letters conflicted with the school's policy of using only lower-case script in the early stages. Thus the child was left even more confused than his parents. Similarly with arithmetic where the differences between the old and new methods were so marked that parents would complain, 'I can't make head or tail of the way they do it nowadays, so I say to him, "You work it out your way and I'll do it mine, and see if we get the same answer." We generally do.'

Mistakenly the emphasis was on getting the correct answer as against the school's encouragement of each child to arrive at its own short cuts to the solution of a problem. Schooled in the traditional rote learning, some parents complained at the lack of drilling in the three Rs, particularly spelling, punctuation and tables. When, as sometimes happened, this was reiterated in front of the children, confidence in the teachers may have been undermined.

It is not pretended here that such out-of-date notions can easily be dislodged, but at least among these parents there is a measure of concern for the way their children are being taught. By very definition an interested but uninformed parent is in need of information. The attempt to impart it should be made.

ADVICE TO PARENTS

The head of an infants' school in North London, when questioned about what sort of advice he gave to parents who asked how they might help their children, replied:

'Just talk and listen to your child, as much as possible. This is the most valuable thing you can do. Ask him to read signs at the bus stop and in shops and other places. Get him to count the change when shopping. Ensure that you read to him, particularly at bedtime. Give him immediate access to mud and tin cans to experiment with. Take him on journeys and visits. Introduce him to the local library and help him to find his way about and make a suitable choice. With regard to arithmetic, ask *him* how it is done. See that he gets plenty of sleep and fresh air. Control and discuss television programmes with him.'

Sound advice though this may be, the likelihood is that those with sufficient initiative to ask may be the least in need of it; and some may hesitate to knock on the head's door in case they seem pushing or interfering. The same advice sent to all parents in a letter might ensure that a larger number receive it, with the additional advantage of economising on the head's time.

Too often, however, letters from schools are delivered in a manner intended to convey more of a warning than a welcome.

'The procedure to be adopted when visiting the school is first to see my secretary. She will deal with enquiries of a purely routine nature, and will arrange for you to see me if necessary. On no account should this procedure be by-passed and a teacher approached directly in or out of the classroom.'

Those on the receiving end of this frosty communication from officialdom must be left in doubt as to whether they are bidden to bring their queries to the head or forbidden to do so. In sharp contrast is the following letter of welcome and advice sent to all parents by Miss Margaret Wright, head of the Hunters Bar Infant School, in Sheffield.

Dear Parents,

Very soon your child, with others, will be starting school, and in order that they may settle quickly and happily in the new environment, I hope you will not mind if I make a few suggestions, with most of which I am sure you are already familiar.

Talk often to your child about this new adventure—never threaten with school. Make sure that you tell them how you will miss them while they are away. Tell them the kind of things you will be busy doing in their absence—cooking, making beds, etc. Assure them that you will be missing them and awaiting their return, and that every care will be taken of their toys and things in their absence. It is dismaying if smaller brothers or sisters are allowed to spoil their toys whilst they are away at school.

Don't be alarmed if, during the first few weeks, there is a sudden breakdown, and your child becomes clinging and doesn't want to be left. Just talk in a reassuring manner and make your departure quickly. Tell the child at what time you will return. I can assure you that if the distress was very real and lasting I should get in touch with you. If you have said that you will be waiting at the gate, make sure you are there—a little child can feel that mother will never again appear if this promise is broken.

I shall probably suggest, if it is feasible, that your child comes in the morning only, or for an even shorter time. Some children find a full school day too much at first, and if we work together we can gradually lengthen this period. Not all children need this form of introduction to school life. If children have been used to leaving mother, and have had lots of contact with other children, they will settle much more quickly. I shall write to you suggesting times for a preschool visit—please try to come and stay with your child. Here is a chance for you to share their new experiences.

If children can cope with all their garments (these should be clearly marked) it helps to make the settling in process much more simple. Most children can, of course, cope with their own toilet needs, and can ask in recognisable terms when they need to visit the toilet.

Often parents ask what they can do about children reading and writing before they come to school. Rarely is a child ready to do any formal learning before starting school, but talking with them and having books available is of immense value. I know you will have all read to your children and allowed them to use pencils and crayons. Counting games are fun, and a great help to us when they begin to learn.

Now for a little about our school. I know many of you will be told by your children that 'we played all day'. Let me assure you that this is not really so. At this early stage the things we want them to learn are presented in a play fashion. To a small child play is work, and we know that you will find yourself surprised what a great deal of knowledge your child is absorbing and learning in this way.

We try to give each child the minimum time of eighteen months with his first teacher. We have found constant change of teacher, who at this stage must be the mother's substitute, is very harmful to the child's progress.

I also want to emphasise that I am here at any time to answer your queries. It helps the school and the child to know of any changes at home which may have disturbed them. Never feel that any problem is too small for you to consult us about. It is only by working together and knowing each other well that we can make sure that every child is a happy, confident, secure little individual, growing up to be a valued member of the community.

Yours faithfully,
MARGARET J. WRIGHT
Head Mistress

Not even the most anxiously diffident could fail to respond to such an invitation as this. How should it be followed up? Some of the ways in which a personal interview might be made more effective were outlined in an earlier chapter, where it was suggested that parents need to be shown as well as told how their children are taught. The most economical way to do this is obviously to explain to the parents collectively at an evening meeting. Here again, however, sometimes the criticism of such meetings is that the parents are unable to obtain the information they want. Take this reaction, for instance, reported in an article in the *Guardian:*

> We have to sit on little chairs and endure talks on things we have known for years, that Johnny will read better if he is read to at home, that Home and School is a good thing because it is a good thing . . . Must I put up with another year of lost evenings, of stalking Johnny's teacher during the social hour and losing her in the crowd because she saw me first? Yet I know quite well that when it comes to the night of the first meeting, a child will come to me at 7.20 and say, 'Aren't you going? It's in our room. Miss Smith will be there. You'll see my drawing—third room on the left as you go in. All the other mothers will be there.'[6]

Though one might sympathise with the teacher's unwillingness to be confronted with so forthright and critical a parent as this, there is some substance in the view that parents' evenings can be a waste of time. This may happen even where teachers are convinced of the need to explain teaching methods to parents, as I was able to observe for myself at a number of meetings in one particular school.

GERARD VANE JUNIOR SCHOOL (F)

Three meetings on Reading were held in the Autumn term. The attendance was reasonably good, nearly half the parents turning up on each occasion. The first two meetings, addressed by Mr Roberts and Mrs Germaine, concerned as they were with the parents of children, in the main, of average or above average attainment, were very different in tone and atmosphere from the third (Mrs Laurie's class) which involved parents of backward children, and for this reason will be considered separately.

The room had been made to appear welcoming with a large fire, daffodils on the table at the front, examples of good writing pinned up on the side, and bright lights shining on the walls. Tea had been prepared to give to the parents on arrival. But in spite of this the atmosphere was very sticky. The teachers were nervous and so were the parents, probably because it was difficult for either to know which role to adopt in relation to each other. If the teachers took the easiest course of behaving to the parents as they did to their children, then the parents would be bound to think them superior and standoffish. If they behaved as though they were parents themselves—on terms more or less of equality—they might have felt awkward and so might the parents, who probably did not quite expect to be treated as equals. After their unsuccessful attempts at a compromise of semi-informality over tea, the teachers retreated defensively behind a row of tables to begin the lesson.

Mr Roberts and Mrs Germaine chose a similar approach: a quick run-through of i.t.a. and the principles behind and objections to the phonetic method; an explanation of 'Look and Say', with examples of the way it was applied in their own lessons; twenty minutes for questions; and a few points of advice on what parents might do in the purchase and choice of books, the use of the local library, the value of play in child-learning, and ways of developing writing skills through letters and scrap books. The rest of the time was taken up with further questions and discussion.

Both teachers had prepared their material with care and presented it in logical and orderly sequence. The content was perhaps too compressed for their audience of working-class parents, and the vocabulary and syntax were too complex. The fact that one or two parents referred to the 'Look and See Method' suggests that the basic principle was not really understood by some of them. More detailed examples together with a recapitulation of the various points, with a pause between each for questions, would have been valuable. Not that there was a shortage of questions; but the answers given were too cryptic. For instance:

Parent: Do they sometimes read words without knowing their meaning?
Teacher: Yes, they do.
Parent: Aren't you relying too much on memory with the Look and See Method?
Teacher: A child has no analytic approach at all. It has to rely on memory.

The replies to these and other questions ought to have been illustrated specifically, possibly with the use of apparatus within the classroom. On the whole the teachers talked too much, the parents too little. Some of the questions should have been thrown back for general discussion. At the end, the parents were asked whether they had benefited from the meeting. There was general agreement among them that they had, the majority being in favour of further talks on teaching methods, particularly in arithmetic.

The value of allowing parents to take part in the discussion actively was demonstrated at the third meeting during Mrs Laurie's talk to parents of backward children. These parents were more obviously concerned, even excited. Though the intention was to follow a similar procedure to the two previous meetings, Mrs Laurie had not got very far before she was interrupted. At this point the meeting became alive and remained fairly so because the parents joined in—one in particular—and for the rest of the evening neither Mrs Laurie nor Miss Curtis, the head, were able to talk for very long at a stretch. This time the parents led the discussion and not the teachers, by deciding for themselves the questions to be raised.

Mrs B. When Merle is reading a book to me at home and she misses the capital letters I get so worked up that I make Merle read the whole passage over and over again . . . I pull her hair when she doesn't read right, and say, 'What's that word?'
Mr F. There's one word in those books I don't agree with: it's 'can't'. You never see the word 'can't', do you? It's 'cannot'.

Though Mrs Laurie made more than one brave attempt to go on with her lecture by talking about phonetics, she'd lost control by then and no one paid any attention, except to her answers to *their* questions. It is doubtful anyway whether any of the parents had the slightest idea what phonetics meant. However, at the end of the meeting when Miss Curtis asked 'Has the meeting been useful?' the reply given by the leader of the discussion, Mrs B., was almost cheered by the other parents: 'I thought my Merle was the only one like it. It makes you more at ease to know that there's so many others in the same boat'. Another mother: 'I have never seen my son's teacher before. Now I've had the chance and really seen you tonight I feel better about it.'

Perhaps because the evening was such an extraordinary muddle and the parents talked a great deal, the atmosphere was better and, even if only to the extent that they were allowed to let the teachers know the strength of their feelings, it was more of a success than the earlier ones.

In all three of the meetings the teachers came along with the intention of presenting the parents with blocks of information that were conceived in terms of what the staff thought to be essential and not what the parents might want to know. The necessity for exploration of what the parents already knew about education was apparent from one of the questions asked: 'At what age does a child leave the primary school? They start at five, I know, but from five to when?'

The teachers talked too much, in the first two sessions at any rate. Though outnumbered, they commandeered three-quarters of the discussion. Too often when a parent was groping inarticulately towards the formulation of an idea the teachers would step in before anyone else had a chance to challenge it or develop it. Parents were not allowed to crystallise their own ideas and the general assumption was that the staff's opinions ought to prevail: a oneway traffic of instruction rather than a mutual exploration of a common problem. It was not that the teachers were intent on displaying themselves as experts versus the rest; rather they were used to providing the answers and couldn't get out of the habit. They had no notion how to conduct a discussion among adults. This reluctance to encourage the audience arose partly because the teachers were on the defensive. All four teachers were sitting at one end of the room, and whenever an implicit criticism was made they all rushed in to defend themselves. It is obviously difficult for teachers to take suggestions from parents about how things should be done; they feel that parents must have confidence in them. However, the comments of the parents at the end of the 'Backward Class' meeting suggested that, when parents were allowed to pursue the points they were interested in, regard for the teachers was increased rather than diminished. At these three meetings, what the parents ought to do and ought not to do wasn't clearly defined. The meetings were drawn to an end too hurriedly and haphazardly, before ascertaining the views of the parents. No attempt was made to find out what suggestions the audience might offer.

A further meeting on arithmetic was arranged, which was attended by twenty-five parents. It began with the head's attempt to explain principles: 'Before the mastery of techniques must come understanding of concepts, etc.' It was obviously too disjointed and abstract an exposition, so much so that one father broke in to ask:

'What I want to know is are you teaching long division in this school, and if so how are you teaching it? We carried the three down. How do you do it here?'

This, as in the meeting of parents of backward children, could have opened up the meeting into a lively discussion based on the parents' own questions. But the father was rebuffed, and this set the tone for the whole of the meeting.

Mr Carter, a first year teacher who spoke after the Head, was more successful because he demonstrated the use of colour sticks and referred to sums written in advance on the blackboard; but he also tended to be too abstract, and the parents' questions were not used to the best advantage.

The most successful was Mrs Furze, who based her talk on an explanation of the apparatus. 'Many parents say that Maths nowadays is nothing but play. But children learn when they are not trying to do it.' She then paraded beads on rings, bingo cards, snakes and ladders, shove ha'penny, picking-up sticks to find how many different colours you could collect together, a wheel that clicked over the floor—one click equals one yard—to give the children an idea of distance, and an electric board where the light came on when the correct answers were given to a sum.

'There's a great field here for clever fathers, in making these kinds of educational toys. Try and create the right sort of apparatus at home and you might make some money as well. We should like any father to contribute something to this table.'

In one respect the meeting was more successful than the ones on reading, because there was more demonstration through the use of apparatus. But the same criticisms levelled at the other meetings applied in some measure to this one: the teachers talked too much; the centre of interest started from the teachers' point of view rather than the parents'; too little interchange of opinion; a concentration on too many aspects of the subject; no recapitulation of the points made; and no attempt to ascertain precisely what information the parents had gained from the meeting. Asked whether the meeting had been any good, a general hum of 'Yes's' went around. One father thought there ought to be four meetings like this in the year, and a mother thought there could be one every month. Perhaps the most important and relevant observation was that offered by another father who said: 'You aren't getting the response you should, because this is the first year and this is the first time some of us have been to this school.'

A more fundamental criticism was that in spite of the insistence that pupils were no longer compelled to remain in their desks doing formal exercises, but instead were encouraged to learn through discovery and experience, the approach to the parents was at odds with everything that was expounded. They were seated in rows facing a group of teachers who delivered a formal lesson. The majority, unaccustomed to applying the sustained concentration required in listening to a lecture of this kind, were restless. Some were bored. Very few, if any, were persuaded to become involved imaginatively in the processes of teaching and learning. For all but a minority, interest in theory and principles was marginal—not likely to be understood or appreciated unless demonstrated to be effective in actual performance. When asked what problems they wished to discuss, invariably from time to time some parent would stand up to ask specifically a question related to his own child's difficulties in reading or arithmetic, only to be disappointed on being told that that was not the particular purpose of their being invited. Hence, this sort of comment: 'I agree with having these meetings to explain things . . . but after all, when you go up to the school it's really only your own child you're interested in, isn't it?'

In order to meet the demands of the parents, a more practical approach is needed, in line with modern teaching methods. The rest of the chapter describes some schools which have been more successful in this respect.

DE LUCY PRIMARY SCHOOL

Roughly 11,000 people occupy the council houses on the Abbey Wood Estate, which, in spite of its proximity to London, is a lonely, isolated community, cut off to the north by a higher sewer bank, to the south by the railway, and on the other two sides by flat featureless marshland along the eastern reaches of the Thames. Hardly the sort of place to attract many visitors. What induced me to go was a brief notice in *The Times Educational Supplement* reporting a 'Maths for Parents' evening at the local primary school, De Lucy Juniors. Since then, on more than one occasion, television crews have been along to film the remarkable experiment in parental education tried out by the head, Peter Bensley, and his staff.

The school has a three form entry, unstreamed throughout, and has a national reputation for successful New Mathematics teaching. On the first evening I visited the school, there was to be a second Mathematics Class for parents. Whose idea was it to hold one?

'It was at a P.T.A. committee meeting. We were talking in one of the classrooms, and there was some Dienes apparatus on a table. One of the parents asked what its use was—we had been discussing that evening what sort of thing the P.T.A. might do—so I suggested they might like to come along one evening to discuss the teaching of Maths.'

How was it organised?

'I don't believe in planning a meeting of this kind to the *n*th degree. My conception of a P.T.A. meeting is that we meet to exchange views. The parents know what they want to find out, and my experience is that if the situation is relaxed and friendly the right questions emerge naturally out of group discussion, just as in teaching children and, if a particular issue does not emerge then, it means either it has not occurred to them or that they are not yet ready to deal with it. It is not our place to tell them what to discuss, but to present them with an educational situation which we hope will provoke them into thinking purposefully about the problems of learning.' Beyond that Mr Bensley was not prepared to go in suggesting what might take place that evening.

Around 7.15 the parents began to drift in, and seated themselves in groups of four or five at tables on each of which was a pile of Dienes apparatus. Other than a greeting or welcome here and there, little was said by the teachers present. No introductory address from the head. Having decided where to sit, the parents played with the bricks, asking questions of a teacher whenever they chose to do so. They were, in fact, confronted with the same classroom situation as their children on first being introduced to the Dienes apparatus. Eventually, when the parents' curiosity was aroused sufficiently to ask to be told the purpose of the apparatus —and only then—the head was prepared to explain to them collectively.

For the next ten minutes, Mr Bensley demonstrated the theories of Piaget by filling beakers and saucers with beads or with liquids and, by means of cards of different shapes, showed how difficult it is for children to grasp the concept of equivalent volumes and surface areas. He then presented an imaginary dialogue between a human being and a Martian with one arm and only three fingers, each endeavouring to explain to the other their respective bases for computations. This was intended to show the parents that the choice of a three or ten base was arbitrary. This of course gives only the bare bones of the head's exposition. His teaching technique was brilliant. Whenever a question was asked, it was thrown back in a different form, thus leading the parents to find their own answers.

After this, parents were invited to solve problems of the sort given to their children. For example:

With a 3 base or a 5 base:

1. Make a 'block' with a tunnel right through the middle, just big enough to put a 'long' through.
2. Make a 'block' with two tunnels right through the middle, each big enough to put a 'long' through.

In this way the parents found themselves working—as their children did—in small groups, learning through the experience of handling the apparatus, discussing difficulties together as they arose, and turning to the teacher when they encountered a problem they could not solve. (At one table there were two newly appointed young teachers also learning how to cope with the Dienes apparatus.)

For the last half hour or so, questions were thrown open for collective discussion.

Mrs A. Do the children not think of these bricks more as a toy than something to learn?

With commendable restraint the teachers withheld the pedagogic impulse to answer the question, and instead asked the parents whether they felt they had learned anything. When they said they had—and enjoyably so—there was little need for the staff to amplify the principles of learning through play.

Mrs B. I get the feeling that my daughter seems to be guessing part of the time. I noticed she used to do that in reading.
Head: Is there anything wrong with having a guess?

After much argument, the parents *themselves* concluded that most words are learned, not by consulting a dictionary, but by guessing their meaning in the context of different sentences.

Condensed and simplified thus, this evening's 'lesson' sounds as if the staff had discovered the formula for instant education. This was not so, any more than the lessons given to the children which the evening was intended to illustrate. Inevitably, not everyone was convinced by two hours of demonstration and practice. The parents' resistance, like that of some teachers in other schools, reflected a fear that so radical a departure from traditional methods might 'hold the children back when it comes to proper arithmetic sums'. A few, aware for the first time how different the new methods were, felt less confident of their ability to help their children at home than before they came. For most of them, the experience of being encouraged to air their views freely and openly was a new one. Discussion about how they might help was rambling and inconclusive, until one mother (cautiously tentative in case her proposal might be misconstrued as interference) suggested she might be in a better position to understand her role in relation to the teacher's if she had the chance to see the children at work during the day. The Head, equally tentative but less cautious, put the question to his staff, 'Would you find it a nuisance if parents wandered into your classroom?'

Unbeknown to the parents, this was an invitation to resume an argument which had taken place in the local public house before the meeting began. One eager enthusiast in favour of parental support said he had no reservations whatsoever.

'As far as I am concerned, parents are welcome to come into my classroom. I have no objection to them sitting in and taking part. There are plenty of jobs parents could do that I'd like taken off my hands.'

Another teacher just as strongly disagreed. 'If we assume that parents can teach the children, well then, what does our three years of teacher training amount to if anyone can do our job?'

After a long controversy the evening concluded with an invitation to the effect that, 'Next term the fourth year children will be studying the Norman Conquest. You can come in and see what the children are doing if you wish. We'll leave the classrooms open for you.'

And the following term, week by week at certain times, classrooms were opened to parents, some of whom took an active part in the children's activities under the guidance of the teachers.

Further evening lessons were given in music, English, and art. The last was run by David Bennett, the deputy head. As the parents came in, they had a choice of rooms, where the materials were at hand for art and crafts: lino cutting, paste and paint combing, ink roller finger patterning, polystyrene block printing, and various kinds of drawing and painting equipment. As before, no introductory talk was given. The difference, however, on this occasion was that the children were present, continuing with the craftwork they had been engaged in during the day. Parents were simply asked to join in and to ask questions if they needed to do so.

Some two hours later, when the equipment had been cleared away, the parents seated themselves in a semicircle to discuss the educational purpose of the evening's activities.

David Bennett: I am sure you must have many questions. Fire away.
Parent: About what?
David Bennett: Well, for instance, do you think this kind of thing is a waste of time for your children?
Parent: When I was at school we had to draw what we could see—say, a bowl of fruit. Can you really call this Art?

In the ensuing argument, what convinced most of them that creativity is not synonymous with producing an exact likeness, was the comparison of their own efforts with those of the children displayed on the walls. More difficult for the parents to accept were the implications of the Work List Day, when it was explained that children were offered a choice of reading, mathematics, art or other subjects. They found it hard to believe that, given a genuine choice of activity, some of the children would not resist the temptation to play about idly. On this and many other issues raised, though not entirely convinced of the effectiveness of the new teaching, the parents were at least beginning to question their assumptions about the validity of the older methods. In any case, the teachers themselves were not seeking unqualified approval of what they were setting out to achieve.

This, I think, was the strength of these 'lessons' at De Lucy—their honesty. Indicative of this was the fact that the doubts about whether to open the classrooms were aired in front of the parents; and what took place really did reflect the day-to-day teaching within the school. Further, the 'lesson' at each stage started from what the parents felt they needed to know. The request to hold such meetings came from them; it was their questions which determined the pace and direction of the discussion (they talked as much as, probably more than, the teachers); and the proposal to be further involved also came from them. By focusing attention on learning through doing, the parents could identify themselves with their own children's problems, at the same time being presented with a situation which enabled them to appreciate the principles of modern teaching. Perhaps the most important principle they learned, applicable to them and their children, was that a truth arrived at for oneself carries far more conviction than a truth foisted upon an audience by others. An additional advantage of the practical approach was that it left the parents relaxed. Intensely preoccupied in their fumbling—sometimes hilarious—efforts to solve problems, much of the restraint and formality which attend so many parent–teacher functions disappeared. Of most significance perhaps was the parents' eagerness for further tuition. What more could any teacher require at the end of a lesson?

PARTICIPATION BY PARENTS

The main concern so far has been to examine the problem of communicating to parents how their children are being taught and to illustrate how various schools have attempted to meet the problem. But is there anything the teachers can learn from the parents? How far should the latter be encouraged to involve themselves in the education of their children on the school premises? I put this question, somewhat hesitantly, to all the heads I visited. Only a minority were resistant to the suggestion; some were in the transitional stage of tentatively exploring ways in which parents might help on the premises; and in a few schools they were already being utilised as auxiliary helpers.

At Stillness Junior School in South London, for instance. According to the headmistress, Miss M. H. Stevens, arising out of a project, 'In the Steps of William the Conqueror', which involved the whole of the upper school, she decided to take the children by coach to Pevensey, Hastings and Battle. A letter was sent out to the parents asking whether any of them would like to join the coach party. Those who did (eighteen of them) were brought up to the school beforehand to talk about the project and were shown the work sheets to be given to the children. On arrival at Pevensey, each of the six groups of pupils was left in the charge of a teacher who was able to call upon the parents to help in the exploration of the neighbourhood. The value of this kind of I-Spy expedition to the parents is that it enables them to see the possibility of adopting a similar constructively educational approach towards their own family outings to places of interest; to the teachers, a chance to talk to adults occasionally above the conversational level of Janet and John, and a relief from the strain of shepherding droves of children. As one teacher at another school said, *à propos* of a visit to the Zoo accompanied by parents, 'This is the first time I have been on a school journey without returning utterly exhausted.'

There were not many teachers, however, who were prepared unreservedly to apply the same principle to parental participation within the classroom. Among those who had no qualms whatsoever was Mr F. W. Wakeford, head of the Dame Tipping Primary, a village school in Essex.

'When parents come up to enrol their children, they are told they are welcome to come into the classroom whenever they wish—yes, at *any time*. They are also informed they may have copies of our schemes of work. Even parents of preschool age children may join us in classroom activities.'

His 'open school' policy was prompted by an exchange visit to the United States. Taken aback at first to find so many parents helping in an auxiliary capacity in American schools, he was eventually convinced by the evidence of their informed interest in their children's education. Very few of the Dame Tipping parents have taken advantage of Mr Wakeford's offer: 'I think this is because, when you say they can come into the school whenever they wish, they feel nothing is wrong, and this makes them less likely to press to come into the school.'

The idea of a *community school* was conceived and developed in practice in the interwar years by Henry Morris in the village colleges of Cambridgeshire. His work has inspired a number of teachers to apply his educational theories in urban areas. One of them is Cyril Poster, head of the Lawrence Weston School. The account given below is drawn largely from a report written by him of his educational aims and practice and from conversations during my visit to the school.[7]

LAWRENCE WESTON SCHOOL

Lawrence Weston is a well-planned postwar housing estate in north-west Bristol, hedged in on three sides respectively by National Trust land, a road, and the River Avon. On the fourth side are the docks, the main source of employment locally. The school is a comprehensive of 1,000 pupils, 80–85 per cent of whom live on the estate (no more than fifty are owner occupiers). Their fathers are manual workers, lower level managers or small shop-keepers. This homogeneity of social class is, in the head's opinion, a disadvantage. In a community where there are no professional middle-class members, there is less likely to be a demand for cultural and communal facilities supportive of education. 'What is the point of encouraging a child to read if he has to walk three miles to a library?' The head knew that the initiative would have to come from the school.

He was appointed in 1959 when the present buildings were still at the drawing-board stage. At the time there was no public library on the estate, and little likelihood of there being one for many years. Mr Poster suggested that the proposed school library 'should be resited, enlarged and designed to meet the needs both of school and community', a proposal which was readily accepted by the Chief Education Officer and the City Librarian. One obvious question to be settled first was the usage of the library. It was decided that it should be 'used exclusively by the school during the morning session, but open to the public (as well) during the afternoons and evenings, on Saturdays and during school holidays'.

The library opened in May 1962, with the advantage to the school of a stock of volumes well above that in the average secondary school, firstrate reading and study conditions for the pupils, and the experience and expertise of a qualified librarian and two assistants who can use the resources of the National Library System. How about the calculated risk of opening the school in this way to the public!

> There were some early misgivings that the presence of adults on the school premises would be a distraction to the pupils, or that adults might be disinclined to use a library that required them to mix with large numbers of young people. In practice, from the outset, a strong sense of communal use rapidly developed, and in many cases there is a 'family' approach to the library . . .
>
> . . . But perhaps the greatest gain is in continuity: the library continues to serve the school's pupils at weekends and during the holidays, school leavers continue as members of the library whose routine and facilities they have grown used to over the years; and, most important, many primary pupils already have a sense of community with the school through the library which makes transition at eleven very much easier.

This was the first major step towards a community school, so successful that there is considerable support for a policy of siting a swimming pool—and perhaps eventually a running track—on the school campus.

In the initial phase, like any other school of its kind, the after-school activities were run voluntarily by the staff. Inevitably, because of the isolation of the estate and the lack of social amenities, these activities began to attract outsiders wandering in with nothing to do. They were looking for leadership. Consequently, in order to meet this potentially much greater demand, it was decided to appoint an Activities Organiser, whose responsibilities were envisaged in wider terms than what is generally considered to be the function of a teacher youth leader. First, he was to be a vice-principal of the West Bristol Evening Institute, centred on the school. Second, he was to be responsible for all school activities which took place in the evening sessions. This was to be a managerial function. That is to say, not to lead the various clubs and groups, but to assess potential needs and to ensure that leadership would be carried out effectively by others. 'Finally, he was to teach five sessions in the school, partly to gain a real identification with staff and pupils, and partly so that his teaching commitment would in overall terms release five teachers each from one day session, in return for the voluntary running of one evening session.'

The objection that this arrangement might weaken the voluntary principle was never accepted by the staff of Lawrence Weston School. My own experience of teaching and observation of many other schools suggests that responsibility for running after-school activities is more often than not unequally shared. Some teachers are disinclined to participate because of pressing domestic commitments, some because they are studying for further qualifications, and others because they have already undertaken evening teaching commitments elsewhere. The advantage of the system at Lawrence Weston is not only that it coordinates the expertise of the staff more effectively but that it actually extends the voluntary principle to include help from outsiders—parents in particular.

The staff are able to contribute in several ways. They may be employed in the evening institute, either in teaching or in youth work. In both capacities they may either be paid additionally for the extra commitment or take an evening session in lieu of a half-day session. Acceptance, which becomes a binding commitment for the year, is entirely a matter of choice. This does not of course preclude teachers from running clubs and groups in a voluntary unpaid capacity. The distinction between paid and unpaid service should be made clear. The latter is concerned with extra-curricular associations, such as the chess club, which requires 'no greater supervision from the teacher who leads it than an occasional look in before he starts and after he finishes a completely different evening activity elsewhere in the school'. On the other hand, 'This "session in lieu" tends to be reserved for the most academic of the evening activities: extended day classes to "O" level in Art and Music, for example, or a Chemistry practical session for Fifth and Sixth year pupils.'

One reason for seeking leadership of various kinds among adults within the community is to provide the young people with a variety of social contacts. On three evenings a week, for example, the three Art and Craft rooms are open for practical work, supervised by 'parents who have some talent in puppetry or pottery or other branches of the subject. A printing club is run by the husband of a member of staff, a pigeon club by a local pigeon fancier, an aeromodelling club by a parent.' Where a pupil feels that his particular needs and interests are not being met, he is told by the Activities Organiser that if he can muster enough support and find an adult to run it, provision will be made. In this way, a Wine Making Club and three 'pop groups' have been formed. A dozen or so adults act as unpaid supervisors of working groups.

None of the school's five youth clubs is directly in charge of a member of staff.

> There are two Upper School clubs, likely soon to merge now that the Sixth Form Centre is nearing completion, for present members of the Sixth, their contemporaries who have left school, and an assortment of boy and girl friends. The three Lower School clubs are run by student teachers from the Redland College of Education, or by Sixth Formers and former pupils, occasionally with the assistance of students on teaching practice from Bristol University.

Links with local secular and denominational youth groups are established through the area youth committee, the leaders of which meet once a month.

The main participation of other adults is through enrolment for classes at the evening institute. Additionally, the school encourages the development of more informal cultural activities—a TV study group, for example.

> In music, this had been done in a number of ways. There is an adult choir, which admits young people: in one family, grandparents, parents and child are all members. Parents and older pupils have joined in the formation of a dance band. The school orchestra is often strengthened for performances by adults—staff, friends, former pupils.
>
> Displays of the school's Art and Craft work make a considerable local impression. A bias towards three-dimensional and functional art forms—pottery, puppetry, design in particular—has, as with the music, led the community to a closer identification with what the school is aiming to do.

This identification has been strengthened further through drama. The plays produced are written for or by the school: there is a strong theatre-goers' club, and a theatre workshop.

Similarly, outsiders are invited to share the school's recreational physical activities.

> The school recognises the decline in popularity among some older pupils of the team game, and sets out to provide a wide range of choice. Judo, fencing, climbing, camping and field crafts, canoeing, trampolining, skating, cycling, badminton, table tennis . . . and for most of these there is some form of continuity for school leavers.

Local sports clubs are welcome to use the school's training facilities. Two local football clubs and one major athletic club have taken advantage of this opportunity.

Links with the world outside the school are established in many ways; through General Studies and Careers Guidance and through the development of social service. Lawrence Weston, incidentally, is one of the four schools selected nationally for a five-year pilot scheme to introduce an 'A' level course in Business Studies. This will necessitate contact with the wider community of industry and commerce in and beyond Bristol.

What is the impact of all this upon the community in general, the parents in particular and, most important, the pupils? Though the effects are not easily measurable, the attempt to evaluate such an experiement as this ought to be undertaken by researchers. How does an estate such as Lawrence Weston compare with others of a similar kind with regard to juvenile delinquency rates, the use of the library, care of old people, relationships between the old and younger generations, the boredom of housebound housewives, and many other facets of community and social relations? Without the evidence, we have to rely on impressions.

The extensive programme of parents' year meetings (visiting speakers, demonstration lessons, mannequin parades, displays, coffee evenings and the like) is well attended. It was estimated that 85 per cent of the parents, from this predominantly manual working-class community, attended the meeting just before my visit to the school; and the Theatre Workshop's presentation played to an audience of well over a thousand. The proportion of pupils staying on in the sixth has increased over the last three years from 20 to 35 per cent of the annual intake.

Once started—as we have seen in other schools—a venture of this kind gathers momentum. Already there are plans for further developments.

> One obvious way in which to meet the needs of housebound mothers is to set up an afternoon crèche for preschool children, professionally staffed but assisted by girls of the school as part of their Home Economics course. This crèche would allow mothers to attend further education classes and courses which could be set up in school: in shorthand and typing, cookery, arts and crafts, woodwork, physical education, and even perhaps more academic pursuits to provide a challenge for lively minds. A large school can usually find reserve capacity in the afternoon without too much difficulty. A tentative beginning has been made with an afternoon cookery class for adults.
>
> There is a more pressing need for a short stay children's home for about ten children attached to the school with a member of staff and his wife as house father and mother. The incidence of temporary family breakdown on the estate is alarmingly high, and in spite of an excellent network of welfare services in the city, situations deteriorate through delay. More important, any provision for children in families when there is sudden or serious illness, desertion or mental breakdown

frequently results in the child's removal to another locality or another school. From the community which he knows and which could best cherish him he is abruptly cut off.

REFERENCES

1. Plowden Report, Vol. 1, p. 42.
2. M. Young and P. McGeeney, *Learning Begins at Home*, Routledge, 1968.
3. J. Downing, 'How your children are being taught to read i.t.a.', *Reading Research Document No. 2*, Institute of Education, University of London, 1964.
4. *Ibid.*, p. 3.
5. I have come across some schools using i.t.a. which do not distribute the booklet to parents. Some had done so when the new alphabet was first introduced into the school as it was felt necessary to allay fears that the children were being used as guinea-pigs; but once the new alphabet was more generally accepted, the distribution was discontinued.
6. R. Wyatt, the *Guardian*, January 1966.
7. C. Poster, ' The head and the community school', in *Headship in the '70s*, ed. B. Allen, Blackwell, 1968.

10

Research on Home–School Relations*

Anne Sharrock

This paper concludes the theoretical contributions of Part Two. It offers a review of significant studies (mainly from Britain) of the relationship between home background and school attainment, parents' attitudes to education and teachers' attitudes to parents, and of modes of home–school contact.

The reviewer's interest in relations between home and school arose from the N.F.E.R. Constructive Education Project which is studying factors in the school and its environment which may affect the attitudes, behaviour and attainment of pupils. It was in the course of looking at the ways in which the home affects these characteristics that the lack of any review of research in this field became apparent. This paper, while not claiming to cover all the relevant material, is an attempt to fill the gap.

Although the importance of home background for success in education has long been acknowledged, it is only within the last twenty years that major studies investigating the operation of this influence have been undertaken. They have been concerned not only to show that children from certain social strata tend to do less well at school, but also to identify precisely those features of the home environment which are the most significant in influencing

* Adapted from 'Relations between home and school', *Educational Research*, Vol. 10, No. 3 (1968), pp. 185–196, by kind permission of the publishers.

this success or failure. While a tripartite system of secondary education was still generally in force and not opposed by most people, interest in the home environment tended to be related to selection for the different types of secondary education. Educational research provided evidence that factors other than ability influenced selection, so supplying ammunition for the arguments in favour of comprehensive schools. Since comprehensive schools have been established in accordance with government policy, the usefulness of such research has not declined since it has become increasingly obvious that an unfavourable home background exerts its influence earlier and more extensively than was thought some years ago.*

Research into the relations between home and school can either be concerned with how the home influences attainment, length of schooling and other aspects of education and occupational choice, or it can study the contacts and interaction between the two. In this article research relating to both categories will be reviewed.

Writing in 1964, Green, the author of one of the most useful studies concerned with cooperation between parents and teachers, said 'there is very little literature on the question of home–school relations which originates in this country or is based on English experience'. Though there have been some significant additions since then this is still a fair comment.

THE RELATIONSHIP BETWEEN HOME BACKGROUND AND ATTAINMENT

Since World War II several major pieces of research have appeared which have contributed greatly to our understanding of the relationship between the child's home background and his attainment in school. Even before the war, attention was beginning to be paid to this relationship (Hughes, 1934), and its importance was underlined by Burt (1947) in the early postwar years: 'What is far more important is the cultural outlook of the parents, the daily

* 'Academic achievement of pupils appeared to be related to their social background even within the more selective groups'. S. Dixon, 'Some aspects of school life and progress in a comprehensive school in relation to pupils' social background', unpublished M.A. thesis, University of London, 1962.

influence that they and their acquaintances will exercise on the child's developing incentives . . . in short, the whole sociological background of the individual child.' A few years later a study by Campbell (1952) showed that 'the home environment affects secondary school achievement', but he suggested that there was a need for more research in this field and that 'close cooperation between school and parents might enable use to be made of these findings in the most satisfactory manner'. This use was definitely within the context of selection for tripartite secondary education. Campbell had concentrated upon the socio-cultural aspect of the home as denoted by social activities, cultural objects in the home and cultural values and attitudes held by the parents.

A much larger project was reported in *Social Class and Educational Opportunity* (Floud, Halsey and Martin, 1956), a book that became one of the most frequently quoted works in the field of education in this country. This inquiry 'into some of the social factors associated with selection for, and success in, secondary education' took place in part of Hertfordshire and in Middlesbrough. The results of the eleven-plus were looked at in relation to home background, and the attitudes of postwar parents to their children's education and future prospects were studied. The authors found that the success of children varied with the distribution of some environmental features, such as material and cultural differences, even at the same social level. Although they were not directly concerned with the question of the influence of environment on intelligence test scores, certain conclusions could be drawn about the part that home environment could play in 'the social distribution of educational opportunity'.

Three years after the appearance of *Social Class and Educational Opportunity*, another important contribution to the study of the relationship between the child's home background and his attainment in school was published—*Home Environment and the School* by Elizabeth Fraser (1959). The author was still able to say that 'in spite of general acknowledgement that environmental factors exert considerable influence on a child's school progress, relatively little scientific research has been carried out to determine which aspects of the environment are most influential and which are relatively unimportant'. Fraser's study of over 400

Aberdeen schoolchildren aimed to discover 'whether environmental factors were related to school progress in greater degree than one might expect as a result of the common factor of intelligence'. The results showed that the home environment was more closely related to educational attainment than to IQ and gave additional support to what was, by then, becoming very strong evidence for the importance of the child's home environment to his progress at school. The assessment of home environment was a composite one, and the three most important characteristics were found to be: abnormal background, income, and parents' attitudes to the education and future occupation of the child.

In the decade since Fraser's book, further evidence has been produced of the relationship between progress at school and certain features of the home background. (Indeed, the home appears to influence not only school attainment but also age of leaving school, and other aspects of life related to education.) The importance of parental interest was emphasised in *The Home and the School* (Douglas, 1964) and its sequel *All Our Future* (Douglas *et al.*, 1968), reports initiated by the Population Investigation Committee. The first report, concerned with primary schoolchildren, stated that the influence of parental interest on test performance is 'greater* than that of any of the other three factors—size of family, standard of home, and academic record of the school—which are included in this analysis, and it becomes increasingly important as the children grow older'. *All Our Future* underlined the importance of the home, following as it did the same children through their secondary schooling.

Education and Environment (Wiseman, 1964), published in the same year as *The Home and the School*, contained the results of a programme of cooperative research in parts of Lancashire and the county boroughs of Manchester, Salford and Stockport. This research had been planned as the first major project of the Manchester School of Education, and it was felt to be essential that its validity and value should be clear to teachers and administrators in the region. The first phase of the project was to be of immediate and practical value to the L.E.A.s concerned. It consisted of the

* That is, 'greater' as judged by the level of the statistical significance of its effect.

construction and standardisation of tests of educational attainment for secondary school children, thus providing L.E.A.s with the tests and the results from the standardisation of the tests in their own areas. The second phase was 'an investigation of the relationship between educational attainment and social and environmental factors'. (The book also contained a valuable survey of research into education and environment.) However, it was *school* environment, of which the home is simply a part, that was under consideration in this northern survey, so that although good school neighbourhood and juror-index were two of the variables, no attempt was made to assess parental interest or to gather other data from individual children or parents. Nevertheless, in writing of the results of the 1951 survey, Warburton stated that three main factors seemed to affect scholastic attainment and intelligence test score: socio-economic level, indicated by good school neighbourhood, high juror-index and good school buildings; progressiveness; and good teaching conditions. Although the homes of the pupils tested were not investigated to see which aspects might have an important influence on attainment, the results do imply the necessity of looking further into the home to try to identify such aspects.

Perhaps the most important recent contribution to the process of studying home background in relation to attainment has been *Children and the Primary Schools*, the report of the Plowden Committee (1967). The Government Social Survey carried out in 1964 the National Survey Among Parents of Primary School Children for the Committee. Over 3,000 parents were interviewed in their own homes about 'their attitudes towards the education their children were receiving and their relationships with the teaching staff of their children's schools'. Interviewers also obtained information on the interest displayed by parents in their children's education, on the socio-economic status of the families, and on the physical conditions of the homes. The report echoes Douglas's findings in stressing the importance of parental attitudes. 'The variation in parental attitudes can account for more of the variation in children's school achievement than either the variation in home circumstances or the variation in schools'. But although there is 'certainly an association between parental encouragement and educational performance', it is not possible yet to say whether 'performance is better where parents encourage more' or whether 'parents encourage more where performance is better'. Not surprisingly, the Committee offer the commonsense suggestion that each factor is related to the other and that homes and schools interact continuously.

Thus, in the last twenty years particularly, educational research has been devoting an increasing amount of attention to the pupil's home environment in an effort to discover what environmental factors could account for variations in educational performance which were not the result of differences in innate ability, in so far as this can be measured (Craft, 1970). It has revealed an association not only with the more material features of the home environment but with less tangible aspects, such as parents' attitudes to education, language 'codes' (dealt with by Bernstein, 1961 and elsewhere) and other socio-cultural features of the home. It is, of course, not easy to isolate such variables and there are considerable problems involved in trying to measure, for example, parental attitudes which do seem to be of the utmost importance, (Sharrock, 1970 b).

If the process of investigating the relationship between home environment and school progress has shown an association between parental interest, encouragement, attitudes to education, and achievement, then one might have expected parallel research into ways of fostering such interest and encouragement and of supporting the 'right attitudes'. Further, one might have expected much research into the whole question of the relations between these two partners in the educational process—the home and the school. That such research has, until fairly recently, been noticeable by its absence has lately been a subject of comment. In subsequent sections some of the main research in this field will be reviewed and suggestions made for future research.

RELATIONS BETWEEN TWO SOCIAL INSTITUTIONS

The study of the relations between two social institutions, such as the home and the school, has comparatively few prototypes, as Blyth points out in another paper in this symposium. Yet to try to increase contact and cooperation between the two without understanding the implications of their relationship may be inviting worse confusion. William Taylor* has suggested four factors that need study as the theoretical basis for understanding the contacts between home and school: traditions of home–school relations in this country; the nature of the teacher's role and task in the school, and the sociology of the school; the psychological factors in the relationships between teachers, pupils and parents; and the interests of the family as an ongoing social unit. The first of these, requiring mainly an historical approach, has been considered in *The Family, Education and Society* (Musgrove, 1966). It does not describe the actual contacts between parents and the staff of their children's schools, but considers the family as an educational agency, contrasting its influence with that of the school. The historical approach has also been adopted in parts of *Home/School Relations* (Sharrock, 1970b) and in an article by Cowen (1966) in *Trends in Education*. So far, however, there does not seem to have been any major work of social history devoted to the historical aspects of home–school relations in this country and this is perhaps unfortunate since the insights it could afford might aid a clearer view of the best way ahead.

There have been numerous studies of the teacher's role in recent years—Biddle, *et al.* (1961), Gross, *et al.* (1958), Wilson (1962)—and much of the material has been reviewed by Westwood (1967a, b) in *Educational Research*. One of the classic studies of this kind was, in fact, written much earlier—Willard Waller's *The Sociology of Teaching*, which first appeared in 1932. The ways in which the teaching and parental roles differ and overlap would appear to be a useful focus of attention for students of home–school relations; possible sources of conflict could be highlighted, and possible areas for collaboration suggested. Waller himself noted that, 'in fact, parents and teachers usually live in a condition of mutual distrust and enmity. . . . This fundamental conflict between the school and the parent is accentuated by the fact that parents and teachers are involved in different alignments of group life affecting the child.'

Floud suggested three levels of research in the sociology of

* In a lecture to the ACE conference, 'Home and School' (January 1968).

education, the first two of which were the study of the relationship between education and the other great social institutions, and the study of the sociology of the school. As has been stated, studies of the first kind are comparatively few and the sociology of the school was described by Hoyle in an excellent article in 1965 as a 'rather neglected field of the sociology of education'.

The third of Taylor's suggested areas of study would include teachers' and parents' expectations of each other's roles and their attitudes to each other. These will be dealt with below. Lastly, the question of the interests of the family in relationship to the interests of the school and, by extension, to society, has apparently not been dealt with in any systematic way.

PARENTS' ATTITUDES TO EDUCATION AND TEACHERS

Mention has been made earlier of the increasing emphasis on the importance of parental attitudes. One of the problems here is that of determining *which* attitudes to *what*. Sometimes 'attitude' is taken to be synonymous with 'opinion', or an expression of a preference for something, e.g. for a particular form of education. Generally the term 'attitude' has been used fairly loosely in the literature and a strict definition will not be adopted here since this would exclude some relevant work. The problem remains, however, of ascertaining whether it is parental attitudes to education, or teachers, or the school, or to children or to life in general, or some mixture of all or some of these that is significant.

Investigation of parental attitudes indicated by the degree of interest expressed in the child's education and preference for type of secondary school was the method adopted in the Hertfordshire and Middlesbrough survey. This straightforward method lends itself to large-scale surveys and interviewing, and similar questions about preferred type of school were asked in PEP's *Parents' Views on Education* (Political and Economic Planning, 1961) and its follow-up carried out by Research Services Ltd and *New Society* (Donnison, 1967). In *Children and Their Primary Schools* (*op. cit.*), the report of the survey among parents of primary school children shows that questions on preferred type of school were used here too, together with others on the responsibility and initiative taken by parents over the child's education, paternal interest and support, the parents' aspirations for the child, etc. (Several variables were classified as attitudes in this survey, but some were tested by getting parents to express agreement or disagreement with a number of statements which formed a scale for the item in question, e.g. relations between parents and teachers.)

The level of interest shown by parents figured too in Douglas's *The Home and the School*, assessed partly from the teachers' judgments made at the end of the first and fourth primary school year, and partly on the records of the number of times each parent visited the schools to discuss their child's progress with the head or class teacher. This is not the only study in which parents' visits to the school have been used as an index of their interest but this method has certain obvious disadvantages. Other indices, sometimes used in combination with this one, have recently been employed in an attempt to overcome these disadvantages.

The use of more sophisticated attitude measures, such as attitude scales, has not been so widespread, at least in this country, although the measurement of attitudes by such means (whether differential, summated, cumulative or other composite scales) has become increasingly important. Some of the problems associated with attitude measurement seem to be accentuated in the case of parental attitudes and this is perhaps why researchers have tended to avoid investigating them. Nevertheless, some attempts have been made to use attitude scales of various types in the study of the relationship between home background and attainment and of relations between home and school. Campbell (1952) used a Thurstone-type scale of forty-five items to measure attitudes to education. Drews and Teahan (1957) used a modified version of a scale developed by Shoben (1949) in their study of the relationship between certain patterns of child-rearing and academic achievement. (Shoben's scale was concerned with parental attitudes in relation to child adjustment.)

We know comparatively little about parental attitudes to education and related topics, and this lack is perhaps felt more keenly now. Some recently completed and current research is devoting attention to this, to a greater or less degree. Current research by Craft into participation in secondary education in Ireland uses questionnaires and Likert-type scales for parents which attempt to chart fathers' and mothers' attitudes to education and to teachers, and which also seek to analyse more basic value orientations (Craft, 1968). Other research with somewhat similar aims will be described later in this article, but more traditional and direct methods are still in use* and will no doubt provide much valuable information.

Parents' attitudes to teachers would be expected to colour their relations with them and it is safe to assume that these attitudes will be affected by parents' conception of the teachers' role. Musgrove and Taylor (1965) carried out an inquiry among 470 teachers in grammar, modern, junior and infant schools 'to establish how widely or narrowly they conceived their role and what elements they gave greatest weight to within it'. A smaller sample of parents, 'gave a list of educational priorities which agreed in substance with the ratings made by teachers', although it was interesting to note that there were some considerable discrepancies between what teachers thought parents regarded as important and what the parents did in fact think. Moreover, if teachers and parents have substantially different ideas about the importance of various school objectives this could be a source of conflict between them. The parents of young school leavers surveyed for *Enquiry 1* (Schools Council, 1968) had views very similar to those of the teachers on many school objectives. Where they tended to differ most was on questions relating to careers and the vocational orientation of school work, with parents tending to give these relatively more importance.

A change in parental attitudes could improve home–school relations and raise the level of attainment, but again little research exists to show how attitudes can be modified. Fleming (1959) notes that now 'it is more readily admitted that changes can be effected in the attitudes of even the most antagonistic'. A study by Garside (1956) has been quoted by both Fleming and Green (1964) as being of importance because it showed how parents' attitudes could be changed. But this is yet another area that needs to be investigated.

* The Plowden Follow-Up Project, currently being carried out by N.F.E.R., as its title implies, is repeating in secondary schools some of the work of the Plowden study.

HEADS' AND TEACHERS' ATTITUDES TO PARENTS

According to Green (1964), 'in selecting certain ways of communicating with parents and rejecting others, the teachers of any school are revealing quite fundamental attitudes to education'. Until very recently, however, there had been little systematic investigation of the attitudes of teachers, in this country at least, to contacts with parents or on broader aspects of education. Yet if the types of home–school contact chosen by teachers reveal attitudes to education, then perhaps these attitudes should be investigated more thoroughly, although possibly one should distinguish between heads and teachers, because the contacts chosen may well reflect the attitudes of the head rather than the teachers. It would seem worth while to consider not only attitudes to education but other attitudes and opinions.

Wall (1947) reported the results of an inquiry by the Committee for Parent–Teacher Co-operation, set up in 1944. The questionnaire used was designed to elicit in a fairly straightforward way headteachers' experience of parent–teacher cooperation. They were also asked at what period in the child's school life they thought cooperation was most valuable, what drawbacks to cooperation existed, the types of cooperation that existed, and what suggestions for further cooperation they had to offer. The one county surveyed reported that 'the need for cooperation between home and school is felt by an overwhelming majority of teachers', although there was no such unanimity about the ways in which it might be achieved.

For many years this was apparently the only survey devoted solely to teachers' opinions or attitudes on home and school contact. Recent publications have begun to change this picture. Spencer (1969), for example, investigated one specific form of contact—P.T.A.s—in an enquiry directed to heads. Later work with broader aims has included data on such opinions, on teachers' attitudes to parents in general, or on specific aspects of education. Studies such as those led by Douglas, the surveys of teachers for the Plowden Committee, *Enquiry 1*, and in the N.F.E.R. Constructive Education Project have all been concerned, in one form or another, with the relations between home and school.

How teachers see their role, and the role of the parent, can indicate their attitudes towards contact with the home. Cohen (1967) describes the use of a role definition instrument in a Likert-type scale form 'to identify and compare expectations held by students, tutors, and headteachers for the occupant of the teacher position on that sector of his role here described as "the teacher as a liaison between school and neighbourhood"'. The responses to the question whether teachers should visit the homes of problem children to discuss their difficulties with their parents showed attitudes to contact with the home in a very direct way. It was interesting to note that there was a great difference between the student teachers' and heads' responses to this item: 64 per cent of students expressed approval, but only 18 per cent of heads expressed approval. Currently more attention is being paid to the teacher's role by researchers and this is likely to add to our understanding of the ways in which parents and teachers relate to each other.

A difference between heads' and teachers' attitudes was indicated also in the data from the Central Advisory Council's questionnaire for teachers in the Plowden Report, which provided information on teachers' preferences about types of contact. Teachers and heads were asked to rank in order of importance, the schools' methods of contact with parents. The first choice of heads was individual interviews of the head with parents, whereas teachers selected individual interviews of the class teacher with parents—a result that could hardly be unexpected, although its implications have not yet been fully realised. Similarly the teachers in the Constructive Education Project showed a strong preference for their individual contacts with parents (Sharrock, 1970b).

Surveys of this kind do not, however, add much to our knowledge of the basic attitudes underlying such views. Oliver and Butcher (1962, 1968) have described the construction and use of attitude scales of the Likert type to measure teachers' attitudes to education, but there seems to have been no attempt to relate those to preferred types of contacts with homes or to study the relation of schools with homes generally.

What is quite clear, however, is that heads and teachers prefer informal contacts to formal ones. This was confirmed in *Children and Their Primary Schools*, in *Enquiry 1* and in the findings of the

Constructive Education Project, although in the first two 'formal' was not strictly defined. If this pronounced preference indicates fundamental attitudes, efforts to bring about greater parent–teacher cooperation by the formation on a large scale of organised bodies of parents may be in vain, and may indeed even increase any latent antagonism between parents and teachers.

TYPES OF CONTACT BETWEEN HOMES AND SCHOOLS

Whether attitudes to education or to anything else underlie the types of contact which heads and teachers choose to have with their pupils' homes, we should know what contacts do exist, their extent and effectiveness. Yet this is another relatively unexplored field. It might seem simple to find out the numbers of formal associations of parents and teachers, such associations being one of the most obvious, though not necessarily most effective, ways of linking homes and schools. Until fairly recently, however, it was not even known how many parent–teacher associations there were in this country. In 1964 Green estimated it at 550, but it was doubtful if this was an exact figure since to date the National Confederation of Parent–Teacher Associations has not kept a record of the exact number of associations affiliated to it. Their most recent estimate was 680. The number of unaffiliated associations is still unknown.

But it is now possible to get a clearer idea of the extent of these associations from data gathered in studies mentioned above. Seventeen per cent of primary schools in the national sample for the Plowden Committee had P.T.A.s; 16 per cent of fifteen-year-old leavers, 30 per cent of sixteen-year-old and 46 per cent of seventeen- and eighteen-year-old leavers were in schools with a P.T.A., according to *Enquiry 1*; 29 per cent of secondary schools in the Constructive Education Project's Phase One sample* (mainly comprehensives and secondary moderns) had P.T.A.s. These averages do conceal quite large variations between types of secondary school (comprehensive schools 50 per cent, secondary modern schools 22 per cent), and variations between different

* This was not a national sample but was fairly representative of urban areas.

regions of the country. There is, as yet, no adequate data* on the range of activities undertaken by P.T.A.s, and it is sometimes hard to distinguish between those carried out under the aegis of the P.T.A. and those for which the school itself (or head) is responsible. The reports previously quoted (*Children and Their Primary Schools* and *Enquiry 1*) provide some valuable information on the opportunities provided for parents to visit the schools, and the extent to which these opportunities were taken. Eight main types of contact were listed and the percentage of parents who had attended was given. In both cases, open days, evenings, seemed to be the most popular, to judge by the level of attendance, but there were some interesting differences between primary and secondary schools; in primary schools, for example, medical and dental examinations were as well attended as open days, but in secondary schools these examinations did not receive as much support. Neither in primary nor in secondary schools were P.T.A. meetings among the most popular functions.

These contacts did not include talks with head or class teachers, which were listed separately. It is perhaps significant that far more parents of secondary school children than of primary school children had had no real talks with their child's head or class teacher (37 per cent secondary, 8 per cent primary).

These figures give us some idea of the various types of contact between home and school, but they do not fill in all the detail nor do they tell us anything about the effectiveness of these contacts in promoting cooperation between home and school. As Ellinger (1961) puts it, 'they have one factor in common—the children; and they will work toward social development of children regardless of whether they have unified their approach'. It is clear from what has been said earlier in this article that the assumption is that the right parental attitudes, and parental interest and encouragement will help to raise the level of attainment, so this cooperation is presumably meant to foster the right attitudes, awaken and increase such interest, and support this encourage-

* Apart from Spencer's survey of P.T.A.s already mentioned there seem to be only small-scale surveys available, e.g. one of its own area carried out by the Cheshire Federation of P.T.A.s, and an even smaller one undertaken by J. Fincham *et al* at the Mid-Essex Technical College.

ment. By so doing one hopes that not only will attainment levels be raised generally but that this will happen in the very cases where it is most needed, which seems to be among the children in the semiskilled and unskilled working class. This desirable state, it is inferred, will be reached if parents are accepted as 'full partners in the educational system'.

There have, in fact, been very few attempts to assess the effectiveness of different forms of contact between home and school, or to introduce changes in these contacts in a school and assess the results. One was Green's (1964, 1968) study quoted above, which covered the development of cooperation between parents and teachers in a London junior school from September 1960 to July 1963. Significant changes in parental attitudes were reported, together with a relationship between children's progress and the degree of cooperation of their parents. More recently Young and McGeeney (1968) have described an 'attempt to introduce a change into a school . . . to make new arrangements for communicating with parents, and to see what happened afterwards'. Following these changes, statistically significant differences (at the 1 per cent level) in non-verbal, reading and arithmetic test results were reported, but the authors point out that these may have been due to practice, better teaching or increased parental encouragement, and that there should have been a longer interval between the test and re-test.*

Both these pieces of research took place in primary schools, and indeed, most development and research in home–school relations so far is in the primary sphere—a fact to be borne in mind when considering what further research is desirable. There has been some dissatisfaction in recent years with the traditional forms of written reports. The need for better methods of communication with parents was stressed in both the P.E.P. pamphlet and *Education and the Working Class* (Jackson and Marsden, 1962), in which the authors show how parents lacked some of the most basic information they needed. It has been felt that substantial changes in report forms would enable parents to learn more about their child's capabilities, personality, relationships within the school

* The reviewer understands that some of this work has been replicated by McGeeney in Devon, but fuller details are not yet available.

and specific areas of strength and weakness. Green describes a change in reporting procedure and the provision of opportunities for parents themselves to contribute something to the reports. The changes produced some significant parental reactions. A recent investigation of the views of parents of first year secondary school children indicated the need for considerable rethinking of some aspects of communications between schools and parents (Sharrock, 1970a). There is still a need for further research in this area.

PARENT EDUCATION

Do schools have a responsibility, not only to educate children, but to undertake some form of parent education? The question was posed to over 1,000 teachers in the Constructive Education Project's Phase Two sample of schools (secondary modern and comprehensive). They were also asked to define parent education, since no agreed definition appears to be in use. Certainly the majority of teachers who responded to this question seemed to feel that parent education is mainly or partly the work of the school. Moreover, just over half of them thought of parent education in terms of informing or educating parents about general aspects of education or parenthood.

If most teachers think parent education is the school's responsibility, is it equally clear to them, as Stern (1960) suggests, 'that any attempt to educate parents leads to a necessity to develop home–school cooperation'? Stern's international survey was a major contribution to the understanding of what constitutes parent education and what is its *raison d'être*. In *Parent Education*, the medical, psychological, educational and social reasons for parent education were explored. The report suggested that the importance of the parent–child relationship, for example, could be made more generally known through some form of parent education; an educational reason was that quite often parents knew 'little or nothing of their children's schooling. The school offers hardly any information or guidance to them. Work at school . . . is not planned in such a way that the parents, too, can make a constructive and consistent contribution.' So if parents were still 'the immediate educational device of society', then it made good sense for schools to undertake the education of parents and cooperation with them 'to make their own work with children more effective'. The report included a chapter on relations between home and school, in which Stern categorised cooperation between home and school in thirty-three countries into four groups, ranging from no organised cooperation to widespread parent–teacher associations and parents' committees. The United Kingdom came in the third group: 'moderately developed' cooperation between home and school. Stern concludes that, 'as elsewhere, close cooperation between home and school is advocated in Great Britain; but compared with those countries where parents go freely into schools, visit classes or make direct contact with class teachers, the contact between parent and school in the United Kingdom is customarily more restricted'.

ORGANISATIONS CONCERNED WITH HOME–SCHOOL LINKS

Two of the principal organisations in this country that have recently been concerned with relations between home and school are the National Confederation (formerly Federation) of Parent–Teacher Associations and the Home and School Council. The N.C.P.T.A. is the descendant of earlier bodies concerned with these relations such as the Committee for Parent–Teacher C-operation. A new Home and School Council was constituted in October 1967, in an attempt to unify the work being done in the field of home–school relations by N.C.P.T.A., the Confederation for the Advancement of State Education (C.A.S.E.) and the Advisory Centre for Education (A.C.E.), but its work as a separate organisation has now ended. Each of the other three bodies is committed to the promotion of better links between home and school and each has been using a variety of methods and approaches to this problem. They are, perhaps inevitably, weighted on the side of the parents and therefore the Home and School Council also, not surprisingly, emphasised the parents' role and urged that they be accepted as full partners in the educational process, on the lines recommended in the Plowden report.

None of these organisations has so far been the object of, or instigator of major research, although both the N.C.P.T.A. and C.A.S.E. have produced some local surveys (such as the study of

P.T.A.s in Cheshire quoted above), and the Home and School Council promoted a development programme for home–school relations in the West Riding of Yorkshire.

CURRENT RESEARCH

It has not been possible to obtain details of all the recent research projects in this country that are relevant to relations between home and school. Some have already been noted: the Plowden Follow-Up Project and the research in Devon under McGeeney. In addition, the School and Community Project under Jahoda at the University of Strathclyde has included some interesting data in its report (Lindsay, 1970). The Central Lancashire Family and Community Project has a School and Home Sub-Project, but this does not seem to be concerned directly with contacts between school and home, but rather the home environment from a casework point of view.

In their study of the relationship between home background and school achievement, Banks and Finlayson have been investigating parent/child relationships and child-rearing methods. Parents have been interviewed in depth on these and other aspects of home background, which need extensive study if we are to have a clearer understanding of parental attitudes. This project, at the University of Liverpool, will be reported on in due course.

The boundary between research and development is not always clear, so it is perhaps justifiable to mention the interest of the Nuffield Resources for Learning Project in the more developmental aspects of home–school relations.*

Earlier references have been made to the work of the Constructive Education Project of the N.F.E.R. The links between home and school are of interest to this project in so far as they constitute one of the factors that may affect the 'attitudes, behaviour and attainment' of pupils. Teachers' attitudes to contacts with parents, parental involvement in the school, and their opinions about the present state of home–school relations have been assessed by a questionnaire administered to all the teachers in over forty comprehensive and secondary modern schools in urban areas.

* A primary school programme to improve home–school relations is being carried out under the auspices of this Project.

This questionnaire also included the questions on parent education referred to above. In addition, the views of the heads of these schools have been sought in interviews, and several items on relations with parents were included in an attitude questionnaire which they also received. Pupil attitudes, too, have been given attention: a questionnaire administered to all first and fourth year pupils included items relating to parental involvement and teacher–parent relations. It is hoped that results from this questionnaire will give some indication of what has hitherto been a neglected and yet very important aspect of home–school relations at the secondary level—the attitudes of pupils to contacts between their parents and the school. Some of the results from this project have already been noted and the rest will be reported in due course.

THE NEED FOR FURTHER RESEARCH

In considering research into the relations between home and school, we have looked at some of the mass of evidence which now exists to confirm the link between a child's home and his performance in school. Since there is little doubt that the two are related, it then seemed logical to look at research on the parent–teacher relationship, and at some of the factors which may determine the type and effectiveness of the contacts in bringing about a closer, more harmonious and fruitful partnership between homes and schools in the education of children.

There are many obvious gaps in our knowledge, particularly in research of the second kind. The present climate of opinion is, in some respects, very favourable to the expansion of such research: the interest in education generally, the emphasis on the needs of educational priority areas and increasing attention to the importance of the parental role in education* are essential components of this opinion. It is unfortunate, therefore, that the economic situation may force a postponement of the establishment of research programmes that could provide vital information.

What research does seem most necessary? It has been suggested

* See for example three articles in *The Sunday Times* (10, 17 and 24 March 1968), entitled 'Success before six'; and chapter 4 of *Children and Their Primary Schools* (Plowden Report, 1967), Vol. 1.

that an attempt should be made to find out what a good parent does that is so helpful and stimulating for a child's education and intellectual progress. A corollary of this would be an examination of the ways in which schools can help parents to fulfil their educational role; this would mean looking further at the whole question of parent education and the school's part in it. We know very little about the attitudes of heads (see Chapter 8 of this volume) and teachers that are significant in their contacts with parents and their conception of the parents' role in education, nor do we know much about the corresponding parental attitudes. We need to know more about why certain types of contact are more popular than others, and why most contacts are generally much less effective in bringing lower-working-class parents into the school.* This is particularly important since it is precisely these parents who may need most help—these are often the parents whom Jackson and Marsden (1962) found 'badly wanted, needed, and yet could not easily come by quite elementary information'.

Should teacher training include some special preparation for liaison with homes or should this be the responsibility of selected teachers only, or teacher/social workers, or social workers who remain distinct from the teaching staff? These questions come to the fore when considering why some teachers and heads have better contacts with parents than others. But a more fundamental need is for a re-examination of the relationship between the home and the school, which would inevitably include much of what has already been proposed.

On the more practical level, less is known about home–school relations in secondary schools than in primary schools so perhaps future research should be biased towards this stage of education.

At both primary and secondary level, however, we need more information about current practices, and the evaluation of programmes of changing home–school contacts in an attempt to raise levels of attainment. The possibilities of further research in

* Data from both the Plowden national survey and the Constructive Education Project showed the attendance of unskilled (Class V) parents at P.T.A. and/or other meetings to be approximately only 25 per cent of that of professional, managerial and intermediate parents (Classes I and II of the Registrar General's Classification).

home–school relations are legion, and any research carried out is likely to be welcomed by teachers and educationists, since it could suggest changes in actual practice.

REFERENCES

(A number of relevant studies which are not referred to in this chapter are included.)

BANFIELD, J., BOWYER, C. and WILKIE, E. 1966. 'Parents and education', *Educ. Res.*, Vol. 9, No. 1, pp. 63–6.

BERNSTEIN, B. 1961. 'Social structure, language and learning', *Educ., Res.*, Vol. 3, No. 3, pp. 163–76.

BIDDLE, B. J., ROSENCRANZ, H. A. and RANKIN, E. F. 1961. 'General characteristics of the school teacher's role', *Studies in the Role of the Public School Teacher*, Vol. 2. University of Missouri Press.

BOYSON, R. 1968. 'Parents and children in the house unit', *Education* March.

BURT, C. 1947. 'Symposium on the selection of pupils for different types of secondary schools', *Brit. J. Educ. Psychol.*, Vol. 17, Pt. 2.

CAMPBELL, W. J. 1952. 'The influence of home environment on the educational progress of selective secondary school children', *Brit. J. Educ. Psychol.*, Vol. 22, Pt 2.

CENTRAL ADVISORY COUNCIL FOR EDUCATION (ENGLAND). 1954. *Early Leaving*. (Gurney-Dixon Report). H.M.S.O.

CENTRAL ADVISORY COUNCIL FOR EDUCATION (ENGLAND). 1967. *Children and their Primary Schools* (Plowden Report). H.M.S.O.

COPLAND, R. E. 1966. 'School reports', *Educ. Res.*, Vol. 8, No. 3, pp. 196–208.

COHEN, L. 1967. 'The teacher's role and liaison between school and neighbourhood', in *Linking Home and School*, ed. M. Craft, J. Raynor and L. Cohen (1st edn., 1967), Longman.

COWEN, N. 1966. 'The place of the parent', *Trends in Education*, July.

CRAFT, M. 1968. 'Social factors influencing participation in secondary education in Ireland' (unpublished Interim Report to Social Science Research Council).

CRAFT, M. ed. 1970. *Family, Class and Education: a Reader*, Longman.

DONNISON, D. V. 1967. 'Education and opinion', *New Society*, 26 October.

DOUGLAS, J. W. B. 1964. *The Home and the School*. MacGibbon & Kee.

DOUGLAS, J. W. B., ROSS, J. M. and SIMPSON, H. R. 1968. *All Our Future*. Peter Davies.

DREWS, E. M. and TEAHAN, J. E. 1957. 'Parental attitudes and academic achievement', *J. Clin. Psychol.*, Vol. 13.

EDMONDS, E. L. 1965. 'Is your Parent Teacher Association necessary?', *Head Teachers Review*, March.

EGGLESTON, S. J. 1967. 'Social factors associated with decisions to "stay on" in non-selective secondary schools', *Educ. Res.*, Vol. 9, No. 3, pp. 163–74.

ELLINGER, B. 1961. 'The interrelationship of home and school: a review essay', *Educ. Res. Bull.*, 8 March, Vol. 11, No. 3.

FLEMING, C. 1959. *Teaching: A Psychological Analysis*. Methuen.

FLOUD, J. 1962. 'The sociology of education', in *Society: Problems and Methods of Study*, ed. T. D. Welford, *et al.* Routledge & Kegan Paul.

FLOUD, J. and HALSEY, A. H. 1961. 'Homes and schools: social determinants of educability', *Educ. Res.*, Vol.3, No. 2, pp. 83–8.

FLOUD, J., HALSEY, A. H. and MARTIN, F. M. 1956. *Social Class and Educational Opportunity*. Heinemann.

FRASER, E. 1959. *Home Environment and the School*. University of London Press.

GARSIDE, A. 1956. 'A study of the wishes as to their children's development expressed by a group of parents of primary school children' unpublished M.A. thesis, University of London.

GOODACRE, E. J. 1968. *Teachers and their Pupils' Home Background*. Slough: N.F.E.R.

GOODACRE, E. J. 1970. *School and Home*. Slough: N.F.E.R.

GREEN, L. J. 1964. 'The development of parent–teacher co-operation in a London junior school', unpublished M.A. thesis, University of London.

GREEN, L. J. 1968. *Parents and Teachers: partners or rivals?* Allen and Unwin.

GROSS, N., MASON, W. S. and MCEACHERN, A. W. 1958. *Explorations in Role Analysis: Studies of the School Superintendency Role*. Wiley.

GURNEY-DIXON REPORT, *see* Central Advisory Council for Education.

HOYLE, E. 1965. 'Organizational analysis in the field of education', *Educ. Res.*, Vol. 7, No. 2, pp. 97–114.

HUGHES, A. G. 1934. 'Discrepancies between results of intelligence tests and entrance examinations to grammar schools', *Brit. J. Educ. Psychol.*, Vol. 4, pp. 221–36.

JACKSON, B. and MARSDEN, D. 1962. *Education and the Working Class.* Routledge & Kegan Paul.

KELLMER PRINGLE, M. 1957. 'An experiment in parent staff group discussion', *Educ. Rev.*, Vol. 9, No. 2.

KEMP, L. C. D. 1955. 'Environmental and other characteristics determining attainment in primary schools', *Brit. J. Educ. Psychol.*, Vol. 25, pp. 67–77.

LINDSAY, C. 1970. *School and Community*, Pergamon.

MARCH, L. 1966. *The Education Shop*, Advisory Centre for Education.

MARTIN, F. M. 1954. 'An inquiry into parents' preferences in secondary education', in *Social Mobility in Britain,* ed. D. V. Glass. Routledge & Kegan Paul, Chapter 7.

MUSGRAVE, P. W. 1967. 'Family, school, friends and work: a sociological perspective', *Educ. Res.*, Vol. 9, No. 3, pp. 175–86.

MUSGROVE, F. 1966. *The Family, Education and Society*. Routledge & Kegan Paul.

MUSGROVE, F. 1967. 'University freshmen and their parents' attitudes', *Educ. Res.*, Vol. 10, No. 1, pp. 78–80.

MUSGROVE, F. and TAYLOR, P. 1965. 'Teachers' and parents' conception of the teacher's role', *Brit. J. Educ. Psychol.*, Vol. 35, Pt. 2.

OLIVER, R. A. C. and BUTCHER, H. J. 1962. 'Teachers' attitudes to education', *Brit. J. Soc. Clin. Psychol.*, Vol. I, pp. 56–59.

OLIVER, R. A. C. and BUTCHER, H. J. 1968. 'Teachers' attitudes to education', *Brit. J. Educ. Psychol.*, Vol. 38, Pt. 1.

PLOWDEN REPORT, *see* Central Advisory Council for Education.

POLITICAL and ECONOMIC PLANNING. 1961. *Parents' Views on Education.* P.E.P.

A PRIMARY SCHOOL HEADMASTER. 1965. 'Parents and the primary school: a survey of parental opinion', *Educ. Res.*, Vol. 7, No. 3, pp. 229–35.

SCHOOLS COUNCIL. 1968. *Enquiry 1.* H.M.S.O.

SHARROCK, A. 1970a. 'Aspects of communication between schools and parents', *Educ. Res.*, Vol. 10. No. 3.

SHARROCK, A. 1970b. *Home/School Relations*. Macmillan.

SHEPHARD, S. JNR. 1963. 'A program to raise the standard of school achievement', in *Programs for the Educationally Disadvantaged*. U.S. Department of Health, Education and Welfare, Office of Education Bulletin, No. 17.

SHOBEN, E. J. JNR. 1949. 'The assessment of parental attitudes in relation to child adjustment', *Genet. Psychol. Monogr.*, Vol. 39, February.

SPENCER, A. E. C. W. 1969. 'Parent–teacher associations in Catholic schools', *Catholic Education Today*, March/April.

STERN, H. H. 1960. *Parent Education: An International Survey*. University of Hull; Hamburg: Unesco Institute for Education.

SWIFT, D. F. 1962–63. 'Analysis of social factors in educational selection at age 11 years in two local education authority divisions', unpublished Ph.D. thesis, University of Liverpool.

VERNON, P. E. 1965. 'Environmental handicaps and intellectual development', *Brit. J. Educ. Psychol.*, Vol. 35, pp. 1–22.

WALKER, A. 1955. *Pupils' School Records*. Newnes Educational (for N.F.E.R.).

WALL, W. D. 1947. 'The opinions of teachers on parent–teacher co-operation', *Brit. J. Educ. Psychol.*, Vol. 17.

WALLER, W. 1965. *The Sociology of Teaching*, 1st Science Editions, Wiley. (First published 1932.)

WESTWOOD, L. J. 1967a. 'The role of the teacher—I', *Educ. Res.*, Vol. 9, No. 2, pp. 122–34.

WESTWOOD, L. J. 1967b. 'The role of the teacher—II', *Educ. Res.*, Vol. 10, No. 1, pp. 21–37.

WILSON, B. R. 1962. 'The teacher's role—a sociological analysis', *Brit. J. Sociol.*, Vol. 13, No. 1, pp. 15–32.

WISEMAN, S. 1964. *Education and Environment*, Manchester University Press.

YOUNG, M. 1964. 'How can parent and teacher work together?' *New Society*, 24 September.

YOUNG, M. 1967. 'Getting parents into schools', *The Observer*, 29 October.

YOUNG, M. and MCGEENEY, P. J. 1968. *Learning Begins at Home*. Routledge & Kegan Paul.

Part Three

Linking Devices and Experiment

11
The Education Welfare Service
A. Dawson

Part Three considers techniques of linking home and school which may be found in contemporary educational practice. This first paper offers an account of the changing role of the 'school attendance officer', a long-familiar agent in relating the school to its neighbourhood.

The Education Welfare Service is one of the oldest statutory social services. It was born shortly after the introduction of the first Elementary Education Act of 1870, when it was realised that although many people passionately desired education for their children it was not sufficient merely to provide the opportunities of going to school.

Many parents then, as now, and largely for the same reasons, showed little interest in education, and compulsory school attendance had to be introduced. In order to enforce attendance, the School Boards which had been set up under the Act, were empowered to appoint School Attendance Visitors, whose job was simply to chase children into school. In Manchester the visitors were provided with a blue serge uniform and were known colloquially in the district as 'the School Board'. In February 1877, in that city, a leaflet was published, quoting the following rhyme—

Who, caused our little hearts to beat,
As Joe and I were on the street,
Vending papers a penny a sheet?
'The School Board'.

Who, forthwith to our lodgings went,
To serve a notice with intent,
Of bringing us to punishment?
'The School Board'.

Who, listened not to Mother's pleading,
That we were clogs and jackets needing,
To get which, she went out a-cleaning?
'The School Board'.

Who, is a terror to each young boy,
And tends to lessen our daily joy,
In tops, whips, kites, and every toy?
'The School Board'.

Who, is there were could do without,
And not feel hurt or put about,
If he were never more seen out?
'The School Board'.

With the introduction of the Education Act of 1902, which abolished the School Boards and made local authorities responsible for education, and the Employment of Children Act of the following year, further opportunities arose for the officer to extend his field of service. Local authorities were given powers to regulate the employment of schoolchildren outside school hours and of children and young persons engaged in street trading, and the officers' duties were extended to protect children from exploitation by employers.

Further development in the service of education, for example, The Education (Provision of Meals) Act, 1906, and the Education (Administrative Provisions) Act of the following year—which for the first time in this country provided for the medical inspection of children at school—widened the scope of the officers' work. By now he was investigating family circumstances—visiting with regard to sick and handicapped children—and was taking upon himself responsibility for welfare work outside his statutory duties, simply because he was the man on the spot at the opportune time. Already he was beginning to forge vital links between home and school.

Many new duties were added by the Education Act 1918 which, with the previous Acts were consolidated in the great Education Act of 1921. One of the effects of this Act, which, with some amendments, set the pattern and standard of education right up to 1944, was that every Local Education Authority had to establish an efficient, properly staffed School Attendance Department. With the introduction of the Children and Young Persons Act of 1933—'The Children's Charter'—many more duties were given to the officer.

With the inception of the 1944 Education Act and the birth of the Welfare State the importance of the welfare side of the officer's work began to be recognised. This was emphasised with a further change in his title. The uniformed 'School Board' with the big stick gave way to the 'Education Welfare Officer' concerned with the whole welfare of the child and recognising that following closely upon the basic requirements of every child to be provided with food and clothing and parental love, comes the next essential —education.

For the vast majority of children, education means regular attendance at school—regular attendance combined with an attitude of mind and a contentment of spirit to enable the child to benefit from all that the school is providing. The officer therefore is concerned not merely with the physical presence of the child in the classroom but of ensuring that whilst he is there, there are no problems hindering his educational progress.

A visit to a home will be concerned with the reasons for the child's absence rather than the collecting of excuses, and because he possesses a greater knowledge of family problems and has wider powers to assist and advise each visit will be an investigation in the truest sense.

Today the officer is able to spend time investigating the causes of truancy and absenteeism, to concentrate his attentions on children who show signs of social handicap. He has developed in the truest sense into a social worker. He comes into contact with the homes and the parents as probably no other municipal officer, with the possible exception of the Health Visitor, and combines with his duties a considerable amount of welfare work.

He must be skilled in social work theory and requires a wide range of virtues such as tact, humour, sympathy, patience, and persistence. He must have an adequate knowledge of education law—of the powers and duties of the Education Authority—when he is so often the only contact which the parent has with the education service. He will be expected to answer questions and offer advice on almost any topic affecting the child from how to get a child into nursery class to how to get a student into a training college. It is this ability to offer help and advice that in innumerable instances leads him to become first a friend of the family and then a trusted adviser.

Because he is often the first to discover a family 'at risk' he must have the ability and the training to assess the difficulties and the needs of such families. He must be able to recognise the symptoms, analyse the causes, and from his knowledge of the powers and duties of other social agencies, know where the case might be referred for appropriate help. At last, after many years of effort by his Association, the National Joint Council for Local Authorities has approved a recommendation of the Local Governments Examination Board instituting a Certificate in Educational Welfare.

So much for his evolution. What is his role today? He has many duties which, if tabulated, would form a formidable list. These duties differ slightly from area to area and from authority to authority. The administration of a small authority is different from that of a large one. The problems to be faced in urban areas differ vastly from those in country areas.

But there are duties common to all officers, the chief one being to ensure that every child receives efficient full-time education suitable to his age, ability, and aptitude, and following this, the provision of welfare facilities such as clothing, school meals, transport and maintenance allowances, to enable him to take full advantage of the education being provided.

Absence from school will therefore be the main reason for a visit to the home but will not be the exclusive reason. Where a call is made because of irregular attendance, the object will be to discover the cause and to ensure that the child returns to school at the earliest opportunity compatible with his safety and the safety of the other children in the class.

A visit to a home may be made, however, where the class teacher has observed some sympton in the child which has given him cause for conern—some material neglect, some lack of concentration, a chance remark by some other member of the class. He will discuss this with the headteacher and the officer, and a visit to the home will follow.

Often parents are faced with problems and have no idea where to turn for help. The whole family is affected by the situation and the child may indicate by his attitude and behaviour at school that something is amiss at home. A visit from the officer may be the means of relieving the situation with skilled help and advice.

It will be seen that the officer is vitally concerned in linking home and school. For the majority of children, school and home work happily together in the interests of the child's education. The parent will seek an interview with the teacher or headteacher, when necessary. He will support the school in every possible way—provide additional equipment—attend open days—join the parent–teacher association—encourage the child to respect the school and to work hard and to make steady progress.

In those cases the head knows that a message to the home will bring an immediate response, but the parents of the child who is socially handicapped, whose cooperation the headteacher and the class teacher are most anxious to secure, make no contact at all. They are often incapable of cooperating. They have so many other problems that the progress of their child at school is the least of their worries. For them school is school and home is home: 'Let the teachers get on with their job; they are paid to do it, aren't they? Why should I care? The sooner he leaves school and starts earning the better.'

It is in this sort of home that the Welfare Officer has to provide the vital link, interpreting to the home the policy, the problems, and the concern of the school for that particular child. In the other direction, he can acquaint the headteacher and the class teacher with the child's background. Teachers are often unaware of the social conditions under which some of their children live. They do not appreciate that some children have no place at home for quiet study, no private possessions of their own, no chair to relax in, and no bed of their own, and know nothing of a warm, comfortable night's rest.

This sort of situation has a marked effect upon many children. They are not neglected according to the law, but their standard of care is inadequate. They certainly receive little practical help or encouragement in tackling the problems of school. When after discussion with the Education Welfare Officer, the teacher realises the family circumstances, he begins to understand why the child is not making the required progress. Some of our children carry enormous burdens of anxiety and worry, and often amaze us by their resilience. Sometimes the burden is so great that the child develops physical symptoms and illness.

The work of linking home and school may begin before the child reaches compulsory school age and go on until he leaves school. In a few cases it develops into the task of linking home and employment. Where it is desirable that a child should be admitted to a nursery class or reception class it is often the officer who brings the parent and the school together, supplying to the headteacher or the authority a picture of the child's background and the circumstances which make it desirable that the child should be admitted to school as early as possible.

He may be approached by the parent when he calls about an older school child or because he is recognised on the street in his district. He may himself suggest to a parent that early schooling could relieve the situation in the home, or some other social worker may approach him for help in this sort of situation. From these early beginnings he seeks to strengthen the link between the home and the school, and does all he can to encourage the parent to visit the school, to cooperate with the staff, to obey the simple rules—after explaining why the rules are necessary.

The problems that face primary school children require the joint cooperation of school and home if the child is to make progress. In social training the development of good habits and personal hygiene are matters which require very delicate handling if some parents are not to be outraged by failing to understand the school's demands, or if some teacher is not to be driven to the point of despair by the failure of the parents to cooperate.

In these circumstances the officer plays a conciliatory role, bringing to the notice of the parents the very practical problems of the teaching staff in dealing with over-large classes, many with children who may be unable to tie their shoe laces or wash their hands and faces, or drawing to the notice of the teacher the problems which face an overburdened mother with several small children under school age at home, in trying to get her child to school suitably clean and properly equipped before the bell goes in the morning.

Transfer to secondary school is another peak period when school–home links need to be strengthened. Sometimes the Education Welfare Officer has to persuade the ignorant parent that a grammar school education, although it will involve him in some additional expense, will nevertheless pay dividends in the long run for, a daughter as well as for a son.

More frequently he has to 'sell' the local secondary modern school to the parent of the child who has only 'just failed' the eleven-plus exam, and who will on no account permit his child to attend that old downtown school. By patient explanation founded upon his knowledge of the school and of the pupils who have passed through its hands, and by arranging for the parent to see the school and talk to the headteacher and staff, he endeavours to forge a link between the home and the school, sometimes so strong a link that his services are not required again during that child's secondary school life.

The first few months of a child's life in a secondary school are often fraught with difficulties. From being 'top-dog' in the small junior school he is reduced almost overnight to being very small fry in a large secondary school, and many children experience difficulties in this situation. It is here that home–school contacts are vitally necessary if the child is to settle down and find his feet. Parental help *must* be obtained, for the child may hide his fears from home yet make it perfectly plain by his behaviour in school that all is not well. It is in this situation that truancy often occurs, but where home and school are brought together to deal with the problem, the situation may easily be resolved. In other cases consideration must be given to measures such as change of school or help from the Child Guidance Service. All the time the one person who is linking the interested parties is the Education Welfare Officer.

Another of the most difficult times in a child's school career when home–school links are of vital importance is the period of adolescence—the third and fourth years in secondary school. It is in this age group that the figures for delinquency show a marked increase.

When problems arise here, the parent often blames the school and the school the parents, and if both sides fail to cooperate, the result may be tragic. If home and school are pulling different ways, each setting different standards, there is little hope for the adolescent. If school is saying 'No' and parents are saying, 'You can if you like'; if school is setting a standard and a challenge but parents couldn't care less, it is no wonder that there are problems.

Whilst we might generally agree that the parents are largely to blame, some schools are not faultless. If teachers can realise the home conditions under which some of their adolescent pupils have to live, with inadequate parents unable or unwilling to give the necessary love and guidance, in homes with no facilities for proper social intercourse, no place to bring friends, they may temper their demands and change their approach to meet the needs of a particular child; and if some parents can be made to recognise that the school has to maintain standards and enforce rules for the wellbeing of all as well as for the welfare of the individual, they may seek to support and cooperate with the school for their child's wellbeing. The task of the Education Welfare Officer in endeavouring to forge links here is formidable indeed.

Handicapped pupils form a category of children who require the services of the officer to link home and school more desperately than any others.

The Education Welfare Officer may be the first contact with the home, and links the parent and the school medical authorities, for he has a duty to bring to the notice of the School Medical Officer any child who might require special educational treatment. Here his personal explanation of the need for the child to be examined, and later on, his introduction of the parent to the special school, paves the way for a happy and close relationship between the school and the home. Where the child has to attend a residential special school, the officer is almost always the only link between home and school when at holiday times he escorts the child to and from his home. In many areas there has developed a special system for the after-care of children who leave special schools, and this usually involves the Education Welfare Officer in linking home and employment.

How does the officer operate in linking home and school? First it must be remembered that he is a representative of the local education authority and not a member of the school staff. Some may think this is a disadvantage, but when dealing with parents who are uncooperative and often hostile to the school, it can have distinct advantages. He is not identified with the school, but is seen in the role of arbitrator. He can listen with unbiased attention to the parents' point of view. Indeed, on some occasions he must agree with it because there are times when the school itself has either caused or aggravated the problem by the unreasonable attitude of the headteacher or some member of the staff. Some of the more sensitive children might suffer greatly if they thought that a member of the school staff were to visit their homes—a child may be secretly ashamed of his home although fiercely loyal to his parents.

The disadvantages of the Education Welfare Officer not being a member of the school staff are minimised where the officer is welcomed in the staff room and joins in the outside activities of the school such as P.T.A. meetings, open days, sports days, excursions, etc., and especially where he has an office situated in the school building so that he can be in frequent and close touch with the school.

Forging links surely means bringing two sides together so that each may appreciate more fully what the other is doing, and in the case of home and school cooperate for the wellbeing of the child. In this work the officer must be the means of interchanging information, of getting each to see the other's point of view, and of persuading one side or sometimes both, to change in the interest of the child.

If the school cannot perform its function adequately because of some social defect in the home, the officer must endeavour to change the conditions. Similarly, if there is some lack of understanding in the school, he must try to put that right. Experience shows that schools are ready and willing to cooperate. Alas, this is not always true of the home.

Forging links can be a formidable task and calls for all the officer's resources, but it is a task which is tremendously important and vitally necessary.

12
The School Care Service
Adeline Wimble

This paper describes a unique and long-established technique for linking homes and schools practised in London, and which incorporates the voluntary element in welfare provision, at a moment when it is undergoing some modification.

[NOTE: On 1 October 1970 the Inner London Education Authority set up a unified education welfare service to take over the functions of the School Care Service and the Authority's arrangements for the control of school attendance. The work will be carried out by teams of social workers and voluntary workers, which will be area-based but school orientated. Besides being concerned with assessments for meals, clothing, school journey grants, uniform grants, follow-up of medical inspections and attendance, the teams will help to strengthen all possible links between home and school and to identify social problems at an early stage. They will cooperate with all the statutory and voluntary social services to enable every child to benefit fully from its education. It will be some time before the functioning of the unified service can be fully assessed and so this paper will seek to describe the operation of the School Care Service as it was at the moment of writing.]

The School Care Service of the Inner London Education Authority was unique. It grew spontaneously at the turn of the century through the concern of teachers, church workers, settlement workers, and others for the wellbeing of children who, from 1870 onwards had to attend school but who in the poorer parts of London were often too hungry to benefit from the education provided. 'Feeding committees' (later called 'care committees') of voluntary workers were formed by these interested and concerned citizens, for the 'necessitous' schools, and they raised money to provide meals and decided which families were in need.

When the 1906 Education Act empowered local education authorities to supply meals for 'any child who by reason of lack of nourishment was unable to take full advantage of the education provided', the L.C.C. decided to use those powers and to delegate to the voluntary care committees the responsibility of deciding which families were in need of such help.

Shortly afterwards routine school medical inspections began, and as the families most in need of help and guidance in obtaining medical treatment were likely to be those whom the care committees were already visiting as needing free school dinners, the care committees were asked to send a member to be present at each school medical inspection so that they could both give the doctor any relevant information about the family's background and difficulties, and ensure that the doctor's recommendations were understood by the parents and the necessary treatment obtained. Many voluntary committees at that time raised the money to provide school clinics where the children could receive treatment at little or no cost to their parents.

As part of the school health service the care committee is still responsible for 'following up' the school doctor's recommendations, and also all cases where clinic or hospital appointments are not kept, or promised private treatment not obtained. Whereas in the early days of the service the care committee worker had to pay many home visits to persuade parents to accept treatment for decayed teeth, defective vision, enlarged tonsils, rickets, rheumatism, impetigo, scabies, running ears, etc., now most of these ailments have either largely disappeared or parents accept treatment almost automatically through the health service. (Immigrant families do of course need a fair amount of advice and guidance.) Such is the improvement in physical health that special investigation clinics that originally spent much time on weedy thin children, now more often are needed to advise on obesity.

Nowadays much of the home visiting, other than enquiries for recommending material help, is concerned with persuading parents that they should accept the recommendation of teacher, doctor, or educational psychologist that a child needs psychiatric help at a child guidance clinic. Many parents do seek such help for themselves through either the family doctor or the out-patient department of a hospital, but many of those most in need do not accept that such help is necessary and have to be patiently persuaded. In these cases the care committee workers prepare the home reports for the child guidance clinics, or for the Problem Case Conference of educational experts who decide what can best be done to help both child and school when parents either cannot or will not accept the need for psychiatric advice.

When the L.C.C. decided to make the voluntary school care committees responsible for recommending free dinners, they appointed two trained social workers as 'organisers' to build up this voluntary service to cover all the elementary schools, both state and church, within the county, and from this grew the present structure. Now each school, primary, secondary, and special, has a care committee of voluntary workers appointed by the Education Committee of the Inner London Education Authority. The voluntary workers are recruited, trained, and guided by professional social workers called School Care Organisers and work from local offices within the Authority's ten administrative divisions, each of which is in the charge of a Divisional School Care Organiser. Each care committee appoints its own chairman and honorary secretary and is fully constituted if it has at least one other member and meets at least once a term. Heads of schools, or their deputies, attend these meetings in an advisory capacity and so do the organisers. There are also Divisional Councils of School Care Committees, and a Central Council to which the Heads' Consultative Committees also appoint representatives, and the chairman and vice-chairman of the Authority's Education Committee are invited to the Central Council.

It is the duty of school care committees, in constant contact with the heads of schools, to ensure that all children obtain full benefit from the education for which they are best suited by age, aptitude and ability; to ascertain the needs of their families and in cooperation with all the available statutory and voluntary services endeavour to prevent or alleviate any physical or mental distress within the family. It is therefore important that a responsible care worker (usually the hon. secretary of the committee) should visit the school regularly to consult with the headteacher and other members of the staff, and that the teaching staff, via the head, should alert the care worker at the first sign that they may observe of home difficulties or behaviour problems, so that action may be taken before these difficulties and problems become insoluble.

Every effort is made to assist and encourage parents to meet their own responsibilities but those who cannot do so must be given constant support and guidance, often over a period of many years. If a school has any reason to suspect cruelty or neglect this should immediately be reported to the care committee worker or the Divisional School Care Organiser. It may be that the worker can herself improve matters (often her friendly, persistent, but non-official contact through many months and years makes her the only acceptable adviser to difficult, suspicious, or neurotic parents), but it may be necessary to call in the N.S.P.C.C. or the Children's Officer. In this type of case it is essential that there should be neither unnecessary overlapping of social services, nor lack of any necessary coordination between them, and it is therefore advisable that only in extreme urgency should a head refer a case direct to the N.S.P.C.C. or any other agency, and that the School Care Service be immediately informed if this has been necessary.

The care committee investigates all requests for free meals and authorises them according to the Department of Education's scale, but also exercises discretionary powers in exceptional cases. The care committee authorises the provision of clothing and footwear (often recommended by the school enquiry officer if a child is out of school owing to lack of either) under Section 5 of the Education (Miscellaneous Provisions) Act 1948, and assesses the parents according to their income, taking good care that the assessment is one that can reasonably be paid within a period of eight to ten weeks. They may provide clothing from voluntary sources if it is not appropriate to use Section 5, or they may refer the case to the National Assistance Board if the Board should be responsible. The care committee also assesses the payments of parents unable to pay the full charge for recognised school journeys, and submits reports on the home circumstances of parents who apply for assistance under the Authority's boarding school scheme.

They also keep in touch (until the age of eighteen) with any young person who needs help and advice after leaving school, and they make available to the youth employment service any information which may assist in the proper placing of school leavers, such as difficult home circumstances, probation cases, etc.; and they undertake any home visiting requested by the youth employment officer. From this aspect of care committee work has developed the Young People's Advisory Service (originally known as the Avondale project) which is available to some secondary schools.* Some care workers who with the head of the school were concerned about the difficulties encountered by the often inarticulate fifteen-year-old school leaver on first starting work, arranged, at the invitation of the head, for one of their members to meet these fifteen-year-olds informally in school over a period before leaving. The worker had teenage children herself and was also very attractive in both appearance and personality. She held small informal weekly discussion groups on any topic of interest to them, and found that they gained confidence and sought her friendly guidance on all kinds of personal problems, readily approaching her on matters that they felt unable to discuss with their parents or their teachers.

Such advisers are now slowly being appointed to secondary schools who wish for them. They are all trained social workers, teachers, or youth leaders; they work on a part-time basis and are paid on the same salary scales as the school care organisers. They work closely with the school care committee, the Careers Officer, the Youth Officer, Heads of Evening Institutes, and all other statutory and voluntary agencies as appropriate. As well as the informal weekly discussion groups in school, they are available for private interviews and visit all the homes before and after the young person leaves school. Guidance is given on relationships with the opposite sex, with parents and employers, and on financial budgeting and grooming, the young people being en-

* This service is particularly commended as a useful experiment in the Newsom Report (paragraph 232).

couraged to express their own opinions and 'talk through' their own problems. Many parents do not understand their teenagers, whilst teachers are in a position of authority and have to consider the welfare of the whole school as well as the needs of the individual. An understanding adult who is outside the home and school setting but in friendly relation to both, can often more easily secure the confidence of young people and discover what is troubling them or causing their irresponsible behaviour.

Having been in existence for nearly sixty years the School Care Service is accepted by London parents as the link between home and school. The voluntary worker is regarded as a 'friend of the family' and is not considered as one of 'them'. However good the direct relationship of schools with parents, there are always parents who have an inferiority complex where teachers are concerned and therefore are automatically suspicious and on the defensive and so do not cooperate or even come near the school or appear to take the slightest interest in what the school is striving to do for their children. In fairness to them it must be confessed that there have been and are schools which dictate too much to parents and which seem to forget that children have home loyalties; they have even been guilty of criticising parents to their children. It is for the parents (and their children) who do not respond to school invitations and suggestions that the care committee link between home and school is invaluable. Very often they can encourage parents to see the school point of view; conversely they can enable the school to realise some of the practical difficulties which may exist and make it impossible for some parents to cooperate.

There is a danger in confusing the role of the teacher with that of the social worker. In a conflict of loyalties the teacher would have to consider the whole school before the individual child and the teacher holds a position of authority. The social worker—professional or voluntary—whilst guiding and advising has always to accept people as they are, and within their own limitations; moreover she must respect her clients' 'confidences' as does the doctor those of his patients. Parents could probably resent teachers visiting their homes as of right; they might regard it as an intrusion and promptly build up a 'barricade' as a defence. Many children, too, would resent their teachers seeing the poverty or other limitations of their homes and getting too close a picture of the ineffectualness of their 'mum'. The average mother's great need is someone that she can just 'talk to' about her problems. Many do of course make confidants of teachers—that is when they make the approach by coming to the school—but they talk much more easily in their own homes to someone who has no authoritative position. Imagine the average child's reaction if 'mum' talked in that way to its teacher!

Outside London, the school enquiry officer, or welfare officer must deal not only with school attendance but also with many of the welfare matters that in London are the responsibility of the care committee workers. But however sympathetic to the families and their problems, he has also to enforce school attendance. He is a paid official and therefore likely to be considered as one of 'them', especially by those so often described as problem families. There are many things that a voluntary worker can do to help even the most serious problem family that it would be impossible for a paid official even to consider. Within the framework of the education service, and with the guidance of the professional worker, the voluntary care worker can potentially cope with any situation and will doggedly persist when officialdom has had to give up. Child Guidance Clinics, Family Casework Agencies and even Mental Health Officers may withdraw from cases when the families will not cooperate, but the care committee must continue to be concerned as long as there are children still at school.

The organiser exercises her professional social work skill by direct contact with some families and schools for which no voluntary worker is for a time available (we have 1,237 schools and over 2,500 voluntary workers but their availability is not evenly distributed), and by training and guiding the voluntary workers. Her expertise is also in directing the right worker to the right school and neighbourhood, and to the type of service for which he or she is most suited. Because the service is trained and guided by professional staff it is accepted by other social workers—family case-workers, medical social workers, psychiatric social workers, child care officers, probation officers, moral welfare workers, etc.—and reports are freely given and exchanged. Also professionally trained, and either employed within the school care service or by voluntary committees working with the service, are specially appointed 'children's workers' who deal with all cases of children and young people who seem to be in moral danger. They also help and advise pregnant schoolgirls and young putative fathers, every effort being made to see that their education is continued and completed to university level if such is their ability.

With the increasing complexities of the social services and the agreed principle that even the most serious problem family should be kept together if possible, and with the development of large secondary schools, it may become necessary to have professional social workers attached to the larger schools. It would, however, be desirable that they should, like the School Medical Service, be independent of school staffing if they are to give the best possible service to the families and so to individual children and the whole school community. If such a development took place in London we should expect them to be part of the School Care Service so that the knowledge, experience, and goodwill of the voluntary workers be used to the fullest possible advantage and the dangers of another 'splinter' service avoided. Social workers are indeed in such short supply that we could never hope to give an improved service by replacing the voluntary workers, only by using both can we maintain and develop our standards. Other education authorities and other social services are also thinking that in order to meet developing needs they too must give serious consideration to using voluntary help.

Perhaps what the School Care Service is able to do may be best summed up by the reading of short accounts of what individual workers have done for particular families—these are all cases that have been quoted in annual reports of the School Care Service to the Education Committee. They also illustrate how the service, as well as helping those in constant need of support, also meets the needs of intelligent families who appreciate having someone with whom to talk over their problems and to guide them in the right use of the education and welfare services.

CASE HISTORIES

1. A widow, after the sudden death of her husband, was left with four dependent children. Her husband had held a good posi-

tion but there was no pension from his firm and as two of the children were already at secondary schools the mother was faced with considerable financial stress. The care committee gave immediate emergency help with free school dinners and some school clothing, and the mother realised that the worker would always be available for advice and help, whenever required. After a short time on National Assistance, the mother obtained a post as a helper in an infants' school. It was, however, still very difficult for her to readjust her expenditure to her reduced income. Again, with care committee help, the eldest boy was able to go on the school journey and, when the mother was accepted for three years' training as a teacher, a grant was obtained through the care committee from a benevolent fund to enable her to meet the family's needs during the period between leaving her job and starting at college. The eldest boy is continuing at school beyond 'O' level and as the mother says, 'they will be a family of students for some time to come'. The care committee's support will continue and enable them all to take full advantage of these opportunities.

2. A grandfather and grandmother legally adopted their grandson after his mother's remarriage. They were an elderly couple and comfortably off until the grandfather died and the grandmother was left with a very small fixed income. The flat, where she had lived for many years, was in an expensive locality but she was worried at the idea of having to leave it. She is managing by taking one or two students for bed and breakfast but finds it somewhat of a strain. The grandson is doing well at grammar school, and with care committee support the grandmother is managing to cope. All she really needs is a willing listener which the care committee supplies regularly. The headmaster reports that this has been a real help and comfort to her.

3. An Anglo-Indian family arrived in England in December 1963, father a labourer, three children aged nine, eight, four, the eldest child being enuretic. Care committee visited and found the family heavily in debt with very expensive furnished accommodation and hardly having enough to eat. Mother was very anxious and poorly, an old T.B. case and fearful of becoming pregnant again. The care committee got in touch with the Health

Visitor and the T.B. Clinic, and the mother is now having advice on family planning. The care committee devoted much time to helping and encouraging the mother to keep appointments at clinics for herself and the children. Help was given with school meals, clothing, and bed linen. Plans are now being made for the youngest child to be admitted to a day nursery when the mother's health is sufficiently improved for her to take light work and so help their financial position. The family is being advised about family allowances and housing, and the care committee will continue to guide and help.

4. In a West Indian family with three girls, the two elder were thought by the school to be ill-treated. When the care committee visitor called she found that the stepfather admitted to beating them because he said he knew of no other way to keep them in order. By regular visiting, discussing the difficulties of bringing up teenage children and the difference of attitudes in the West Indies and England, she has been able to help. The girls seem happier, and though sometimes naughty they are no longer treated so harshly.

5. Father a polio victim and confined to a wheel-chair, the care committee arranged a family holiday for the mother and the five children aged three to fourteen when, through the hospital, the father spent a month in a convalescent home. This was the first holiday that any of them had been able to have since the father's illness. Not only was a considerable amount of money raised to pay for the cost but the care committee saw that the family had suitable clothes and enough money for the little extras that make such a difference to a holiday.

6. Parents and five children aged eight to sixteen had been rehoused from another district under the 'problem families' quota. The intensive case-worker who had been visiting them prior to rehousing supported them through the move and for some time afterwards, but a year later the Housing Department reported rent arrears of £50. This was mainly due to the father, it is said, being 'work-shy'. The care committee arranged for one of their men evening visitors to tackle the situation. This he did with great energy and persistence, backed by advice from a psychiatric social worker in the Public Health Department. Father had

developed a grudge against a former employer, maintaining that he had been wrongly dismissed. The care committee worker was eventually successful in persuading him to forget this. The worker looked out suitable advertisements, provided him with a decent suit and cajoled him into applying for jobs and finally saw him safely through a rehabilitation course. The family were visited weekly for over a year; the visitor even mended the TV set on Christmas Eve and so forestalled the family buying a new one on hire purchase. Father now has a regular job, the rent is paid promptly and arrears are almost cleared. The wife, who in despair had secretly consulted a probation officer about a possible legal separation, seems a different woman. Recently the care committee visitor was an honoured guest at the eldest daughter's engagement party.

7. A family was brought to the care committee's attention because of Mary's poor school attendance and inability to work when she did attend. This was due to her mother's emotional disturbance and distrust of authority. A psychiatric clinic had been treating the mother and her sister but had given up because they could not get their cooperation. Many of the mother's problems were financial, she was separated from her husband and received a small maintenance allowance supplemented by National Assistance. Help was given with meals and clothing and application made to a charity which met a large outstanding electricity bill. This help won the mother's trust and she herself sought advice when her eldest daughter became pregnant. The care committee made all the necessary contacts and helped the daughter to manage her affairs independently of her mother, which was very necessary for both of them. Summer holidays were twice arranged for Mary, and this year she went to a S.C.M. camp with help from a voluntary fund. A care worker took her shopping to spend her uniform grant. Her self-confidence has so much improved that she now attends school regularly, takes an active part in all school life, and also goes to a youth club. The mother has lost her feelings of distrust and now turns to the care committee with any problem that arises—recently the cost of dentistry and chiropody for herself.

8. At the beginning of 1963 a family of parents and three children

was about to be evicted once more on account of rent arrears. On investigating, the care committee worker discovered that their total debts, including rent arrears, amounted to just under £200. These had accrued partly through the parents' illness and partly for maintenance of the children in care following a previous eviction. The family was again in danger of breaking up and had completely lost heart. A small grant from a voluntary fund staved off the immediate danger and avoided the expense of court action. Free meals, clothing for mother and children, and a recuperative holiday for the children all helped, but for the next eighteen months the care committee visited regularly and through their support and practical help the family in that time cleared all but one small debt. Recently one child was referred to a child guidance clinic owing to lack of progress at school and it was encouraging to learn that in the psychiatrist's opinion 'this is a worthwhile family, not very expert at accounts, that has responded well to the supportive action of the Care Committee Service'.

9. Irish family, six children under twelve, father indolent, mother devoted and hardworking but a poor manager, housing appalling —two small rooms. One child epileptic and now in a day special school as the parents will not accept boarding school placement. The care committee was in close touch, but the mother did not reveal the fact that debts were mounting until eviction was threatened. The father then took a labouring job and the mother asked for help. With a grant from the Children's department (given under Section 1 of the 1963 C.Y.P. Act) the care committee provided the father (slightly crippled) with suitable working boots, cleared the electricity and grocers' bills so that the family was able to reduce, and by now will have cleared, the rent arrears. They have also been recommended for priority rehousing.

10. Mrs R, a Liverpool girl, after many separations finally left her husband and came to London in 1959 with two young children and expecting a third. Since 1960 the care committee has been her main support, providing clothing, arranging holidays, including a free one at Butlin's for Mrs R and the baby. There have been times when Mrs R has been very depressed and

even threatened suicide, and the care committee called in the Mental Welfare Officer but the psychiatrist who saw Mrs R decided that it was friendly interest and support that she needed rather than psychiatric treatment, so the care committee worker has continued to give that and arrange for material assistance when required. Mrs R did a part-time job for a time but had to give it up owing to arthritis; whilst working she undertook various hire-purchase commitments (she keeps her home and children very nicely) and in trying to meet them neglected the rent. This debt was cleared by the care committee obtaining help from several sources. Mrs R once wrote, 'I am ever so sorry to take my worries to you, I do hope you can help me', and there is no doubt that the necessary support will always be available when required.

13
The Social Education Team
Derek Birley

An important innovation in school welfare provision is the 'social education team', recently developed in Liverpool. The City now has five such teams, and the thinking behind the scheme is sketched here by Liverpool's former Deputy Director of Education.

Social education teams were not conceived as an organisational device. They were created because of an organisational problem, but one that we saw as a symptom and not as the disease itself. The problem that sparked off the development was, in fact, a familiar one: to which department should certain additional staff belong if appointed? It happened to arise in Liverpool and the year happened to be 1966, but it could well have been anywhere else and any time in recent years. So, too, could the situation revealed by the more detailed study that followed. There was tremendous activity amongst those educationists and social workers concerned about children with handicaps. An ever-growing range of problems was being tackled by many different agencies, each with its own traditions and techniques. Some owed administrative allegiance to education, some to other services; some were statutory, some voluntary. Most had been set up in earlier days to meet specific needs as they had emerged. Their paths crossed frequently, but more by accident or impromptu effort than design. There were, for example, remedial teachers assigned to schools for short periods on an *ad hoc* basis; education welfare officers concerned mainly with attendance; doctors largely involved with medical inspection and the process of 'ascertainment' for special education; school nurses engaged on their own inspections and visiting homes as health visitors; a few psychologists and social workers dealing with child guidance by withdrawing children from school to attend clinics. Communication among them, and with the schools they served, was erratic.

All these were specialists disciplined to look at people from a particular angle, belonging to an administrative set-up that encouraged selection or rejection of 'cases' according to narrow terms of reference. Add to them the child care officers, housing officials, probation officers, police and various family case-work agencies, all of whom might be concerned with a particular child, and there was every chance of confusion. A more fundamental weakness, though, was that this welter of specialisms tended to conceal the need to look at children's problems in the round. Children are human beings, not cases. They are also, of course, members of families and residents of particular districts. Here we could see another weakness. Certain areas of Liverpool had more than their share of social problems. The same districts came highest on the problem lists of several departments—in, for example, educational standards, housing, child care, health, social and psychological adjustment, school attendance and observation of the law. Yet the logic of this had not been followed: the weight of tradition and compartmentalism sanctified prevailing practices with little regard for their relevance.

Most field-workers saw the need for closer links with other agencies and many took the trouble to make personal contact with opposite numbers. But goodwill and individual effort were nowhere near enough to surmount the enormous obstacles: different allegiances, different methods, different objectives (or assumed objectives), different professional attitudes. And sometimes, since the people concerned were human, these attitudes seemed to conceal vested interests. More was needed than tinkering with the organisation. It was not enough to ensure that educational psychologists were attached to the 'right' department: it had to cease to matter which had nominal responsibility for them. The most serious problems and the areas affected most had to have concerted, skilled attention. Children needed help early enough for it to do some good. In short, there had to be cooperation, not merely coordination, and this meant turning sterile interprofessional tensions to constructive ends. For we were not only dealing with a multiplicity of separate problems; there was an interrelationship between them that added a new dimension to the task. Social and psychological factors, emotional and behaviour difficulties led to educational mishaps, and vice-versa. For many children there was a vicious circle of deprivation and performance, with the human and physical environment of home and school interacting to their increasing disadvantage. Any expert involved had to see particular handicaps as indicators, facets of a whole.

The social education team tried to meet this exacting requirement. A pilot exercise in a small part of the area in greatest need brought together a school doctor, a school nurse, an educational psychologist, a psychiatric social worker, a remedial teacher, and a group of education welfare officers. Initially, they worked with fourteen schools in a concerted attempt to seek out handicaps of every kind that came between children and their education. Their brief was to discover the source of trouble rather than clear up particular symptoms, to do so, if they could, at the incipient stage, and then collectively to decide what action to take. We tried as far as possible to use existing resources. (We had, as it happened, little choice, but in any event an unrealistic level of staffing would have reduced the experiment's predictive value.) Nor did we wish to threaten traditional allegiances. So the team members were part-time, spending much of their week on their usual duties. However, there had to be someone whose first allegiance was to the team, to see that it operated smoothly and to see that its purposes were kept before the members. It so happened that a long felt need of the education service in Liverpool was for expert attention to the effect of social influences on educational performance; so the opportunity was taken to appoint a full-time Education Guidance Officer for this work, and to ask him to act as leader of the social education team.

The team then began meeting once a week to discuss certain children from families thought to need special attention, to decide on lines of approach and, if necessary to call on other agencies. The Children's Officer, Probation Officer, Chief Welfare Officer, Director of Housing and Chief Constable were informed of the venture and asked to send representatives to join in the work.

Once a month the team enlarged itself to meet these colleagues. This, as well as forming a simple, organised link between social work departments, also offered a much easier channel of communication between schools and the various agencies; instead of wondering which one to approach they need only turn to the Education Guidance Officer. He was also a permanent link between meetings for all participants.

Aside from his function as team leader the Education Guidance Officer's role was an extension of that of the Education Welfare Officer. Poor school attendance is at once a handicap and an indicator, often the first, of something more seriously wrong; something that could stem from trouble at home, at school, in the child himself or all three. Legal sanctions, even if effectively applied (and they rarely are), are usually irrelevant to this sort of situation. For these children it is much more important to find out the cause of the trouble. Many E.W.O.s had long accepted this, but had to reconcile it with the traditional duty of keeping up a high average attendance at schools. The social education team could not, of course, resolve this dilemma, but by showing the importance of attendance as an indicator it helped make the E.W.O.s' role a coherent one rather than an uneasy amalgam of police and welfare functions. Thereafter it tried to make systematic use of their considerable skill and experience in identifying and treating the small proportion in greatest need.

Apart from detection, the E.W.O. also had a key role in linking home and school which the team saw as the first practical step to be taken. The E.W.O. tried to build up a good relationship with the parents of a child in trouble, to create an atmosphere in the home in which parents would at least talk about the difficulties. Then, if possible, he tried to bring home and school closer together. He and the Education Guidance Officer were the main means of communication in this: they tried to make contact not only with heads but with class teachers, not always a simple matter, particularly in primary schools. They were not, it must be emphasised, forging these links as an end in themselves. They were acting as essential links in a chain.

Because this contact had a specific purpose it seemed more likely to succeed (and more likely to happen) than generalised attempts to improve communications. This principle was applied in all team-working, internal and external. Thus the connection regularly being demonstrated between learning and emotional or behaviour problems constantly reminded psychologists and their social workers of the importance of providing schools with reports on the progress of children receiving treatment. Children still had to be brought out of school to attend child guidance clinics and psychologists were rarely able to get into schools; but the remedial teacher made regular visits, which, programmed by the team, were a useful link between psychologist and class teacher. (This worked so well that when a much enlarged remedial service was later set up it was organised in district teams corresponding with the social education teams, with which they were linked through the psychologist-members.) It was naturally hoped that when more psychologists and social workers could be appointed they would visit schools themselves, but this would not lessen the specific value of the remedial teacher in demonstrating practically how intellectual, emotional and social factors were interrelated.

The role in the team of the school doctor was naturally related basically to the effect of physical factors. Medical knowledge can sometimes put an entirely new complexion on a problem, and the doctor was often able to give valuable guidance. But most doctors learn a good deal of the families in their areas, about other than medical matters, and the pilot team were fortunate in having a doctor member who contributed substantially in this way. Similarly, the school nurse's visits to schools (for eye and cleanliness inspections, for instance) and her quasi-health-visitor relationship with many homes in the area made her an important contributor. These medical colleagues helped to enlist the aid of general practitioners and hospital services on many occasions.

There were no formal procedures of referral: it was left to the discretion of individual team members to decide what they could handle alone in conventional fashion and what to refer to the team. Nor were full team-meetings the only means of operation. The Education Guidance Officer could pass on a problem to an individual member or to an agency outside the team. Within the first few weeks, for instance, he consulted voluntary agencies such as the Family Service Units, the Young Volunteers of Merseyside, the Liverpool Personal Services Society, and such obvious sources of help as the Hospital Service and the Ministry of Social Security. In short this was not another new agency, competing for custom, but a cooperative association supporting and strengthening what existed.

A team is not a committee. This one did not demand that all problems be brought before the whole group and wait a week for the privilege. Nor, conversely, was it thought necessary for meetings to be held if there was nothing to discuss. Its terms of reference related to objectives rather than administrative frontiers. Of course, it was hoped that there would be operational advantages. Less time might be wasted passing pieces of paper or telephone messages to the various headquarters and back; there should be less confusion if left hands knew what right hands were doing. It would be a step towards common boundaries for the various field-workers' districts: there would be easier links with schools and with other agencies. Team-working should make more effective and economical use of staff. But, beyond this, the team was the embodiment of an attitude, built up from the concept of collective solution of problems at the point of impact.

This short account inevitably omits a good deal. Most serious, perhaps, is that little can be said about the place of ventures like this in educational personal services as a whole, for they make no sense unless they form part of a comprehensive and consistent approach towards redressing inequalities of educational opportunity throughout the whole of an authority's education service.* Another serious omission is the absence of any attempt at *evaluation*. One can say that the Education Committee were so enthusiastic about the early results that they expanded the scheme to provide five teams covering between them the whole city. One can add that the Corporation's management consultants were sufficiently impressed to recommend that complementary teams be set up for the authority's personal health and social services work. But no objective measures can be applied: it is too soon, particularly as throughout its life so far the scheme has never been free of

* For a further discussion of this and related questions the reader may wish to consult *An Equal Chance* by Derek Birley and Anne Dufton (Routledge & Kegan Paul, 1971).

change. Nor is it clear what criteria can fairly be applied to such a venture—connected with education, concerned to emphasise complexities and interrelationships, feeling its way—nor who will be entitled to apply them. Bearing in mind the principles of self-analysis and capacity for change built into the social education team idea, the answer is probably that the teams themselves will be in the best position to judge and that, properly supported by sensitive administration, they will evaluate the scheme by the way they themselves change and develop in the years to come.

14
Attaching Social Workers to Schools—I*

Pauline Avery and Robert Adamson

A developing means of linking home and school is through the appointment of school social workers. This is an account of the work of these specialists, based on the authors' experience as school social workers at two secondary schools, as part of the Central Lancashire Family and Community Project.

Schools seek to help children with problems in different ways. Head and assistant teachers sometimes undertake home visits and discuss cases with statutory and voluntary agencies. They prepare reports for courts and child guidance clinics. Education welfare officers, as their change in title indicates, have gradually come to work with many problems affecting the attendance and performance of the child. Educational psychologists and psychiatric social workers from child guidance clinics may visit home and school to reach an assessment of a problem. The school nurse may also be the health visitor who has known the family for a period of years.

This summary indicates that, in general, the welfare aspects of education are covered by members of the teaching staff who lack specific social work training and experience; or by workers based outside the school, unfamiliar to some degree with the climate and functioning of the school concerned. In this paper we discuss the appointment of social workers as school staff members, with particular reference to appointments made in the Central Lancashire area.

* Adapted from 'School social work and crime prevention', *Howard Journal*, Vol. 12, No. 4, 1969, pp. 264–70, by kind permission of the publishers.

A social worker appointed to schools offers a casework service to individual children and to families. He needs a room of his own, readily accessible to children, and a telephone within easy reach. Unfortunately small rooms are not generally available in schools and telephones are usually situated where conversations can easily be overheard.

Referrals come from different sources—headmaster, teachers, parents, education welfare officers, and local clergy. Children come of their own accord for help and the social worker himself may observe boys and girls in difficulties. Contact with primary feeder schools and routine interviewing of first year children may alert the secondary school social worker to incipient delinquency or maladjustment. A child who is already the responsibility of another agency (such as the children's department or probation) will have his own caseworker; but a social worker in school can sometimes supplement this service.

Children often come to the notice of the school social worker because they are anxious about lessons or about relationships with teachers, the peer group or members of their families; or because they exhibit the symptoms of such anxieties—headaches, sickness and dizziness, lack of concentration, poor attendance and truancy. Amongst other reasons for referral are disruptive and withdrawn behaviour in school, pilfering, poor material conditions and also the sort of problems normally associated with adolescence.

Wherever possible, the child concerned is first interviewed in school so that his initial perception of the social worker is of a concerned and non-threatening person. Home visits, discussions with teachers, referrals to other agencies can then be seen as part of a helping process, undertaken with his knowledge and co-operation. Giving notice in advance of a first home visit may help towards acceptance by parents.

Another service which the school social worker can offer is group work with deprived or delinquent children. Where the group works with some activity (rather than discussion as its obvious task), the proportion of more normal children who will want to come hiking or make toys or play table football should help to prevent the group from becoming too easily identifiable.

Sometimes a child leaves school with a problem unsolved.

The school social worker can offer an after-care service in such cases.

The role of any social worker is broadly defined by the setting in which he works, and by the structure of his local agency. This is especially true where the social worker is seeking to become established in an organisation that has built up its own separate expertise over a lengthy period. Schools have over generations developed their own ways of coping with the problems posed by individual children. It is asking a lot to expect all teachers to welcome as a colleague someone from another profession, who seeks to supplement what is being done for the pupils by methods that are sometimes so similar and in other respects so different from these now used in education. How far the social worker can become established, with a clear identity as the member of staff offering a specific casework service, depends on the combined effect of a number of factors.

Some teachers are orientated more towards their subject than towards the children. They feel that it is no part of a school's function to be concerned more than is absolutely necessary with the wider aspects of the children's development. It would seem to them unnecessary and irrelevant to employ a social worker within the school. Other teachers and local education authorities may feel that for a school to have a social worker immediately brands it, in the eyes of the public, as a 'problem school'. They may seek to avoid such an appointment, or alternatively to take steps to disguise the real purpose of the job by changing the title and the role of the worker in some way.

Perhaps in most secondary schools there is a willingness to assume responsibility for the all-round development of the pupils. Much help is given with individual problems. Many headmasters are justifiably proud of the interest taken in the children and their families. Headmasters have themselves tended to lead and direct the welfare aspects of the school's work, liaising with families and local social workers. As schools are getting bigger, however, there is inevitably a need for greater specialisation. More and more schools are starting to appoint teachers as housemasters, school counsellors, and home-liaison officers, to be responsible for improving links between home and school, and to ensure that the difficulties of individual children are not overlooked. There are some factors here that will necessarily limit and define the role of the school social worker. In the first place, his position will be affected by the extent to which class teachers feel undermined and threatened by his presence, in their own professional desire to get to know their pupils well and to give help and guidance. Moreover, the social worker attached to a school is dependent on how far his headmaster is prepared to delegate the welfare elements of his own job; and how much this aspect of the school's work is being catered for by other specialist 'counselling' appointments within the school.

Helping teachers to greater awareness leads on from understanding the causes of personal difficulties and behaviour problems to looking for solutions. Here the social worker's expertise is put to the test. Teachers may think in terms of quick and easy solutions. When these are not available they may conclude that no solution is possible. They have to be helped to appreciate that, in some cases, a slight modification must be regarded as a major improvement. The damage done by years of insecurity or lack of self-esteem cannot be overcome in a matter of weeks. Frequent setbacks must be tolerated. It is difficult for some teachers to accept that the aims of social work may appear to conflict with their own. When a withdrawn child tries out his newly experienced relief of tension, or when a child lacking in confidence gains in self-reliance, his conduct in the classroom may be markedly different from his previous, inconspicuous (and therefore satisfactory) behaviour. Schools may have to acknowledge problems which have always existed but which have only recently been adequately diagnosed.

Heightening staff awareness of the personal problems of children affects the climate of the school. The gradual development of concern and esteem, of acceptance and informed compassion brings a response from all children, including the socially deprived and inadequate. A school social worker can represent the interests of this section of the school community when discussing policy with the headmaster, during staff meetings or in informal discussions in the staffroom. Function and structure of a house system, use of merit and demerit marks, sanctions applied in school, place (and even nature) of school uniform, approach to sex education, use of prefects, appointment to positions of responsibility of the less intelligent, promotion of after-school activities—these are areas where a social worker may help headmaster and staff to appreciate the problems of those he endeavours to help.

In the recent White Paper *Children in Trouble*, the Government envisages regular discussion between the services working with children: 'Teachers . . . will take part in these meetings, and children's departments will maintain close liaison with schools when considering the action to be taken in individual cases.' We feel that discussion at coordinating meetings is not enough to bring about cooperation and understanding between teachers and social workers. How far it is possible to break down the barriers that exist between the two professions depends on how much those who train social workers get together with lecturers from colleges of education, to study their respective courses, to agree on what prospective teachers and social workers need to be taught in common about child development, possible methods of dealing with difficulties that occur, and the various sources of help available in the community.

Appointing social workers to individual schools at least means a daily confrontation between members of these separate professions. This in itself will not necessarily bring about understanding between workers from the two fields. But it should at least highlight the areas of overlap between them, point out some of the difficulties that stand in the way of real coordination, and perhaps provide a few examples of effective cooperation between teachers and social workers for the benefit of the children.

The White Paper also stresses the importance of early recognition and treatment of problems. If we accept that preventive work has an important part to play in countering delinquency and other forms of social breakdown, then we should remember the potential of schools to help in this respect. Elizabeth Irvine (*New Society*, March 1966) points out that 'once a child has entered school, his teachers probably have more opportunity than anyone but his parents to observe the signs of incipient emotional disturbance or character disorder'. A school social worker provides a casework service for children and their families who might benefit, but would not normally be reached, by other social workers.

But the school social worker's role is not only affected by the staffing arrangements in his school and by the attitudes of the teachers. It is also influenced by the social work provision in the area, and by the way he is viewed by his colleagues in these outside agencies. Overlapping and duplication must be avoided. It is obvious that the social worker attached to a school served (for example) by a well-staffed Child Guidance Clinic, will have a different job from one working in an area without a clinic.

It is not possible to talk about the role of the school social worker in the abstract, as if this referred to a single clearly defined concept. The social worker attached to a school is given a specific area in which to operate. His work is also shaped by the pressure of feeling that surrounds him. On the other hand, he does not necessarily have to submit to being passively moulded by these outside influences. The exact job he is given to do, and the way it evolves, will also be affected by how he himself regards his role, the strength of his feelings about his work, and by his ability to persuade people to his point of view.

There are five of us working as school social workers in Central Lancashire.* We have all had very different forms of training, and our functions within our schools are not identical. Only one of us is employed solely as a social worker. Three of us have about a quarter of a teaching timetable in addition. The fifth does some teaching and is also a housemaster, with special responsibility for helping first-year children with problems of adjustment to a new school. Each version of the school social worker's role seems to have its own peculiar advantages and disadvantages.

A school social worker with no secondary duties is perhaps less likely to be initially acceptable to teacher colleagues. On the other hand, he has the possible advantage of being able to establish gradually a clearly defined role. He can get on with his primary task unhindered by other duties. His problem is that he is in danger of not being able to make contact with the wider school population outside his own caseload. There are ways round this difficulty (group work, club activities etc.). But unless some such measure is adopted the worker is not well placed for spotting early signs

* Written in 1968.

of disturbed behaviour by his own observation. He faces the possibility of being outside the normal school routine, at the end of a referral system which could tend to isolate both himself and his clients.

The teacher/social worker hybrid, by comparison, is more likely to gain acceptance from his teacher colleagues, will appreciate their problems, and is in a position to observe, and make contact with, children who might never be referred to him. On the other hand, the more forms he gets to know by teaching, the less time he has for casework and home visiting. Furthermore, there may be some role conflict which is confusing for everyone. The child perhaps cannot understand why his social worker allows him to behave in a very uninhibited manner in interview, but has quite different expectations in the classroom. If the social worker teaches, there may be less need for teachers to think about the use of casework in schools. At times of staff shortage especially, there is likely to be pressure on the social worker to hide his separate identity and become just another teacher.

Education at its fullest is concerned with the total development of children—intellectual, physical, social, emotional and moral. The conveying of information is structurally organised: there are heads of departments, departmental discussions, prepared syllabuses, a system of record books, etc. Responsibility for the physical development of children is shared by the physical education specialists and the school health service. The social, emotional and moral development of the children is promoted through many different media. All teachers, through their approach to their subjects, can make an important contribution. By their general expression of concern, both headmaster and staff can provide a helpful atmosphere. More specific provision is made through religious instruction, social education courses and through guidance and counselling facilities. The appointment of a social worker to the staff represents one further way in which the school can show concern for the less tangible aspects of the development of children, stressing particularly the possibilities of growth through relationship.

The school social worker has the opportunity to arouse and increase the sensitivity and awareness of other staff members in their approach towards children in difficulties. Teachers often know the obvious problems only in an intellectual way. There is the child getting free meals or a uniform grant, the child on whose behalf school reports have to be made to the children's department, the child who persistently comes late and has to struggle with inadequate facilities and lack of encouragement over homework, the immigrant child with his problems of understanding and integration, the child of low intelligence with special needs for achieving his limited potential. The academic acknowledgement of these difficulties can be extended into a deeper realisation of their implications and a warmer, more understanding approach to the children concerned.

In addition to increasing awareness of obvious problems, the social worker can introduce increased sensitivity to children with behaviour problems. Some examples are the attention-seeking child whose behaviour may be ingratiating or descriptive; the child who lacks motivation or powers of concentration; the withdrawn child; the isolated child; the precocious child; the bully. Teachers may be helped to a greater acceptance by an outline, or deeper discussion, of the factors involved—health, marital disharmony, family background, personality development, etc.

Passing on to teachers information acquired during home visits, individual interviews or agency contacts involves questions of confidentiality. Some social workers do not give details at case conferences, others are guarded in the information they give to a mutual register, and refrain from cooperating because they fear it may be misinterpreted or misused. Since this issue is still a matter for debate by social workers with common training and aims, there are difficulties for the school social worker in relation to teachers. If staff members are to be helped to greater awareness of their pupils' problems and the impact of these difficulties on behaviour and performance in school, some details must be conveyed. But how much and to whom? If the social worker decides to withhold information, how does he justify his reservations when challenged, without appearing to be pretentious? Teachers may expect that, in a two-way process, all information will be shared. Some may see the conveying of such details as the social worker's main justification for including him on the staff.

15

Attaching Social Workers to Schools—II

Margaret Auld

In this paper Miss Auld describes a scheme for the attachment of social workers to schools which has run successfully for a number of years, and is continuing within the reorganised pattern of Scottish welfare services.

The Sub-committee on School Attendance, on behalf of the Education Department, in 1944 presented to the Corporation of Glasgow a report on juvenile delinquency, in which it was stated that there were cases and situations where home influences adversely affected the child, but were capable of correction, and that specially trained officers who would form a valuable link between the school and home appeared to have a place in the modern school. In 1945 steps were taken to make such appointments, in the first place on an experimental basis. The service lapsed in 1948, but was reinaugurated in 1950.

In 1957 the Committee considered the whole position and concluded that the evidence obtained justified the retention of the service as a permanent feature of the corporate life of the school in which this type of assistance was necessary, and agreed to develop the service as opportunity presented itself. Since that date there has been expansion and development, and by 1967 there were sixteen school welfare officers and one Senior Welfare Officer in the City. It is fitting that one should pay tribute to the Education Committee for initiating and supporting the School Welfare Officer Scheme in Glasgow, and acknowledge the enlightened administration which has nurtured the Service since its inception.

With the implementation of the Social Work (Scotland) Act in November 1969 a complete reorganisation of Scottish welfare services has begun. The administration of the Glasgow School Welfare Officer Service has passed from the City's Education Department to its new Social Work Department, and although the School Welfare Officers will probably remain school-based they will in future be known as 'school social workers'.

Appointees to this kind of post must now be professionally qualified in social work, i.e. holders of a university diploma or certificate in applied social studies or, alternatively, a certificate in social work awarded by a college of education. Two of the appointees are graduate teachers as well as being social work trained, and another is at present on secondment to an advanced course in Applied Social Studies at Queen's College, Dundee. Each social worker is a member of staff within a secondary school, directly responsible to the headteacher for the conduct of social work from within the school, and in future to be administratively controlled by the Director of Social Work.

The school social workers are supplemented by a number of welfare assistants who were previously employed as school attendance officers but were seconded to a modified course of social work training. They assist the social workers by undertaking work related to clothing, late-coming, or neglect, or on cases supervised by the social worker. The contribution made by the welfare assistants has enabled the service to encourage case referrals from the primary territorial schools and offer a limited service to 'outwith area' schools. One of these welfare assistants has since successfully completed a professional course on secondment and has returned to the Department as a qualified social worker. The service is used as a practical training placement by the University Social Study Course and the Probation Officers' Course.

A broad outline of the duties of the former school welfare officer was originally set out as follows:

To make contact with the pupils in the school; keep in touch with the homes of the pupils with whom the Officer is dealing, and by various means direct them, the pupils, into interesting and profitable ways of spending their leisure time. It is not intended that the Officer should concentrate wholly on the delinquent or the potential delinquent or truant, but on those conditions which will effect a reduction in the incidence of juvenile delinquency and truancy.

The wide range of duties may have presented difficulty in that the work undertaken by the Welfare Officers showed some diversity from school to school, dependent on the interpretation of duties as determined by the headteacher and the varying needs of the schools. Nevertheless, it also afforded the opportunity for both teaching and social work staffs to consider function and inter-relationships in the light of experience and, as we have clarified our thinking in this respect, so has greater uniformity been achieved without ignoring the distinctive characteristics of a school and area.

The early development of the service has been that of social case work within an educational setting, directed towards prevention and correction, in the belief that if symptoms are recognised by the teaching staff as an early warning of social maladjustment, attention given at this stage may prevent the more serious problems from developing or becoming established as an antisocial or inhibiting pattern of living. Only recently have we endeavoured to consider objectively the particular aspects of school social work, and we would now define our function as one of specific concern for the pupils whose social and environmental difficulties are such as to prevent them from gaining full benefit from the educational system without special help and guidance.

New ideas are not always easily acceptable. In the early years, perhaps, the emphasis on delinquency and truancy, possibly exaggerated, created some unwarranted suspicion that the appointment of a school welfare officer questioned 'professional proficiency'. The charge is made that school authorities are traditional and obdurate, but no stronger evidence is required to refute this statement than the fact that the schools have come to accept the social worker as an integrated member of staff with a recognised place in the team of school personnel.

Basically, the social worker will be concerned with the children who are delinquent, who truant, who are presenting behaviour problems, or who appear to be neglected. On referral of a case, the social worker will endeavour to establish the closest possible link between the school and the home, not merely as a liaison but in a case-work relationship, through which it may be possible to see wherein the difficulty lies. He will visit families in which there is a multiplicity of problems or possibly defective personal relationships requiring care over a prolonged period and involving assistance from both statutory and voluntary social services; or families with lesser problems who may be passing through a crisis, when advice and help may be given and visitation continued in order to give support; or families wherein one or two visits may be sufficient to resolve the problems of clothing or footwear, perhaps, or difficulties within the school–home relationship.

Most parents want their children to do well at school and only a small minority are completely hostile. Parents do bring their doubts and perplexities to school, often in the pathetic hope that the school will succeed where the parents have failed. Apparent lack of cooperation may be due to lack of interest or to apathy, but may sometimes be unwitting, arising from misunderstanding of the school's concern, or from feelings of inferiority. It may be the very practical difficulty of organisation which prevents a mother with perhaps two or three children under five years of age from coming to school, and work commitment too often excludes father from the picture. Often the parent most in need is the parent who finds the greatest difficulty in coming to school, and it may be necessary for the social worker to interpret the needs of the school, to the home, and the needs of the home to the school, possibly preparing both parent and teacher for the school interview.

To return to the particular duties of the social worker: within the category of delinquency one would consider not only the children who have appeared before the courts, but the pupils who have been detected pilfering within the school, or who are involved in incidents of theft reported by the local shopkeepers, etc. Not all of the pupils who appear before the courts are potential criminals. Many of them are there because of silly pranks which have caused annoyance and inconvenience to the community, and it is often found that the parents of such children are fairly responsible people, quite capable of exercising the necessary supervision; one can feel confident that steps will be taken to ensure that there will be no further incidents of this kind. On the other hand, if the teacher reports deterioration, perhaps in application to class-work, in attitude and demeanour, or in attendance, then this is the pupil at risk, and an effort must be made to correct this trend and to direct his energies into more constructive channels, particularly with regard to the use of leisure time. Here may be found the parents who are too involved in their own personal affairs, or who feel that their duty to the child is met by providing for material needs. The understanding and attention of the teacher and club leader may be sufficient to enable this boy or girl to cope, whilst an endeavour is made to stimulate a sense of greater responsibility in the parents. These are the endangered children—the children who have appeared at court and perhaps been fined or admonished, delinquency-prone rather than the true delinquent. The school social worker works in close association with colleagues concerned with probation, often keeping a friendly eye on the probationer in school, and where necessary reporting irregular attendance or lack of school progress; but the social worker does not visit the home of a probationer unless so requested. If he has previously been visiting the home, he will continue only if it is considered expedient to do so, and in consultation with those colleagues concerned.

There is little doubt that truancy is closely associated with delinquency, although not all delinquents truant. One is reminded of a lad, delinquent, backward, an awful nuisance—although everyone liked the character—of whom the staff said at times rather wistfully: 'If he would just stay off for a day or two to give us peace!' But regular as clockwork he appeared at 9 a.m. and 2 p.m. It is possible that the school provided the only stable factor in this lad's life. The routine check of irregular attendance is not the province of the school social worker. Yet investigation of truancy is emphasised as a duty of the school social worker and also concerns the school attendance officer. Irregular attendance is often 'condoned' truancy. The whole question of irregular attendance should be looked at more closely and recognised as perhaps a first indication of social malaise.

One constructive step has been taken in recent years in relation to pupils brought before the courts by the Education Department for truancy or failure to attend school. Previously, these pupils were committed to an approved school, but the School Social Worker Service, on behalf of all such children, now provides a social enquiry in which recommendation is made either for committal to approved school or into the care of the local authority, or that a supervision order be granted to the social worker. Of the many court supervision orders, only a small number has been so unsatisfactory as to warrant breach, and one wonders if the pattern of irregular school attendance could be reversed if case-work help were available at an earlier stage.

It is not suggested that every pupil who misbehaves in class is either socially or emotionally maladjusted, but the boy or girl who is constantly a disruptive and disturbing influence in class, unresponsive to normal class discipline or school sanction, is recognised by the good teacher as a pupil experiencing difficulties with which he is unable to cope. The stress may be expressed as dullness and apathy, failure to relate to other children and adults, or in insolence, aggression, or bullying. From the report and assessment of the home and environmental influences much may be learned which will throw light on the child's development, and this may lead to a greater understanding of the pupil's needs. It may be, with this new insight and awareness, the teacher will consider a different approach or method in class. The attention of the teacher alone may ease the situation, or in consultation it may be decided that the teacher will make more effective use of the group situation, whilst the social worker will see the pupil individually for a time to support what is being done in class. The teacher may concentrate on the child, whilst the social worker continues to work in the home. Where the difficulties are such that they can hardly be modified, then perhaps all that can be done is to help the child to cope more effectively and with less distress. There should be no hesitation in referring to the Child Guidance Clinic the pupil who is emotionally disturbed. The question of respecting confidence appears to be one which occasions anxiety to social workers, but within the teacher–social worker relationship there grow trust and respect, and relative and helpful information should be shared.

Cases of latecoming, neglect, illness without physical cause, extreme anxiety, and many other related matters are also referred to the school social worker. The miscellaneous duties accepted by the social work staff used to include visitation of the new intake and the escort to hospital of children who have sustained an accident. But this latter work is now increasingly being carried out by 'teaching auxiliaries,' and the pastoral care by the house-masters/mistresses who have been appointed to many City schools. It is important that the welfare officer should not present the image of one concerned only with the awkward, delinquent or truant children, and for this reason the social worker should participate in school functions and activities—attendance at church, prizegiving and sports day, school camps, and excursions abroad.

In brief, the aim of the Service is to offer aid to the pupil who, by reason of social handicap, is unable to make full use of the educational system. The method is case work, preventive and remedial in intent, offered to children and/or their parents. The school social worker provides a link between the school and the home, collaborates and consults with other school staff and, where the problems demand outside resources, seeks the coopera-tion of other social agencies and community organisations.

How does one attach a social worker to a school? In Glasgow the newly appointed officer is given a four-week period of train-ing, or orientation, with an experienced officer. Part of this time may be spent in a comprehensive school in a new housing area, where the difficulties may be those of personal adjustment, community adaptation, or economic stress, whilst a further period may be spent in an area of poverty, poor housing, grim and dismal surroundings. Yet the atmosphere within the two schools may not be dissimilar. This is not in any way to deny the right of teachers and pupils to decent buildings with good accommoda-tion and equipment, but merely to stress that the school in the depressed area may be as happy, purposeful, and satisfying as that of the new area, since the atmosphere of the school will depend, not on buildings alone, but on staff.

During this period of training the social worker will be expected to acquire some knowledge of the organisation of a school, recognise that there is a hierarchy and accept that there is authority. Identification with the school is necessary if one is to function as a school social worker. It will be learned that referrals are seldom formal but arise from casual mention or staff-room conversation, and that consultation can be as constructive in a corridor encounter as in formal discussion. Referrals must be sanctioned by the headteacher. There should be as little interruption as possible to the work of the class, and when the social worker wishes to interview a pupil arrangements should be made with the teacher. The social worker must learn to plan her day and establish a routine so that staff and parents are aware of the times when she will be available.

What should one expect of the school? Perhaps it is of primary importance that the social worker be accepted as a person and as a member of staff. Inconvenience will be minimised and efficiency increased if the school will provide accommodation for the social worker. The teacher must not interpret social work as merely distributing largesse or 'spoon feeding' families. Social work is not just good common sense, but a profession founded on knowledge, and with its own principles, skills, and techniques. It does not threaten the teacher's authority or security, but is offered in support of what is being done in class to promote the development of the potential within every child. 'Discipline' is not an unseemly word in social work vocabulary. If a pupil returns to class from the social work interview via a 'smoke in the lavatory', this minor indiscretion will be frowned upon by the social worker as much as by the teacher, but it should be recognised that the interview with the social worker is as legitimate school practice as is the visit to the clinic or school doctor. Social workers do not perform miracles. Growth may be slow and there are frustrations and despondency in social work as in teaching. Perhaps the social worker may be envied his freedom of movement—a day not wholly controlled by a bell—but it should be recognised that the only time to see the father at home is in the evenings.

It has been said that the 'two professions of teaching and social work share a common belief in the potential within the individual and in the ability to grow and change'. School is the normal environment of all children during their formative years. In the field of social work there is an ever-increasing emphasis on prevention and early diagnosis but prevention is not possible without early detection. A school-focused, school-based service provides the means by which both detection and prevention may be practised and it offers a readily available link between the school and the home.

Every effort and experiment which succeeds in bringing greater understanding and cooperation between teacher and parent must be welcomed. In Glasgow, whilst we frankly admit that much is still to be learned, there is evidence that the two professions of teaching and social work can work in harmony and understanding; and the service of school social workers is based on the belief that the gap between the home and the school can be bridged.

16
Attaching Social Workers to Schools—III

A. R. Chorlton

This third account of a scheme for attaching social workers to schools offers a number of comparisons and a detailed evaluation of considerable interest, particularly to Local Education Authorities.

The merit of what I have to say may perhaps lie in the approach of a largely rural Authority to the problem of the child socially handicapped and failing to benefit from school, and the experience it has had in trying to bring about changes in this approach on the part of both teaching and of welfare staff. Our experience has not been a particularly encouraging one, but this may be a result of our own failures of approach or of a lack of persistence in getting over the sense of the new outlook to those concerned.

Oxfordshire, despite the growth of the motor industry and the increase in recent years of extra-metropolitan overspill, is still largely a rural area. Of its 172 primary schools with about 20,000 children on roll, over 100 are of three-class size and less; for a secondary population of 12,500 it has thirty-one schools. This is a factor which conditions many aspects of the education service which it seeks to provide.

I would not for one moment claim that our attitude to these children is more enlightened than many other Authorities. All we have possibly done is to travel a little further than some along the road to a more positive, and at the same time preventive, approach to the treatment of the socially handicapped child.

For a school population of about 24,000 at the time of the change (some ten years ago now) we had a staff of nine full-time school attendance officers. None of them had any special training. Their backgrounds were various. Whatever their previous experience and outlook, all responded loyally to the change of approach.

An analysis of the time spent on their various duties revealed that 50 per cent of the attendance officers' time was taken up in routine attendance visits and 24 per cent in consequential clerical work. The effectiveness of the service tended to be judged by attendance figures and percentages and the officer's efficiency likewise. Yet if one included absences due to unavoidable illness, attendance week by week in almost all schools was between 95 per cent and 100 per cent and the hard core of persistently poor attenders which all schools have, represented not more than 2 per cent to 3 per cent of the school population at any one time.

We felt—this was in 1960—that the time was ripe for changing to a service in which a greater emphasis was placed on welfare and prevention than on enforcement. Three attendance officers were dut to retire, and we were trying at the same time to create among headteachers the image of a single closely knit support service for children with behavioural or other difficulties. A team of professionally trained specialists were working together to provide a support service in which the welfare officers—or, as we decided to call them, school social workers—had a central role to play, and of which physiotherapists, speech therapists, psychologists, school nurses, were all regarded as members; with the help of this team the school would be armed to deal quickly and effectively with almost every type of need or problem.

I can perhaps indicate the shift in emphasis by quoting a paragraph of the memorandum which was sent out to headteachers at the time:

> The emphasis of the future service should be on the welfare of the child of school age in the context of the total educational process in which home and school share responsibility and not primarily on the enforcement of his attendance at school, the time and efforts of the officers concerned being redirected accordingly. The chief function of the service should be that of

helping and advising the schools, teaching staffs and parents with those children who for one reason or another are not deriving benefit from school, in many of whom the first symptom of a difficulty may be irregular attendance.

Such an alteration of emphasis and function implied:

1. that the routine work connected with the attendance of the normal child at school should be reduced to a minimum;
2. that a mixed staff of men and women would in future be desirable since there would be problems of a personal kind concerned with both sexes to be dealt with;
3. that the concept of a mixed team of professional equals—social workers and teachers—required professional training for the social worker posts and a professional scale of salary; (proper professional training remains, as the Younghusband report pointed out, the key to substantial improvements in the service);
4. that an essential qualification for officers would be a good knowledge not only of the education service but also ancillary medical and welfare services, since an important factor would be the ability to know when and to which specialist agency to refer.

Our experience had shown that the majority of children requiring help and attention were to be found in the non-selective secondary schools. For this and for geographical and administrative reasons we felt that these schools were the most convenient bases of operations, and we decided that several of them, together with their contributory primary schools, should form the social worker's service area.

It was explained that in these areas the social worker, ex-attendance officer, would normally be the first contact and source of reference and advice in cases of difficulty. As general purpose welfare workers they would act as the first 'sieve' dealing with the straightforward cases, calling upon specialist staff as and when required for the more complex cases.

The school social worker would also act as case conference convener, since we felt that periodic case conferences, possibly two or three a term, would serve a useful purpose in ensuring regular contact between the various members of the team. There was nothing especially original or out of the ordinary in all this; it is mentioned mainly to fill in the background.

The type of cases which we wished social workers to concentrate on, and which we explained to headteachers in presenting for them the new angle which we wished to emphasise, included:

children whose behaviour in school gives cause for concern;
children who are continually late to school for no apparent good reason;
children who appear to be inadequately clothed or shod or who appear undernourished;
children engaging in unsuitable employment out of school hours to their detriment;
children persistently kept at home for domestic duties;
children whose record of progress in school is unaccountably poor;
children who present behaviour problems with which the school needs outside help;
children who appear tired in school and persistently late;
children believed to be in moral danger;
and so on.

The list is indicative, of course, and not exhaustive.

It would rest, we made plain, with the headteacher to decide which cases to refer.

From close knowledge of the families in areas where we expected the social workers to be working, we felt that they should also concern themselves with the welfare and after-care of:

1. educationally subnormal and seriously retarded children about to leave school and in their first two years of employment;
2. handicapped children attending schools away from home.

We were able to fill the three posts vacant in 1960 with two men and one woman, all with appropriate qualifications and a useful and varied background of previous employment. If we had got over the message of the new approach, all seemed 'set fair'. Much would depend, we realised, on the effective explanation of the altered emphasis in the service and on the understanding and support of headteachers.

Eighteen months later we met the social workers to review progress. 'What had been their experience?' we asked. 'What difficulties had they encountered?' 'What was the attitude of heads?'

Here are a few examples which provide the gist both of their replies and of the extent of teacher understanding:

1. Heads are not referring cases as intended; appear to be concerned with routine absentees only; a failure to appreciate spirit and intention of new service.
2. Headteachers coming new into the county fail to make themselves aware of the new approach.
3. There is an attitude of indifference in the schools. 'In the past twelve months I have had only four cases reported to me.' Heads do not like to refer cases on paper. Heads would not bother to operate the scheme.
4. Heads appear to appreciate the scheme but are reluctant to adopt new methods.
5. The social worker has a feeling of inadequate status and of non-acceptance by professionally trained colleagues and fellow workers. Not being treated as professional.
6. Professional status is impaired by having to do other outside and somewhat menial tasks. 'One does not expect the man who deals with coaches to deal with neurotic children as well.'
7. The apparent failure of headteachers to explain the changed role of the school social worker and to secure the cooperation of the form teachers, the form or class teachers really being the people in possession of knowledge about the child with behaviour or other problems.
8. Too much was being left to the school secretary.
9. Tendency of headteachers to refer cases direct to children's officers and to Family and Child Guidance Clinic and not follow the channels of reference laid down.

This was disappointing. We therefore held meetings with Heads and senior teachers in various parts of the county to explain the service we envisaged and the kind of cooperation we sought from them. Progress was clearly going to be slow, and so it has proved. It was going to depend, as do so many aspects of the work of schools and of the education service, on the enlightened attitude of individual heads and the personality and competence of the social workers themselves. We could not enforce changes. The reveiw which I have mentioned, and others, subsequently threw light on a number of issues which the local education authority itself had to face and find a solution for:

1. The problem of who was to deal with the work not requiring professional training and which detracted from the status and acceptance of the social worker, i.e. bus routes, checking on children moving to the area of other L.E.A.s, issue of transport season tickets, census requirements, etc.
2. The problem of the social workers' status *vis-à-vis* the teachers' in the school and in the school staff room, where it was essential that they should be accepted as equals.
3. The very poor subsequent response from qualified applicants to vacancies, which suggested the need to alter the field of recruitment.
4. The number of schools with which the social worker could effectively deal. A group of 3 or 4 schools and contributory primary schools with a roll of 3,000–4,000 children was too large. Our experience has been that the number of referrals increases as the form teacher's understanding of the service and his role grows.

We can hope to move only gradually to a satisfactory answer to these.

We ourselves did not lay down or prescribe for schools a pattern of procedure for school social workers and teaching staff within the school's four walls. But in the event certain patterns have emerged which, with variations to suit differences of size and internal organisation and the heads' convenience, are being followed increasingly in the larger schools. I give one of these as an example, choosing a secondary school because it is here that the social worker's efforts and time are chiefly concentrated. At the same time there remain a number of heads who cling to the old system with great tenacity and the picture is by no means one of overall improvement.

It should, perhaps, be mentioned here, by way of background to the social worker's role, that we are strongly encouraging:

1. continuity of planning in syllabus and teaching methods between the top forms in the primary school and the lower forms in the secondary school, with as much movement of staff between schools as possible;
2. the avoidance of streaming in the first one or two years of the secondary school, and greater emphasis on the pastoral role of the form teachers, who shall have primary responsibility within the school for their pupils' welfare and for securing a full picture of the child;
3. staffing our schools on group staffing concepts as opposed to individual school staffing, with the added flexibility that this brings and the added ability to see the child's growth and upbringing through from his early beginnings to school leaving age or later.

The social worker's link and counterpart on the teaching staff is the year tutor. The year group, composed of all pupils of the same age and at an approximately similar stage of social, physical, and emotional development, fulfils the need, particularly in larger schools, for a sub-group within the school. Amongst the year tutor's responsibilities are psychological and physical welfare, academic progress, including transfer between sets and forms, contact with parents on admission, keeping the pupil's record card, the organisation of parents' meetings, the encouragement of social and 'out of school' activities. Elsewhere this link is with the house tutor or, in smaller schools, with the lower school tutor, the upper school tutor, and so on.

The social worker meets year tutors in pairs, every Friday morning, for a case discussion, first- and second-year tutors together since this enables the welfare of children passing from first to second year to be followed through. The responsibility of referral in the first case rests with the form teacher, who discusses with the year tutor any case in his form where he feels that attendance, work, behaviour, health, gives rise for concern and needs further investigation. Together they fill in details on the case referral form and this is discussed with the social worker who takes the appropriate action and reports back at the following weekly conference, or earlier if the matter is urgent. The social worker also regularly meets the headmaster to discuss cases of particular difficulty or complexity.

The social worker attends parents' meetings to discuss the L.E.A.'s school welfare service and periodic staff meetings to explain his responsibilities and work, for it is essential to the success of the scheme that all participating, particularly the form teacher and teachers new to the staff, should thoroughly understand it, and that the lines of communication should be clear.

Through this procedure, a satisfactory conclusion can be reached to the majority of cases referred by the personal contact of the school social worker, and an improved relationship is established between home and school. The tendency under the old procedure would have been for the attendance officer to have been regarded and received as a policeman, calling at the house to cause trouble and to take the child to court, and an atmosphere of non-cooperation and resistance established from the outset.

Where, as in a proportion of cases, it was necessary to refer to or seek the help of some other agency, an intensive follow up was maintained, which the weekly case conference at the school encouraged in any case, so that individual cases were not lost in the labyrinth of welfare agencies. This improvement of lines of communication is of great importance. We had earlier found that, because of a lack of 'feed back' of information to the school from the specialist welfare agencies, heads and form teachers too often felt they were working in a vacuum, and were discouraged from making further referrals.

Our school social workers are attached to secondary schools; but they are not members of the staff of an individual school. That has been found to have certain disadvantages, apart from the lack of time the social worker has to give to each of his schools. I have referred to the great difficulty we have experienced latterly in recruiting the kind of staff we wanted. More and more schools are finding the need for help and for follow-up facilities to be immediately available in other directions, for example with such tasks as: persuading the parents of children who would benefit to allow them to stay on at school and making known the available forms of financial help; persuading parents to support the periods of residential education which are a feature of Oxfordshire's secondary school system; acting as a liaison and channel of information about misbehaviour out of school leading on occasions to trouble with the police, which parents and school may be quite unaware of, and so on. Furthermore, about 30 per cent to 40 per cent of parents do not attend school functions; in these and other cases correspondence is time-taking and ineffective. The only successful way is through personal link and contact for which the majority of teachers have not the time, and they are often not best fitted for the work.

We are in transition from the old type of service to one that we hope is more enlightened. We are perhaps no more than half-way along the road. The direction of further travel is, however, becoming fairly clear. It was discussed in the Department of Education and Science Report on Education No. 22 on this very subject, *Education under Social Handicap*. It is not to use the staff of the Children's Department more fully as some have suggested; it is not to rely more on the school nurses, who often have the best of all entries to the pupil's home; it lies in those areas of the county where the Heads themselves see the kind of service we are aiming at and will use staff effectively. Here, where the schools are sufficiently large, the solution is either to appoint to the school staff a teacher with an aptitude and interest in social work and with appropriate training, or a trained social worker with an interest in teaching. I envisage this as a gradual process. With the development of Newsom-type studies and courses, particularly for the older pupils, there is a useful role in a school's programme and timetable for both: in Social Studies, in Health Education, in liaison work with School Careers staff, and so on, and in assembling information about children useful to those concerned with counselling on choice of courses and placement on transfer from primary to secondary school. Their service area would, as at present, be that of the secondary school and its contributory primary schools, enabling them to maintain contact with problem families from the time children start school, and to act, as now, as the school's own link with outside welfare staff and agencies.

This will overcome the difficulty of assimilation of the present social workers on school staffs; it will help with the problem of professional status and career structure with which this is connected, and which is a real deterrent to recruitment in the Education Welfare Service as it is at present and it will add to the school's own power to deal directly with its partners in the growing-up process, the parents, not only with school failure cases but in other sides of the school's role as a social force.

17

*Counselling in Schools**

John Raynor and Tony Atcherley

The introduction of counsellors into some of our schools offers one way of systematically dealing with the personal, educational and vocational needs of children, and, at the same time, of bringing the home and the school into greater contact.

Within the last decade we have witnessed a series of changes which have affected the secondary education of our children. Among them we should note, particularly, the gradual abandonment of selection for secondary education at eleven-plus; the trend towards staying on longer at school and the imminent raising of the school leaving age; and the swing towards the reorganisation of secondary education along comprehensive lines. These movements within the organisational structure of education have been accompanied by the recognition of a variety of problems which have been noted in a series of postwar researches and governmental enquiries. Amongst these problems are the identification of groups of young people who, for a variety of reasons, either have limited educational opportunities or reject those which are offered to them; the call for closer parent–school relationships; the general inadequacy of vocational guidance within the school; and the need for help to be given to young people who are growing up in an exceedingly complex and rapidly changing world.

The coalition of organisational changes with the identification of a series of new problems has produced a variety of responses,

* Adapted from 'Counselling in schools—some considerations', *Educational Research*, Vol. 9, No. 2, 1967, pp. 93–102, by kind permission of the publishers.

one of which is the introduction of the school counsellor into our schools. Within the last few years we have seen new training courses set up in several universities to train school counsellors, a slow penetration of the idea into colleges of education; and a developing interest in the movement by workers in the youth and community area. The field has been ploughed, the seed sown; what we wait to see now is what kind of plant will grow.

In our view all this is healthy enough, but a number of problems are in urgent need of clarification. In the first place, we know little yet about how best school counsellors can be deployed in our schools. Secondly, we need more information on the relationship between counselling and the curriculum. Thirdly, we need to know more about the role problems experienced by such workers. Finally, we need to construct a theory of counselling, applicable to schools in our culture, and not to rely upon concepts and theories imported from North America.

This paper seeks first to examine some prevailing theories of counselling, and goes on to consider some of the problems involved in the appointment of counsellors in schools.

GUIDANCE OR COUNSELLING?

All too often the terms guidance and counselling are used as if they were logically equivalent. The failure to distinguish between them can be seen in the literature and one of the problems of research in this field lies in ensuring that the terminology and objectives are the same. The term counselling in our education system is of recent vintage; traditionally guidance* has been the term used. It is essential to make clear from the beginning that we see a real distinction between the two.

Guidance, however it is practised, logically implies directing and can be applied to objects as well as to human beings. Counsel-

* The term 'guidance' has been used—technically and officially—in three connections, *viz.:* child guidance, vocational guidance and educational guidance. Of vocational guidance there has been comparatively little, really, in the schools; and 'educational' guidance has been largely biased towards 'selection' (e.g. at eleven-plus). In the present discussion, the term is used largely with the last two applications in mind; 'child guidance' in its technical sense is not involved, and it is realised that this approach is not usually directive.

ling, on the other hand, seems to us to be applicable only to human beings and to be closely connected with two fundamental assumptions about them. The first is that they are, or should be, autonomous, that is self-directing. The second, that human personality and behaviour are both unities. The counsellor has to be aware that he is not just dealing with an educational occupational, or personal problem that has to be solved, but that these problems and the individual's adjustment to them affect other aspects of his personality too. In other words the counsellor deals with a person and not just a problem.

Historically, it would seem that the development of the counselling movement in the U.S.A., has reflected the above distinction. Starting as vocational guidance and then increasingly taking into account the application of psychometry, it was strongly influenced by an expansion of knowledge about personality development, which was largely derived from psychotherapy with its emphasis on the motivational and affective aspects of behaviour. The counsellor 'was first either a teacher who helped people explore the world of work, or a psychologist who gave and interpreted tests. Then he, who might or might not have been a psychologist was a user of community resources, of occupational information, and psychological tests. He has now emerged as a psychologist. He is, however, a psychologist who uses varying combinations of exploratory experiences, psychometric techniques, and psychotherapeutic interviewing, to assist people to grow and to develop' (American Psychological Association, 1956).

While there is a distinction between guidance and counselling it by no means follows that they are incompatible and mutually exclusive. Whereas counselling is to us a more developed and inclusive term than guidance the counsellor is not prohibited from giving guidance. To insist that a counsellor should always be non-directive seems to us to be doctrinaire and unrealistic. Work with children or adolescents who for a number of good reasons, psychological, social or economic, have not yet reached a stage of autonomy may well require more guidance than counselling. It is interesting to note that this same point of the need to be directive was made by Dr Ratcliffe when writing on the problems of Youth Counselling. Similarly, since external reality, or environment, in its various material and social manifestations, be it the labour market or the law, exercises constraints on persons, there may arise situations where talk of autonomy is empty, and the counsellor working under the same constraints must be directive. As Callis (1960) puts it: a client's 'behaviour repertoire may be inadequate for any of three reasons: lack of experience, distortions in perception, or erroneous generalisations. . . . Lack of experience is most effectively dealt with by the method of counsellor discovery and interpretation. The Counsellor supplies the client with proper information (experiences) and the client can correct his inadequacies in a straightforward learning situation. . . . Distortions in perception are most effectively dealt with by the method of client self-discovery.'

It is undoubtedly the growth of knowledge about personality that has led to the change from guidance to counselling in both aims and methods. The method has been strongly influenced by the realisation that many problems of adjustment are not merely the result of lack of experience but of distortions of perception, including 'self' perception. And that these distortions are not necessarily haphazard but frequently result from attitudes which fulfil a function, usually defensive, for the personality. The fact that human beings are not aware of having distorted perceptions, with their underlying attitudes, means that the mere provision of information and advice is incapable of changing them, and this in turn leads to a modification of method. Likewise, because the attitudes fulfil a need there is a resistance to change and this dictates a more sophisticated and supportive approach than mere guidance.

In this paper then, guidance refers to a more directive approach while counselling refers to a non-directive approach. To repeat: the essential aims of the counsellor are (1) to enable the client to be, or become autonomous and (2) to deal with him as a total personality, and not merely as the manifestation of a particular problem. If these aims were clearer, much of the confusion between directive and non-directive counselling would be dispelled.

The arguments over directive and non-directive counselling are less marked today than once they were. The ends to be served, as seen by Williamson, whose name is associated with directive counselling, and Rogers whose name is closely concerned with the non-directive approaches are not fundamentally opposed. The means used are certainly different, but for both the ends of 'Helping the client achieve an independent and autonomous way of feeling and acting, and at the same time helping him overcome the specific and immediate needs that made him consult in the first place' remain the same. And the proponents agree too that the practitioner develops his own approaches suitable to his own personality as well as to his own theoretical orientation.

If counselling is concerned primarily with changes in the client's self-concept, how then is it to be distinguished from psychotherapy? In essence any counselling situation is a learning situation and, being so, it is concerned with both the cognitive and affective side of personal development. In psychotherapy, the patient has come for help, and though he remains self-directing in many aspects of his behaviour, he is to some degree incapacitated and his power to direct himself is diminished, at least temporarily, so that the emotional aspects come to dominate. In the stress situation, where the problem which presents is likely to be more apparent, then the therapist must immediately intervene and become more protective; it is only later that the client can expect to be more self-directing. In school, though a similar situation might arise from some children undergoing stress, the counsellor will be predominantly concerned with children developing normally, and the cognitive aspect comes to dominate. The normal child's problems will, as likely as not, be environmental ones, or ones arising from uncertainty of choices. Here the task is to help the child to think logically and constructively about himself and his relations with other people and things.

The closeness of counselling to psychotherapy may bring about dangers, however. This evident affinity between counselling and psychotherapy should lead to caution against over-optimism about the effectiveness of the counselling process. Eysenck's (1952) salutory shock over the effectiveness of psychotherapy, Levitt's (1957) work on the effectiveness of psychodynamic child guidance treatment, plus the *Cambridge-Somerville* (Powers and Witman, 1951) study of delinquency, and the whole vexed problem of how to measure improvement, cure or change through psychotherapy must lead one to consider how effective the counselling of the normal child in school can be.

The school counsellor with his own particular theoretical orientations may come to use definitions that approximate to clinical types when classifying children. And this becomes particularly dangerous when the counsellor, anxious about his own professional status, absorbs such classifications as used by social workers, psychologists and psychiatrists. There is much truth in the comment of Cicourel and Kitsuse (1963) that:

> teachers and counsellors of an earlier period characterised and interpreted student problems in everyday terminology and related them to everyday problems of the classroom, the peer group and the home. Students might be called 'lazy', 'indifferent', 'wild', 'girl crazy', 'unhappy at home' and the like. A clinical approach to these same problems would presumably describe them in terms that imply more serious roots and consequences. In terminology of clinical types a child may be 'rejected', 'overly-dependent', 'weak in egostrength', 'have an unresolved Oedipus problem' and the like.

In so far as these latter concepts when contrasted with the former, imply a diminution of responsibility on the part of the child (i.e. a lazy child can become diligent, but a rejected child cannot necessarily become accepted) they suggest a subtle change in attitude on the part of the adults concerned. They might imply an essentially passive role on the part of the child and this itself raises the question of a contradiction between such terminology and the whole idea of counselling as leading to self-determination.

There is no time to consider this vitally important question. While realising that classification is essential for diagnosis and treatment, it would seem important to avoid classifications which have deterministic elements built into them. It is interesting to recall that Rogers, in the Rankian tradition, accepts the general principle that therapy can proceed without an analysis of the client's past, and that a diagnostic orientation on the part of the therapist could interfere with his intuitive understanding of the patient's feelings.

Pursuing the distinction between guidance and counselling further, whereas guidance implies a directive approach, which could be given from a position which is emotionally distant and, therefore, theoretically more objective, counselling, on the other hand, rests to a large extent on a close relationship between counsellor and client. The counsellor must show a basic empathy, experiencing and showing interest, understanding, acceptance and respect. There is in the relationship an identification between counsellor and client which falls just short of emotional involvement. (An analogy here would be with an actor who in order to act well must 'live' the character who he is portraying, and yet at the same time must be able to stand outside himself so that he remains in control of the part that he is playing, and of himself.) Only by the existence of this empathy can the supportive elements of the relationship prosper. It is clear too that in this situation listening, by the counsellor, is more important initially than verbal responses. Listening, however, should not appear to the client as mere passivity. As Rogers (1951) writes:

> Some Counsellors—usually those with little specific training—have supposed that the Counsellor's role was merely to be passive and to adopt a *laissez-faire* policy. . . . He feels that his faith in his client's gain is best exhibited by a passivity which involves a minimum of activity and of emotional reaction on his part. This misconception of the approach has led to considerable failure in Counselling—and for good reasons. In the first place, the passivity and seeming lack of interest or involvement is experienced by the client as a rejection, since indifference is in no real way the same as acceptance. In the second place a *laissez-faire* attitude does not in anyway indicate to the client that he is regarded as a person of worth. . . . Many clients will leave both disappointed in their failure to receive help and disgusted with the Counsellor for having nothing to offer.

It is also essential that the counsellor must be, as far as possible, neutral, for the client must be able to approach the counsellor without the feeling, which seems to be a built-in part of all social relationships, that his behaviour and personality are being judged. It is this difficult problem of neutrality which leads to the ineffectiveness of the personal tutor system in many colleges. The tutor is nearly always given the task of assessing the student's ability and personality while at the same time being expected to act in a counselling capacity. And the student, realising the dual nature of the tutor's role, fails to make use of him for advice because of fear of revealing himself in such a way that the tutor will take note of this in his evaluation of him.

The counsellor, then, must be neutral, and any evaluation that must be made in order to help the client should be free as far as possible of either rejection or condoning. As Jung (1959) writes:

> If the doctor wants to offer guidance to another, or even to accompany him a step of the way, he must be in touch with this other person's psychic life. He is never in touch when he passes judgement. Whether he puts his judgement into words or keeps them to himself makes not the slightest difference. To take the opposite position and to agree with the patient offhand is also of no use, but estranges him almost as much as condemnation. We can get in touch with another person only by an attitude of unprejudiced objectivity. This may sound like a scientific precept, and may be confused with a purely intellectual and detached attitude of mind. But what I mean to convey is something quite different. It is a human quality—a kind of deep respect for facts and events and for the person who suffers from them a respect for the secret of such a human life.

This brings in a further distinction between counselling and guidance, for the advice given in a guidance situation arises to some extent from a judgement being made. The adviser has to take sides if direction and advice giving are to follow.

Facing the counsellor too is the critical problem of time. The counsellor's task of teasing out the real from the apparent problem necessitates both client and counsellor having sufficient time to pause and reflect. Whatever the level of maturity and however rational the client may be, any process which involves haste inhibits the chances of the self-directing process being made possible.

To sum up, all types of counselling seem to have the following common elements:

1. The counsellor should be aware of the unity of personality and behaviour. He counsels people rather than problems and is aware that it is a person who needs help rather than merely an educational, occupational or personal difficulty to be resolved.
2. The counsellor has to help the client to deploy his resources in such a way that he determines for himself what he is seeking, what his needs are, and how best to make satisfactory relationships with others.
3. To do this effectively, the relationship of counsellor to client should be one of empathy and neutrality with sufficient time available for the process to work fully.
4. The process should be such that any evaluation made is simply to guide the judgement of the counsellor on the kind of help needed in order that the client's needs and aspirations are fully met.

If these conditions are to be met much hinges on the personality of the counsellor himself; it is a problem that cannot be settled entirely by a professional education. The counsellor must have reached a stage in his own personal development where the conditions listed above can be met. His own attitudes must not impede his relationships with the client, and he should be aware of himself enough to realise the part they play in the developing relationship. The counsellor must avoid being emotionally dependent on his client, in respect of affection or status or power-seeking. Self-awareness is an essential quality that all counsellors need to strive for, and this may necessitate the counsellor himself having a supervisor or consultant who is in an uninvolved relationship to him, so that he avoids the analytical dangers of counter-transference, or even over anxiety on the client's behalf.

We have attempted to indicate some of the distinctions between guidance and counselling. If we now turn our attention to the English schools, it is difficult to recognise any procedures followed that resemble counselling, for our approaches are more eclectic, less homogeneous and thus difficult to characterise. In Britain, as in most West European countries, it is rather guidance that is being practised with its concern for diagnosis, assessment and classification leading to more direct advice-giving.

THE SCHOOL COUNSELLING MOVEMENT

The term 'school counsellor' has been commonly adopted to apply to the specially trained teacher. As was indicated at the end of the previous section, the work undertaken is guidance rather than counselling, but it seems undesirable at this stage to invent a new term. Therefore, the term school counsellor will be used in the following section, even though it is something of a misnomer.

There are numerous reasons for the growth of interest in school counselling; these can be classified as:

1. Pressure external to the school.
2. Organisational problems of the school and its bureaucratisation which serves to meet pressures under 1 above.

External pressures

Just as High School counselling in America has received considerable support from what has come to be called the 'crisis in education', that is the search for and the maximisation of the talents of all children in schools, a similar concern in this country has led to the counselling movement in our schools. This has manifested itself in two ways: a plea for more effective educational guidance and a demand for more productive vocational guidance in our schools. There has been a growing awareness of the school's relationships to the needs of a changing society. In particular it has been realised that the educational system, being now the main avenue of social mobility, is linked inextricably to the occupational structure of the country and hence to the life-chances of each individual child. Similarly, the apparent appreciable increase in mental stress in adolescence, brought about by rapid and extensive social changes has led workers in the Youth Service to consider the possibility of incorporating counselling in their tasks.

After the 1944 Education Act, 'guidance', as Burt (1955) says, 'was envisaged almost of necessity as a problem of classification'. Personal guidance of the child, in theory at any rate, has always been regarded as part of the pastoral duty of headmaster, form and subject teacher. Educational guidance has appeared in its most developed form at eleven, but after this period has rested more on divination than on a psychological analysis of the pupil's abilities and aptitudes. Vocational guidance is the responsibility of the careers master, if the school possesses one, working in conjunction with the Youth Employment Service. Superficially, it appears that we have a comprehensive guidance system but, as we know, glaring inadequacies are evident. Personal guidance of the child is often poorly attended to in our schools. The schools grow in size and headmasters cannot know, even if they ever could, all their pupils; the form teacher's work has become little more than nominal with the growth of specialist teaching, and, if we add to this a frequently rapid staff turnover and the reconstitution of forms, it is difficult to ensure a continuous awareness of the child's personal needs. Educational guidance, too, is episodic with too great a reliance on the teacher's judgment of the child's abilities and aptitudes, as being more valid than objective tests. Finally, vocational guidance is often something that takes place in the final year at school, if it takes place at all, and of a process emerging through courses instead tailored to what Wiseman (1964) calls 'particular patterns and profiles of abilities'. As for the Youth Employment Service, its effectiveness seems to be very limited as revealed in the researches of Chown (1958), Jahoda (1952), Carter (1962), Maizels (1965) and others.

A further external consideration which is leading to the initiation of a school counsellor service is the concern for help to be given to young people during the turbulent years of adolescence. Compulsory education to fifteen, and soon sixteen, mandates the school to extend its period of secondary socialisation. But further years of education do not necessarily lead automatically to greater maturity; help, it seems, has to be given in fostering the young person's self-discipline and self-responsibility. As Wall (1964) writes:

> The adult's task is to help the young person to perceive exactly where the choice lies, to help him to get or provide him with information about alternatives without which choice is impossible, to suggest trial solutions and to help predict likely outcomes—and then to allow the child or adolescent to choose, and if necessary, to choose wrongly. Then the youngster should abide by the consequences—unless these are unbearable or too destructive.

And it must be realised that, even after the implementation of the Industrial Training Act, many young men and women will receive no further education, even part-time, and will thus be denied any access to any institutionalised counselling service, unless there is a rapid development of Young People's Advice Centres throughout the country.

The final external force which is pressuring us to incorporate a counselling service is the move towards comprehensive education. At a simple level, the size of the units makes counselling more necessary and more possible. And in so far as the comprehensive school ideally engages in 'contest' as opposed to 'sponsorship' mobility the more likely it appears that counselling will be needed if the school is to 'avoid being dominated by an over-evaluation of intelligence as opposed to other abilities' (Wiseman, 1964, p. 151). The school must not fail to guide the child towards courses that develop his particular talents and interests. Comprehensive schools will, ideally, be obliged to offer a wider range of courses in order to cope with wider ability ranges. And at the same time, if we try, as Wiseman (1964, p. 151) suggests, to avoid 'the tendency . . . to identify whole forms for G.C.E., and with an adequate system of testing and guidance, allocate to sets in individual subjects, then this will give opportunities to those children whose interests and talents lie in one or two fields only, instead of restricting opportunities to all-rounders'.

It also appears that the forms of comprehensive education that are emerging will need guidance for children (and parents) at key points in the school years. Guidance, it would seem, will be essential when changes of school arise. Transfer, within the two-tier system, or to the sixth-form college, means that many children will need help in making decisions or choices at this critical period.

The more open the educational system we enjoy, theoretically, the greater occupational possibilities are available to all children whatever their social class, and the better the chance of avoiding damage to the child's self-esteem. A soundly based guidance system will help the child to make the most of the opportunities afforded.

APPLICATION PROBLEMS

If then the school counsellor works in the inextricably interrelated areas of educational, personal and vocational guidance, certain practical difficulties manifest themselves within the society of the school.

If instead of the aggregation of assessment of different teachers based on impressions of behaviour and performance in traditional tests, counselling is introduced, it will entail a much more rigorous and continuous record of the child's progress. It implies seeing the child as a whole person and not merely as a performer in certain academic contests: so that inevitably there comes within the counsellor's purview, personal aspects of the child's life including his family and other social relationships.

And here, perhaps, is one of the most difficult aspects of the counsellor's role. There is evidence to suggest that the child's self-image is, to some extent, determined by the attitudes of the school, teachers and peers towards his behaviour in schools, and this may mean that the teacher/counsellor may have to intervene, not only to correct the child's self-image, but also to improve the attitude of others, perhaps his fellow teacher-colleagues—aspects of his role which bristle with dangers overlooked by those who think one can simply institute such specialists in our schools. If children have a negative self-image of themselves which is at odds with their real ability, and there is evidence that numerous children in the school are affected negatively through what Taylor (1963) calls 'the climate of expectations and possibilities transmitted by the schools through its curriculum and traditions and the pupil's perception of its place in the educational and social structure', then, the problem arises as to how the counsellor intervenes. Does he align himself with the head and his colleagues against the child, or vice versa? Clearly, his tendency is to align himself with the latter, though this may not be in the best interest of the child. Conversely, if instead of a teacher/counsellor we have later, full-time counsellors then this professional worker will be less well equipped than ever to gain support of the head and his colleagues.

This brings us into the field of organisational analysis and its application to the schools, and in particular to the administrative relationships existing within the school. Getzels (1952), borrowing Weber's model of forms of authority and applying it to the school, concludes that it is the 'rational-bureaucratic pattern based upon professional expertise which was the most functional type for educational administration'. But the headmaster's role in the British school is to a large degree charismatic and instrumental in that while his authority is based upon personal and non-rational powers, he is concerned in the process of reaching goals, i.e. selection and differentiation of talent of the children in his school. The professional school counsellor on the other hand has his authority determined by legal, i.e. bureaucratic and rational, forms, but acts in his relationship to his task in an expressive way, i.e. maintains harmony and integrative relations between the child and the counsellor's fellow colleagues, while resolving the personal problems of the child himself. And the further the professionalisation of the school counsellor goes, the greater, as Hoyle (1965) suggests, 'professionalisation in the bureaucratic sense may lead to conflicting loyalties between the "executive" with a loyalty to his organisation, and the "expert", with a loyalty to his profession and professional standards'. Again, if we follow Parsons's pattern variables as applied to teaching and accept his conclusion that the roles likely to be followed by the teachers are likely to lie in the direction of neutrality and universalism—that is, he pursues his teaching instrumentally, judging the child according to some universal criterion such as academic performance—the counsellor on the other hand, one could hypothesise, is more likely to be directed by affectivity and particularism, i.e. there is an affective relationship between himself and the child, judging him on his (the child's) own unique individual qualities. Role conflict seems, therefore, when these models are applied, to be endemic to the situation where professional or for that matter, teacher/counsellors exist, and this may have dysfunctional effects on the schools where such specialists are employed. As Gross (1959) suggests 'when viewing school systems as organisations there are two major organisational barriers to effective functioning: lack of agreement as to organisational goals and lack of consensus on role definitions associated with educational positions'.

We said earlier that evaluation of the child is an essential part of the teacher's role, and even in informal classroom situations this cannot be avoided. But the process of evaluation of the child does not, because very often it cannot, lead to particular treatment of the individual child. As Parsons (1962) writes: 'The school class is structured so that opportunity for individual treatment is severely limited. Because there are so many more children in a school class than in a family and they are concentrated in a much narrower age-range, the teacher has much less chance than does a parent to grant particularistic favours.' Any expectation of concentration by the individual teacher on the problem child is often unrealistic, and it is as well to remind ourselves of Peters's point, that the teacher is mainly concerned with teaching within the educative process and is not primarily a socialiser or a therapist. If this is true, then it would seem to follow that counsellors in schools are a necessary and useful institution to balance the narrower pedagogic role of the teacher.

It is in this evaluation aspect that perhaps the distinction made earlier between guidance and counselling, can be seen. Essential to the practice of counselling is the non-judgemental element of his role, where the counsellor is to be seen neither judging nor condoning aspects of the child's behaviour and performance. How realistic would this be in the office of a teacher/counsellor? It would seem that there would be for him a real problem in role conflict in attempting to be both teacher and counsellor. He would have a non-judgemental attitude in one situation and a judgemental one in another. What is required, it would seem, is guidance which by its nature involves judgement and evaluation.

And is there not a great danger that the very existence of this specialist may effect the rest of the staff in that they could come to look upon him as the expert to whom they could turn over their problems? No counsellor can be expected to be entirely responsible for personal, educational, and vocational guidance of all the children, nor, it is argued, should it be so. If one of the traditions of our schools is teacher responsibility for pupils, it would be a pity to encourage teachers to sidestep such responsibility by introducing school counsellors. What we need are teachers who are sensitive and aware and practise their pastoral duties more effectively. The counsellor should not be the person to whom all problems are referred no matter how trivial, and he should not be a substitute for the continuous guidance which only those teachers in constant contact can offer.

Finally, there are several sociological considerations that need to be borne in mind if school counsellors are to be introduced into this country. Parsons's view of social class membership as a determinant of the aspiration and achievement of young people makes the family and the schools into primary and secondary agencies of socialisation whereby the child learns and internalises the culture, the organisation of the social structure, and the differentiation of his role types. But what Parsons omits to mention, and what is the important thesis of Cicourel and Kitsuse's (1963) study is that the differentiation of students is a consequence of administrative organisation and decisions of personnel in the high school. Just how far do the routine decisions of guidance and counselling personnel, they ask, relate to college/non-college decisions and, by implication, to the occupational choices made by students? In other words they see as problematic 'Parsons's view that the "virtually ascribed" college-going expectation among middle and upper class segments of the population accounts for the higher rate from these social classes who do in fact go to college' (*op. cit.*). Indeed, they conclude that student and parental aspirations are made more problematic by the existence of counselling services within the school. They suggest that as counselling itself becomes bureaucratised then the gap between parental aspiration on the one hand, and the child's actual ability on the other, leads to 'many children being identified as a "problem" within the organisation', where 'the students' records may become the object of intensive review by the counselling personnel, in the course of which not only the students but the parents may be subjected to interpretation and analysis' (*op. cit.*). In other words the school, responding positively to the twin aims of differentiating and developing talent, and helping the individual development of the child, institutes counselling, but in doing so throws up many problems, not the least of which is the classification of children by the counsellor, so that progress through the schools is made upon the ascription principle of placement implemented by a set of bureaucratic procedures.

If American experience is anything to go by here, then, ascription may replace achievement by the child. It seems likely that the use of counsellors may take root first in our comprehensive schools which are likely to be those schools where 'contest' mobility (to follow Ralph Turner's classification) in which 'elite status is the prize in an open contest' replaces 'sponsorship' mobility where elite status is given on the basis of some criterion of supposed merit and cannot be taken by any amount of effort and energy. If this happens, then counsellors could serve to 'curtail students' own course programmes . . . include or exclude students from the "contest" so that aspirants own efforts are neither the only nor the critical determinant of the qualification of the contestants' (*op. cit.*). We may feel that by instituting a counsellor service we are rationalising procedures in order to produce greater objectivity, but as the above authors say:

> examination of how students are assigned to college and non-college curriculums distributed among different ability group courses and identified as various 'problems', suggests that the progressed ideal of equal access to educational opportunities for those of equal ability is not necessarily served by such procedures.

The counselling system can incorporate the concepts and methods of psychiatry and psychology into the school and can make more relevant and valuable the interpretation of students' performances as measured by objective testing procedures. But equally well 'a student's mobility may be more than incidentally contingent upon the sponsorship of organisational personnel who certify him to be a "serious", "personable", well rounded student with leadership potential'.

We said earlier that it is guidance rather than counselling that is the practice in our schools and any move, or plea, for a less directive approach fails to appreciate that guidance is a more feasible proposition because it is closer to and more in accordance with the present climate of the English school than is counselling. Non-directive counselling seems to presume a progressive school climate, flexible timetables, an elective system and cooperative head and staff. No doubt this is possible in some schools but one would not expect at the moment that this picture is in any way representative of all secondary schools, though there is no reason why they should not become so.

It is not difficult to make out a case for the provision of such specialists in our schools, and we feel in sympathy with this case. Nevertheless, there are short term difficulties, as we have tried to illustrate, not the least being getting clear just what kind of counselling should be offered. There is much we agree with in Dr Still's (1966) comment:

> There is still a strong and widespread feeling that some personal counselling falls within the proper scope and responsibility of the teacher . . . and many accept this responsibility and regard their own training as having fitted them in large part to undertake it. Many of these, and many engaged in some forms of counselling work recognise the existence of gaps and inadequacies in their resources for dealing with some of the problems that arise and would welcome the existence of specially trained or specially gifted colleagues in dealing with some of the more specialised or difficult problems.

Though we have drawn attention to problems of application we do not consider them to be insurmountable or such as to lead people to prevent the introduction of such specialists into our schools. Our task has been to show that such innovations will entail adaptation and consequent reorganisation on the part of the school. But this is, after all, what happens to any social organisation when new methods and approaches arise. If counselling in schools leads to a more effective implementation of the values to which our education system is committed, then short-term dysfunctional effects will have to be tolerated. The fact is that the state system of education is in a near monopoly position, and it is incumbent upon it to meet the needs of its clients more effectively. With this in mind it will be interesting to watch the effects of counselling services, in various forms, in our schools.

REFERENCES

AMERICAN PSYCHOLOGICAL ASSOCIATION. 1956. (Committee on Definition; Division of Counselling Psychology). 'Counselling psychology as a speciality', *American Psychologist*. Vol. 11, pp. 282–5.

BURT, C. 1955. 'The guidance movement in England', in *Year Book of Education*, 1955. Evans p. 98.

CALLIS, R. 1960. 'Towards an integrated theory of counselling', *Journal of College Student Personnel*, Vol. 1, pp. 2–9.

CARTER, M. P. 1962. *Home, School and Work*. Pergamon.

CHOWN, S. M. 1958. 'The formation of occupational choice among secondary school leavers', *Occupational Psychology*, Vol 32, No. 3, pp. 171–82.

CICOUREL, A. V. and KITSUSE, J. I. 1963. *The Educational Decision Makers*. Bobbs-Merrill, p. 82.

EYSENCK, H. J. 1952. 'The effects of psychotherapy: an evaluation', *Journal of Consultant Psychology*, Vol. 16, pp. 319–24.

GETZELS, J. W. 1952. 'A psycho-sociological framework for the study of educational institutions', *Harvard Educ. Review*, Vol. 22, No. 4, pp. 235–46.

GROSS, N. 1959. 'Some contributions of sociology to the field of education', *Harvard Educ. Review*, Vol. 29, No. 4, pp. 275–87.

HOYLE, E. 1965. 'Organizational analysis in the field of education'. *Educational Research*, Vol. 7, No. 2, pp. 9, 99.

INTERNATIONAL ROUND-TABLE IN EDUCATIONAL AND VOCATIONAL GUIDANCE. *Conclusions*. Neuchatel, January 1966.

JAHODA, G. 1952. 'Job attitudes and job choice among secondary modern school leavers', *Occupational Psychology*, Vol. 26, No. 4, pp. 206–24.

JAHODA, G. and CHALMERS, A. D. 1963. 'The youth employment service: a consumer perspective', *Occupational Psychology*, Vol. 37, No. 1, pp. 20–43.

JUNG, C. 1959. *Modern Man in Search of a Soul*. Routledge & Kegan Paul, p. 270.

LEVITT, E. E. 1957. 'The results of psychotherapy with children: an evaluation', *Journal of Consultant Psychology*, Vol. 21, pp. 189–96.

MAIZELS, J. 1965. 'Entry of school leavers into employment'. *British Journal of Industrial Relations*, Vol. 3, No. 1.

PARSONS, T. 1962. 'School class as a social system', in *Education, Economy and Society*, ed. J. Floud, A. H. Halsey and C. A. Anderson, Free Press of Glencoe.

POWERS, E. and WITMAN, H. L. 1951. *An Experiment in the Prevention of Delinquency* (The Cambridge Somerville Youth Study). Columbia University Press.

ROGERS, C. 1951. *Client Centred Therapy*. Houghton Mifflin, p. 27.

STILL, R. 1966. Comments on International Conference at Neuchatel, 1966.

TAYLOR, W. 1963. *The Secondary Modern School*. Faber, p. 69.

WALL, W. D. 1964. *Guidance in Adolescence* (Charles Russell Memorial Lecture). The Trustees, 17 Bedford Square, London, W.C.1.

WISEMAN, S. 1964. *Education and Environment*. Manchester University Press, p. 151.

18

The School Welfare Team

Maurice Craft

This paper concludes Part Three. It seeks to review the range of needs, and the present range of provision, in the field of home–school relations and school welfare, and considers the emerging concept of a 'school welfare team'.

Over the past two decades, a now well-known series of reports and researches, many of them discussed in this book, have sketched the outlines of educational inequalities in modern Britain. This is not a new situation, but one about which we have become increasingly concerned, with accelerating national needs for skill, and with changes in our political and moral beliefs about individual opportunity (Craft, 1969a). In more recent years, researches have tended to move away from large-scale studies of educational opportunity and have begun to focus more upon 'educability', responsiveness to schooling, and the analysis of the complex *mechanisms* of disadvantage has begun (Craft, 1970).

But while it might be argued that the postwar reports and researches have reflected changing societal needs, and have sometimes possibly even acted as a catalyst of social policy (in the case of the 'educational priority area' programmes, for example), our present, evolving pattern of school welfare provision has far more diverse roots and owes much to national traditions of problem-solving. Our preference, for example, for political decentralisation; for down-to-earth practical solutions to social dilemmas rather than for large-scale reform; for consensus by compromise between competing interests, rather than for decision by hierarchy; and, above all, for gradualism rather than cataclysmic change, has meant that national needs have traditionally been met on a local, pragmatic basis, and school welfare is no exception.

The picture is therefore an extremely varied one, and is further complicated by the fact that school welfare provision serves a diversity of functions, ranging from the largely 'educational' to the largely 'therapeutic'. This may be an unreal distinction in many ways; but for the purposes of argument it is broadly, perhaps, a workable one, and it is used in this chapter as a means of analysing the range of welfare tasks now recognised, and of welfare techniques now to be found in British schools.

We begin with a brief sketch of the range of ends and means, going on to outline current proposals for change, and to hypothesise a possible 'team' model.

PRESENT PROVISION

The Education Welfare Service, established in the 1870s (and described in Chapter 11) is still probably the most widespread form of school welfare provision, and its function may range from a relatively limited concern with school attendance, clothing, school meals and transport, to a form of social casework. But in recent years the area-based E.W.O. has been supplemented by a growing number of school-based specialists, teachers often with additional training whose roles may range very widely indeed. Some may be appointed to foster links with parents, to bring them up to date with curriculum changes and to involve them more fully in the education of their children (McGeeney 1969, Cave 1970), and there have been numerous published accounts of experimental forms of parent–teacher cooperation (Department of Education and Science, 1968a; Inner London Education Authority, 1968; Green, 1968; Lang, 1968; Haynes, 1969; Midwinter, 1970). In some cases, the 'home–school liaison officer' (or 'teacher/social worker') may have a particular interest in 'parent education', discussing with parents the value of conversation, reading, and particular kinds of toys and activities at home, and perhaps going on to deeper aspects of child-rearing (Stern, 1960; Kellmer Pringle, 1970). Another kind of specialist, the 'school counsellor', may have an even more therapeutic function involving casework with individual children on personal problems (see Chapter 17). All these kinds of welfare role can involve home visiting.

Then there are welfare roles of a more instrumental sort which tend, on the whole, not to incorporate home visiting: careers teachers, for example, who may organise visits and work experience, provide careers information, and teach careers courses to ease the transition from school to work. Where a trained counsellor also undertakes work of this kind ('vocational guidance'), he may administer tests of ability, interest and aptitude, and be responsible for an elaborate record system covering the whole of a child's school life and not simply the final year. Educational and vocational guidance then merge. Form teachers and house tutors are the traditional specialists in these areas and will continue to outnumber counsellors and teacher/social workers in secondary education for many years to come (Monks, 1968).

An even more recent area of development in schools is 'compensatory education'. Like the growth of closer parent–teacher relations and the rise of guidance and counselling, compensatory education has tended to inherit the value commitments of the older mental health movement (which have also gained a wide currency in primary education through the spread of the developmental tradition). Compensatory education has a range of interpretation, concerning itself with problems of physical, emotional and cognitive deprivation, and compensatory programmes range correspondingly widely. In one direction there is an overlap with individual counselling which may involve contact with parents and with local welfare services; or there may be a focus on 'social education', seeking individual fulfilment and social competence through the medium of group processes. In another direction compensatory education is preoccupied with learning difficulties, the curriculum, and teaching methods, and looks very much like a modern counterpart of the older tradition of remedial education* (Schools Council 1968, 1969, 1970a, 1970b).

* This more 'traditional' remedial education is another important segment of school welfare provision, and the debate here is about the grave deficiency of remedial services in some areas; and whether such services should remain firmly based in the schools, or be part of the school psychological and school health services.

Some schools also have a *community* involvement though the appointment of a teacher/youth leader; or by designating themselves 'community schools' and creating a focus of cultural, recreational, or ameliorative activities (Poster 1968, Gillett 1969). With the changed orientation of youth work towards community organisation and development, the appointment of teacher/youth leaders may be expected to increase an appointing school's community involvement (D.E.S. 1969, 1970).

These are some of the welfare specialists now to be found in British schools. All except the E.W.O.s are teachers, and some are specially trained for this work. But there is also a group of welfare specialists who are not teachers but social workers. The appointment of 'school social workers' is discussed in Chapters 14, 15 and 16, and is considered further below; then there is the youth employment officer (now called 'careers officer'), the school nurse (who may be a health visitor in the locality and a valuable source of information about the area and its families), and the child guidance and school psychological services.

The total range of provision is therefore quite extensive, but it varies from L.E.A. to L.E.A. (Plowden Report, 1967) and indeed from school to school, for traditionally, welfare services have depended very largely upon the interests, abilities, and available time of individual heads, class teachers and education welfare officers. This is not to argue against variety *per se*, or to suggest that freedom to experiment should be curtailed. But where experimental roles tend to be laid alongside or superimposed upon existing ones there is likely to be stress, duplication and inefficiency. As counsellors emerge, for example, the precise role of the housemaster/mistress in a comprehensive school (or of the traditional pastoral function of the form teacher) will require some redefinition. Similarly with careers teachers, a vociferous and fast developing group of specialists whose role is being increasingly regarded as complementary to that of the careers officer, and not in conflict with it (D.E.S. 1965; Ministry of Labour, 1965; Roberts, 1969, 1970). It may be some time before the five E.P.A. research projects and other studies can offer any evidence on the most functional patterns of organisation.*

* See, however, Fuller (1967), Schools Council (1967), Rose (1970).

So much for present provision *within* the school. There has also been some relevant innovation *outside* the school in the last few years. The main proposal for change arose from the Seebohm Committee's (1968) plan for a unified social service department in each Local Authority, embracing all neighbourhood welfare provision and including school social workers based in individual schools or serving groups of schools. The proposal argued that this pattern would considerably clarify channels of referral from the school outwards; but there was sharp disagreement among L.E.A.s as to whether the new school social workers, recruited from the present E.W.O.s should become part of the social service department or remain with the education authorities (Clegg, 1968; Cook, 1968), and the *Local Authorities Social Services Act 1970* leaves this question open and for local authorities to decide. In those authorities which decide to transfer education welfare to the social service department we may therefore expect to see new patterns of school welfare provision developing, possibly utilising the Seebohm notion of school/area-based school social workers.

At much the same time as Seebohm was being debated, the I.L.E.A. was reviewing its long-established system of school care committees (described in Chapter 12) which channelled school referrals through the Divisional School Care Organiser. The controversy here centred on whether this system should remain at L.E.A. level or be brought within the Seebohm concept of a social service department in each borough. The final outcome, based partly on the recommendations of the Jefferys Report (1967), is that a unified education welfare service is to be set up (incorporating the School Care Service, and school attendance), operating through area teams of social workers and voluntary helpers.

Liverpool has also recently established new machinery, and, as described in Chapter 13, is now operating five area-based 'social education' terms through which school referrals are channelled. Each team is coordinated by an 'educational guidance officer' and links the child guidance and school psychological service, remedial teaching teams and educational welfare officers. Other L.E.A.s, Southampton, for example, have experimented with less formalised coordinating mechanisms (Luckhurst, 1969).

At the *training* level, the proposal that teachers and social workers should in future be trained alongside each other in an 'interprofessional' setting has found widespread expression in the current reappraisal of teacher education (Craft, 1969b, 1971), and Professor Tibble considers this area in Chapter 19. Such a development might well enhance the school's preventive function and it seems nearer today than at any time in the past; but this is very much a long-term proposal and cannot be relied upon as the only strategy for future welfare provision. Similarly, the 'Seebohm' rationalisation of local social services and such far-sighted school welfare schemes as those of London and Liverpool are to be welcomed, but they cannot completely meet the need. However efficient the neighbourhood provision, it can only complement provision *within* the school; it is no substitute for it, and there is no escaping the necessity to scrutinise intra–school provision whether on grounds of economy (to avoid duplication), functional efficiency (to provide a better service, or to meet needs not hitherto met at all), or organisational efficiency (to streamline the staff role structure and reduce tensions arising from over-lapping 'territories').

THE SCHOOL'S WELFARE TASKS

It will be clear from this sketch of the present range of school welfare provision that even when due allowance has been made for terminology (different titles describing essentially the same role, or 'modernised' titles describing long-established roles), there remains a wide range of *tasks* which fall into this category, and there can be little doubt that this is a category which has grown in the 1950s and '60s. The reasons for this expansion are possibly to be found in the structural and ideological changes referred to earlier, the need for skill and concern for the individual, changes which have been reflected in the growth of an affective dimension to many professional roles (particularly teaching) and in the normal corollary of this—a splitting off of new welfare roles. Thus, while the average teacher is now expected to possess an expertise that is psycho–social as well as academic, it is recognised that specialisation must occur in this as in other fields, leading, for example, to the appointment of counsellors, as well as of academic team leaders.

When we come to review the range of welfare tasks it is evident that not all are alleviative. As suggested earlier, the distinction between 'educational' and 'therapeutic' roles is not always a clear one, but in the following threefold classification this broad distinction is maintained for the purposes of argument. First, and perhaps foremost, school welfare provision seeks to offer effective systems for the identification of the *seriously disadvantaged* and for their treatment, whether by referral to outside specialists, or (as is more likely in many cases, given the present chronic shortage of remedial and psychiatric facilities) by a supportive therapy within the school, perhaps in consultation with outside agencies. For this group, welfare provision will also involve a compensatory curriculum, particular techniques of educational and vocational guidance (terms which are considered below), and relationships with parents of a 'therapeutic' as well as an 'informational' kind. Whether this group of children 'at risk' comes from as large a proportion as 20 per cent of all families, as Kellmer Pringle (1970) has suggested, it is impossible to say. But numerous reports and researches in education (Mays, 1962; Newsom Report, 1963; Plowden Report, 1967; Wiseman, 1964, 1967), housing (Taylor and Ayres, 1969), poverty (Abel-Smith and Townsend, 1965; Ministry of Social Security, 1967; Coates and Silburn, 1968; Townsend, 1970), and nutrition (Lambert, 1964; Yudkin, 1967; Land, 1969; Lynch, 1970) leave no scope for ambiguity about the existence of a seriously deprived minority whose children require special help within the schools.

Provision for these children immediately raises some major ethical and economic problems which can only be touched upon here. For example, does the devising of more systematic school welfare provision imply the more effective adjustment of children to what is generally regarded as an intolerable social environment? Can the post-Plowden provision of special salary allowances, ancillaries, playgroups, nursery school and day nursery places, reception and language centres, and new school buildings in 'educational priority areas' be extended to meet the need, by governments committed to reducing public expenditure? Is the urban land shortage, the preference for city living, and the consequent building of 'high-rise' flats going to provide new generations of problem children for the future? These wider policy issues are beyond the scope of a chapter concerned with the tactics of prevention at school level.

The second area of school welfare tasks is less obviously 'therapeutic', and concerns the needs not of a deprived minority but of the *overwhelming majority* of normal schoolchildren. This is the dual and interrelated category of educational and vocational guidance which seeks to identify abilities, interests and aptitudes, and to provide for their fulfilment in school and beyond. Probably the majority of parent–teacher programmes fall into this second category; they are largely concerned to provide information about school progress, courses and careers, and such 'parent education' as they involve is aimed at fostering supportive attitudes rather than at more basic matters of attitude change (and even value change) which may be entailed with deprived families. The comprehensive reorganisation of secondary education and abolition of selection at eleven-plus in many L.E.A.s has given rise to larger schools, more extensive curricula, and delayed and more flexible selection for an increasingly complex academic and commercial market, and these changes provide the more obvious rationale for more elaborate systems of guidance to facilitate informed educational and vocational choice.

Thirdly, there are the normal stresses of *adolescence* and the need to provide personal counselling, a somewhat more 'therapeutic' service, for those children who seek it. This is a need which is often overstated by psychotherapists. Nonetheless it is real enough for a number of children who could not be regarded as seriously deprived or disturbed, in a context of larger and more complex schools, smaller and more mobile families, and an accelerating rate of economic and social change which may foster an 'inter-generational gap'; and in an ideological setting in which the parodoxical commitments to individualism and to collective responsibility maximise freedom but set the adolescent a major learning problem. With this third group, home–school relations might be more casework oriented.

PROPOSALS FOR A WELFARE TEAM

So far this chapter has argued that the present pattern of school welfare provision is complex, first, because it has grown up piecemeal to meet the changing needs of a society which prefers local, gradual adjustments rather than large-scale, radical reform; and second, because it embraces a wide range of 'educational' and 'therapeutic' functions. It ought also to be added that the educational system of England and Wales with its 33,000 schools, situated in regions of contrasting levels of economic development, and divisible into numerous categories by age of pupils, type of curriculum, and form of government, is hardly likely to produce a tidy pattern. Nonetheless, this chapter has suggested that this range of school welfare functions can be grouped according to three broad categories of need: the needs of a small minority, the seriously disadvantaged; the need of the great majority of schoolchildren for educational and vocational guidance; and the need of a minority of normal adolescents for personal counselling.

It will be obvious from this tentative grouping of welfare tasks that there are no neat divisions either of clientele or of processes, in this field. 'Disadvantage' is a relative term and the size of this minority group fluctuates with time and place; and similarly with the proportion of young people who feel in need of help and advice as part of growing up. Secondly, the processes of guidance and counselling (themselves neither conceptually nor operationally distinct) can be applied to all three groups. Nonetheless, this composite classification is felt to offer a workable basis for considering the shape of day-to-day machinery. This machinery, given the range of tasks, the growing size of secondary schools in particular, and rising standards of pastoral care, is increasingly being thought of in terms of a *team*, an idea that has been more widely implemented in the United States where the classroom teacher may be assisted, for example, by counsellors, a visiting teacher (or school social worker), a psychologist, and perhaps a psychiatrist, in a given school or school system (Arbuckle, 1966, Strang, 1968).

In Britain, vocational guidance, for example (as suggested earlier), is now thought to require the complementary skills of both the careers teacher and the careers officer. As the Albemarle Report (Ministry of Labour, 1965) put it:

> The future of careers counselling in schools will be best served through the development of a *team* approach. . . . Guidance given by the Y.E.O. [careers officer] without relevant information from and consultation with the school is likely to be based upon an inadequate knowledge of the young person. Guidance given by a teacher without the coöperation of the Y.E.O. is likely to be based on too narrow a knowledge of the field of employment and the requirements of occupations.

The C.B.I. Report (1969) similarly recommended that each school should have a 'strong team of teachers' responsible for careers, working in conjunction with the careers officer who should 'supplement the careers teachers' understanding of the individual's personality, interests, and attainments, with a detailed knowledge of careers in all areas of employment and the physical and psychological requirements of particular occupations'. Hoxter (1964) has proposed a slightly more elaborate team structure for vocational guidance. He suggests that each school should appoint a counsellor responsible for educational and vocational guidance who would be assisted by an area-based 'vocational guidance counsellor' (the equivalent of the present careers officer but with more specialised training), and by an L.E.A. appointed 'vocational guidance adviser' who would plan and coordinate the work of the school counsellors.

These different schemes place a varying emphasis upon the school-based/area-based elements in educational and vocational guidance; but although they argue for a *team* notion the team they propose is to have relatively narrowly prescribed welfare functions. How are those needs which cannot be neatly classified as educational or vocational to be dealt with, for example? With the Scottish Education Department's Report (1968) we have the recognition that even if counselling for personal problems is offered by a school, the counsellor would still need the assistance of other staff to cover careers work; and Daws (1967a) draws the important distinction between *therapeutic* counselling on the one hand and *educational and vocational* counselling on the other. He argues that together, both elements would comprise too demanding a role for a single welfare specialist and has elsewhere (1967b) considered a three-man team: careers teacher, careers officer and counsellor, in which the counsellor would have a therapeutic concern. Clearly, this three-man team with its increased range would be likely to draw in form teachers, housemasters, and others on occasion (Daws, 1968).

An additional dimension is added when the necessity to provide for home–school relations is taken into account. This adds yet a further role demand, a further caseload, and a further set of techniques to those of a counsellor who might already be trying to combine 'therapeutic' and 'educational/vocational' commitments; and it has led to the suggestion of a further specialisation, the school social worker (Fuller and Juniper, 1967; Juniper, 1967) and to the proposal for a four-man team: careers teacher, careers officer, counsellor, and school social worker (Daws, 1968; Vaughan, 1970). Lytton's (1968, 1969) notion of a four-man team is very similar: he sees educational and vocational guidance being carried out by teachers (with some additional training) working in collaboration with the careers officer; home–school links would be maintained by welfare officers rather like the present E.W.O.s; and personal counselling, diagnosis, and referral to outside specialists would be the function of a 'pupil personnel worker'.

All these schemes are an improvement on those considered earlier, for they recognise and seek to provide for a wider range of needs. But none take the school health service into account and this neglects a valuable source of information about the individual child, about family histories, and about the local subculture. Secondly, none of these proposals makes specific provision for remedial education. 'Educational guidance' would probably embrace a compensatory curriculum in the educational priority area, but what of the average suburban school? Here, remedial education is often a largely self-contained area of work; but in any overall review of school welfare provision is it justifiable for it to remain so, for there is certain to be a welfare dimension in the work of most remedial classes, and conversely, the work of welfare specialists will often have implications for remedial education?

The Report of the National Association for Mental Health Working Party (1970), which also feels that school welfare is 'essentially a team function', puts forward a more flexible team concept in which different members of staff and outside welfare specialists would be consulted by a school counsellor in particular cases. Thus, matters of 'educational choice' might involve consultations with departmental heads, parents, personal tutors or house tutors, and perhaps, the educational psychologist; 'vocational choice' would bring in tutors, parents, careers teacher, careers officer, and even employers; and 'critical developmental problems' would embrace the house tutor, form teacher, E.W.O., parents, and members of the Child Guidance team. Organisationally, the Report suggests, this pattern might be achieved by provision at two levels. At a senior level within each school, a counsellor would be responsible for coordinating an *overall programme*, including liaison with outside agencies, and he might be one of two key assistants to the headteacher (the other being a senior administrative colleague). At the second level, there would be a number of assistant counsellors who would undertake *specific tasks* in the educational, vocational and personal areas.

As the Report suggests, this kind of scheme has the merit of providing a career structure for school welfare specialists; and it makes the important proposal that a single, trained specialist at a senior level should be responsible for coordinating a rational welfare policy within each school. The 'second level' provision also allows for an admirable flexibility in the consultation of all colleagues concerned in each particular case. But it could easily be woolly (and more expensive in personnel) at this level; and a clearer role definition, involving, if possible, the incorporation (and enhancement) of existing posts of responsibility might be thought to have some advantages.

ELEMENTS OF TEAM PROVISION

Circular 10/65 (D.E.S. 1965) with its six basic alternatives for the reorganisation of secondary education, and its subsequent withdrawal by the present Secretary of State has introduced an almost bizarre variety into the forms of British schooling. It is therefore clearer than ever that no single blueprint for school welfare provision could possibly meet the varied circumstances of more than a proportion of the schools. However, if the broad categories of need outlined earlier are accepted as valid; and if current trends in thinking (sketched in the previous section) are any guide, it seems that three essentials in any future model must be, first, the establishment of a single, clear focus of welfare efforts, an *internal coordinator*, within each school; second, the elements, at least, of a *team* within each school; and third, the establishment of a *clear channel* out of the school to neighbourhood welfare services. Naturally, the interpretation of such a model would vary with local conditions.

The appointment of a *coordinator* to design, facilitate and contribute to a comprehensive programme of guidance and counselling, home–school relations, relations with local social workers, and the maintenance of appropriate school records does not imply an abandonment of the class teacher's traditional responsibility for pastoral care. On the contrary, having a specialist on the staff is claimed to enhance it (Whale, 1969). As the N.A.M.H. Report puts it:

> The counsellor with specific duties is seen by himself, and certainly by those who run courses in counselling, not as usurping the general counselling function of other members of staff but as complementing their work by a service—which he can offer by reason of extra time, knowledge and facilities.

The counsellor's role, as the Schools Council Report (1967) noted,

> is rather to strengthen, by providing a focal point [his colleagues'] already active endeavours. Many teachers, therefore, in this cooperative situation, are likely to take on further pastoral duties, or to exercise them more effectively, rather than to abdicate from them. This at least seems to be the experience in a number of schools so far.

At the same time, to leave pastoral care *entirely* to class teachers would be asking more than is realistic at a time when, for example, the rising tide of curriculum innovation is greatly extending the intellectual and emotional demands being made on teachers; and so it is felt to be essential that the special appointment of an internal coordinator is made.

In a large comprehensive school the internal coordinator might be a full-time (i.e. non-teaching) counsellor. Elsewhere, a part-teaching specialist might meet the need. Secondly, in large schools the range of welfare duties would obviously be too great and too conflicting for a single person to carry out alone and the co-ordinator might therefore concentrate on the most demanding personal counselling while coordinating a *team* of part-teaching colleagues who were responsible for educational and vocational guidance, for home–school relations, and for remedial work; and responsible, above all, for acting in a consultant capacity to colleagues wherever required (Diagram 1).

Diagram 1. The school welfare team—basic roles

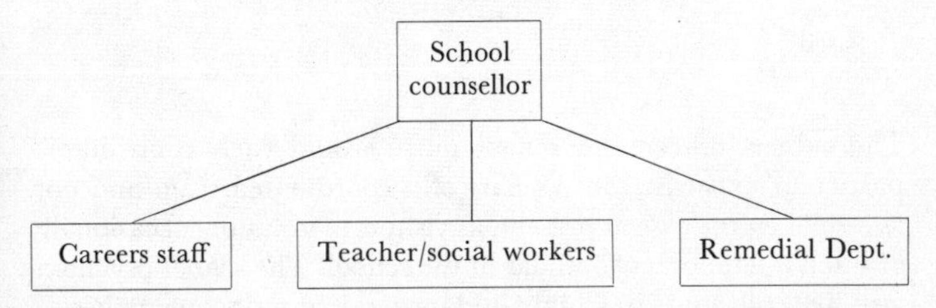

This is the basic team. Appropriately trained careers teachers would be capable of administering psychometric tests as part of their work in educational and vocational guidance; but if not, this could be done by the counsellor. Teacher/social workers (or 'home–school liaison officers' as they are sometimes called) would foster links with parents, mainly in connection with educational and vocational guidance, and they would have a timetable adjusted to allow for this. Home visiting is so time-consuming that it is doubtful whether any of the other roles could be combined with it. In educational priority areas the teacher/social workers might also be involved in community work (Gulbenkian Foundation, 1968), for this is a role which might lend itself to this line of development. In a small school, on the other hand, a teacher/social worker might have a less specialised role and might well be the internal coordinator. To these basic roles must be added the school's remedial teachers, and, of course, the outside specialists who would work with the team (Diagram 2).

Diagram 2. The school welfare team—internal and external specialists

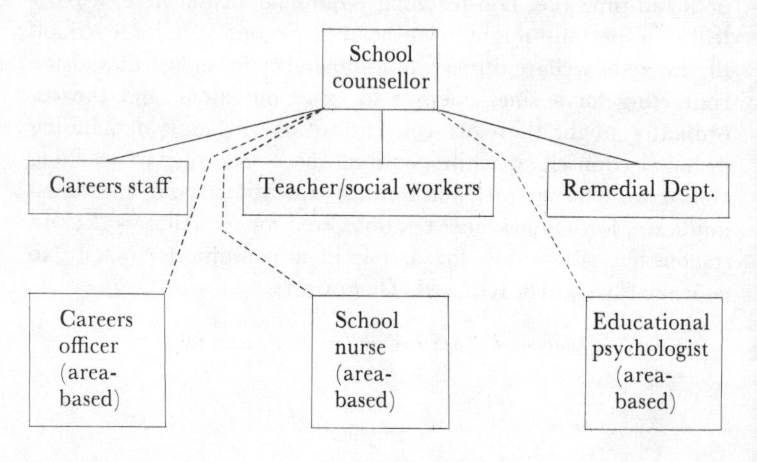

The careers officer and school nurse would each contribute a particular expertise, but as part of a coordinated team and not, as is so often the case at present, as visitors in isolation, occasionally granted a temporary foothold in the school. The school psychologist, like colleagues in Child Guidance, might well come to have a consultancy function in many areas, as suggested earlier. The traditional scheme of referral for specialised treatment combined with a supportive therapy in school may be the ideal relationship with area psychological and psychiatric services; but where these are seriously overstrained (if not actually non-existent), 'the schools' (as the Schools Council Report (1967) put it) 'have in large degree to contain their difficulties as best they can'. Where a school has a trained counsellor on the staff, and the rudiments of a welfare team this containment could offer a constructive solution in many L.E.A.s.

There would be much informal contact between members of the team and regular consultation with housemasters and other colleagues. The role of housemaster would probably centre upon traditional administrative and extra-curricular duties, facilitating the normative climate of a large school, and a pastoral concern at 'general practitioner' level with referral to the school welfare team wherever necessary. The coordinator would be responsible for calling regular case conferences which the outside specialists would attend as necessary.

The *internal coordinator* and the internal *team* are two essential elements in this model. The third is a *clear channel out of the school.* This might be thought to be the most ambiguous element, for Diagrams 1 and 2 have already indicated several channels: the relationship of the school-based members of the team with their area-based colleagues (i.e. careers officer, school nurse, psychologist) will obviously be a flexible one and will embody clear and efficient channels as the occasion arises; similarly, the teacher/social workers who will be involved in conveying information about courses and careers, discussing learning or behaviour problems, and in some areas, in aspects of parent education, will also maintain flexible 'channels' out of the school for these purposes. But when it comes to the most serious cases of deprivation or disturbance involving family casework, probation, child care or other welfare services, this will be more appropriately a matter for the local social service department. As suggested earlier, the Seebohm Report recommended the establishment of a school social worker who would liaise between the schools and the department, and this would provide the channel whereby referrals of this kind were made. The school social worker, area-based and serving several schools (and possibly recruited, with additional training, from the present Education Welfare Service) would be responsible for convening case conferences of colleagues and might also be involved in casework with a child's family.

The need for a clear and effective channel in these more serious cases has often been stressed (e.g. Wedge, 1965), and some have argued that the *counsellor* (in our model, the internal coordinator) could provide it (Lytton, 1969, D.E.S., 1968b). This would certainly seem to be a logical solution in smaller schools. But in larger ones, the coordinator of a large team who is also carrying a personal case load would hardly have the time to undertake liaison with a variety of specialists within the social service department; nor would it be right for *him* to decide which was the appropriate point of contact. Furthermore, there are those welfare tasks at present carried by the Education Welfare Service (meals, clothing, transport)* which will continue and whichever member of the social service department takes care of these could also provide the point of referral (Diagram 3).

Diagram 3. The school welfare team—A possible model

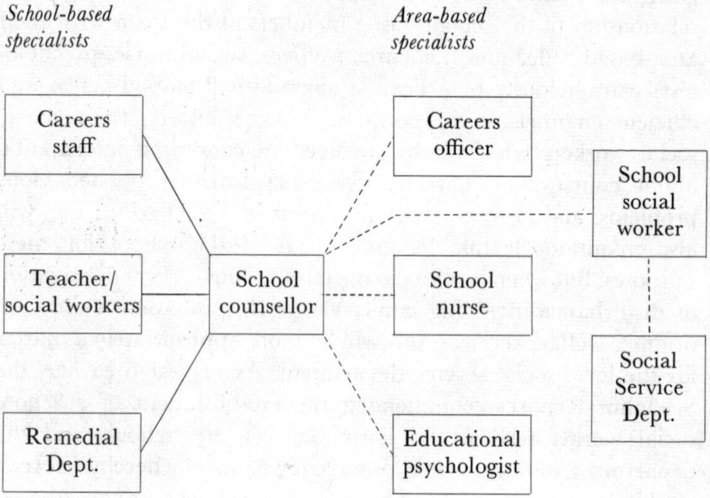

School-based specialists

Area-based specialists

Careers staff

Careers officer

School social worker

Teacher/ social workers

School counsellor

School nurse

Social Service Dept.

Remedial Dept.

Educational psychologist

Note: The school social worker and all the other area-based specialists would, of course, serve *several* schools and not just one.

A CHANGING PATTERN

Diagram 3, it must be stressed, presents a purely hypothetical model the purpose of which is to illustrate the range of functions involved in a modern conception of school welfare provision, and the model could be adapted to meet the pressures of local conditions. It is not argued that each school must have this particular blend of components. But *coordination, team* functioning, and a *clear channel* for referral are basic concepts. The emergence of a more rational and coordinated pattern of neighbourhood social services will help little if schools do nothing to rationalise *their* internal resources.

* Attendance might easily fall to the teacher/social worker as being related to other home background problems, but not necessarily.

Secondly, this chapter has attempted a tentative exploration of techniques only. More basic organisational issues relating to role analysis, and a more theoretical concern with the social functions of schools and the social process of education have been left on one side. However, some theoretical assumptions have been made and these were referred to earlier. Our society's growing need for skill and its ideological commitment to individual fulfilment have, particularly since 1945, contributed to the greater emphasis placed upon developmental aspects of the educational process. *All* teachers are being increasingly exhorted (and to some extent trained) to take on a wider and more diffuse range of tasks, including those of social welfare. But however desirable this may be thought to be, it is functionally impossible given the increasingly demanding pedagogic aspects of the teacher's role, and the wider range of 'educational' and 'therapeutic' tasks now included under the heading of school welfare provision. Although all teachers may therefore be expected to be capable of identification and referral at 'general practitioner' level, the emergence of school welfare specialists of one kind or another is inevitable, and in terms of functional efficiency, highly desirable.

There remain many issues for research and for educational and social policy. What the most functional team pattern should be for schools of different types and in different localities is clearly a foremost question. What our national policy should be, is another; now that we have the *Local Authority Social Services Act 1970*, are school welfare and the position of the E.W.O. to be forgotten about for another generation? More important, perhaps, is whether the coordination of training is adequate to the national need. Is it possible, for example, for the Universities Council for the Education of Teachers to support university proposals for advanced diplomas in guidance, counselling and school social work (and for the D.E.S. to approve such courses for secondment purposes) without some broad, national guidelines on school welfare policy? For sub-diploma courses there is even less co-ordination.

Finally, this chapter has tended to assume that school welfare provision is largely a secondary school phenomenon, but as Moseley (1968) has argued, there are obvious grounds for claiming that preventive measures should most logically be sited in the *primary* school. This, too, is something which needs close scrutiny at a national level.

REFERENCES

ABEL-SMITH, B. and TOWNSEND, P. 1965. *The Poor and the Poorest*, Bell.

ARBUCKLE, D. S. 1966. *Pupil Personnel Services in the Modern School*, Allyn & Bacon.

AVERY, P. and ADAMSON, R. F. 1969. 'School social work and crime prevention', *Howard Journal*, Vol. 12, No. 4.

CAVE, R. G. 1970. *Partnership for Change: Parents and Schools*, Ward Lock.

CENTRAL ADVISORY COUNCIL FOR EDUCATION. 1963. *Half Our Future* (Newsom Report), H.M.S.O.

— 1967. *Children and their Primary Schools* (Plowden Report), Vol. 2, H.M.S.O.

CLEGG, A. 1968. 'Seebohm: a sorry tale?', *Education*, 11th October.

COATES, K. and SILBURN, R. 1968. *The Morale of the Poor*, University of Nottingham.

CONFEDERATION OF BRITISH INDUSTRY. 1969. *Careers Guidance*, C.B.I.

COOK, D. 1968. Comment on Clegg (1968), in *Education*, 25 October.

CRAFT, M. 1969a. 'Guidance, counselling and social needs', in Lytton and Craft (1969).

— 1969b. 'Developments in interprofessional training', *Higher Education Journal*, Vol. 17, No. 3.

— 1970. ed., *Family, Class and Education: a Reader*, Longman

— 1971. 'A broader role for colleges of education', in *The Future of Teacher Education*, ed. J. W. Tibble. Routledge.

DAWS, P. P. 1967a. 'What will the school counsellor do?', *Educational Research*, Vol. 9, No. 2.

— 1967b. 'The guidance team in the secondary school', *Abstracts of the Annual Conference of the British Psychological Society* (Education Section).

— 1968. *A Good Start in Life*, C.R.A.C.

EDUCATION AND SCIENCE, DEPARTMENT OF. 1965. *Careers Guidance in Schools*, H.M.S.O.

— 1965. *Circular 10/65: The Organisation of Secondary Education*, H.M.S.O.

— 1968a. *Parent/Teacher Relations in Primary Schools*, H.M.S.O.

— 1968b. *Psychologists in Education Services* (Summerfield Report), H.M.S.O.

— 1969. *Youth and Community Work in the 70s*, H.M.S.O.

— 1970. *Circular 3/70: Basic Training of Youth Workers and Community Centre Wardens*, H.M.S.O.

FULLER, J. A. 1967. 'School counselling: a first inquiry', *Educational Research*, Vol. 9, No. 2.

FULLER, J. A. and JUNIPER, D. F. 1967. 'Guidance, counselling and school social work', *Educational Research*, Vol. 9, No. 2.

GILLETT, A. N. 1969. 'Teachers for community schools', in *Towards a Policy for the Education of Teachers*, ed. W. Taylor, Butterworth.

GREEN, L. 1968. *Parents and Teachers: Partners or Rivals?*, Allen & Unwin.

GULBENKIAN FOUNDATION. 1968. *Community Work and Social Change*, Longmans.

HAYNES, J. 1969. *Schools and the Community*. Kent County Council.

HOXTER, H. Z. 1964. 'Fresh thinking on guidance and counselling', in *Yearbook of Events, 1963–64*. Institute of Youth Employment Officers (London and S.E. Branch).

INNER LONDON EDUCATION AUTHORITY. 1968. *Home and School*, I.L.E.A.

JEFFERYS REPORT. 1967. *The Social Welfare Services of the I.L.E.A. 1965–66*, Bedford College.

JUNIPER, D. F. 1967. 'School social work', in *Abstracts of the Annual Conference of the British Psychological Society* (Education Section).

LABOUR, MINISTRY OF. 1965. *The Future Development of the Youth Employment Service* (Albemarle Report), H.M.S.O.

LAMBERT, R. 1964. *Nutrition in Britain, 1950–60*, Bell.

LAND, H. 1969. *Large Families in London*, Bell.

LANG, P. 1968. 'A school with a department for home/school relationships', in *Parents and Schools*, Vol. 2, No. 4 (C.A.S.E.).

LUCKHURST, C. 1969. 'Experiments in welfare', in *Trends in Education*, January.

LYNCH, G. W. 1970. 'Can two in three be malnourished?', *Education*, 2 October 1970, p. 311.

LYTTON, H. 1968. *School Counselling and Counsellor Education in the United States*, N.F.E.R.

— 1969. 'An integrated approach to counselling and social work', in Lytton and Craft (1969).

LYTTON, H. and CRAFT, M., eds. 1969. *Guidance and Counselling in British Schools*, Arnold.

MCGEENEY, P. J. 1969. *Parents are Welcome*, Longman.

MAYS, J. B. 1962. *Education and the Urban Child*, Liverpool University Press.

MIDWINTER, E. C. 1970. *Home and School Relations in Educational Priority Areas* (Occasional Paper No. 4), Liverpool E.P.A. Project.

MONKS, T. G. 1968. *Comprehensive Education in England and Wales*, N.F.E.R.

MOSELEY, L. G. 1968. 'The primary school and preventive social work', *Social Work*, Vol. 25, No. 2.

NATIONAL ASSOCIATION FOR MENTAL HEALTH. 1970. *School Counselling*, N.A.M.H.

NEWSOM REPORT, *see* Central Advisory Council for Education.

POSTER, C. 1968. 'The head and the community school', in *Headship in the 1970s*, ed. B. Allen, Blackwell.

PRINGLE, M. L. KELLMER. 1970. 'Co-operation in child and family care', *Concern*, No. 5 (National Children's Bureau).

PLOWDEN REPORT, *see* Central Advisory Council for Education.

ROBERTS, K. 1969. 'The changing functions of the Youth Employment Service', *Social and Economic Administration*, Vol. 3, No. 3.

— 1970. 'The Youth Employment Service, the schools, and the preparation of school leavers for employment', *The Vocational Aspect of Education*, Vol. 22, No. 52.

ROSE, G. 1970. 'Central Lancashire Family and Community Project', (unpublished paper).

SCHOOLS COUNCIL. 1967. *Counselling in Schools*, H.M.S.O.

— 1968. *Compensatory Education: an Introduction*, University College of Swansea.

— 1969. *Children at Risk*, University College of Swansea.

— 1970a. *Cross'd with Adversity*, Evans-Methuen.

— 1970b. *Teaching Disadvantaged Children in the Infant School*, University College of Swansea.

SCOTTISH EDUCATION DEPARTMENT. 1968. *Guidance in Scottish Secondary Schools*, H.M.S.O.

SEEBOHM COMMITTEE. 1968. *Report of the Committee on Local Authority and Allied Personal Social Services* (Seebohm Report), H.M.S.O.

SOCIAL SECURITY, MINISTRY OF. 1967. *Circumstances of Families*, H.M.S.O.

STERN, H. H. 1960. *Parent Education: an international survey*, University of Hull.

STRANG, R. 1968. 'Guidance and the classroom teacher', in *Readings in Educational Psychology*, ed. V. H. Noll and R. P. Noll, Collier-Macmillan.

TAYLOR, G. and AYRES, N. 1969. *Born and Bred Unequal*, Longman.

TOWNSEND, P. 1970. ed., *The Concept of Poverty*, Heinemann.

VAUGHAN, T. D. 1970. *Education and Vocational Guidance Today*, Routledge.

WEDGE, P. 1965. *Preston Family Welfare Survey*, County Borough of Preston.

WHALE, H. 1969. 'The school counsellor from the headteacher's viewpoint', in Lytton and Craft (1969).

WISEMAN, S. 1964. *Education and Environment*, Manchester University Press.

— 1967. 'The Manchester Survey', in Plowden Report (1967), Vol. 2.

YUDKIN, J. 1967. In *The Times Educational Supplement*, 28 July.

Part Four

Overview

19
Interprofessional Training
J. W. Tibble

Part Four presents two papers, each offering a distinctive 'overview'. In the first, Professor Tibble discusses the overlapping viewpoints of teacher and social worker, and considers the possibilities offered by joint training.

Some years ago, in 1958, there was held at Keele, thanks to the inspiration and energy of Professor Paul Halmos, a conference which brought together trainers of teachers, social workers, clinical and educational psychologists, and nurses, to consider the possible common ground in the content, aims and methods of training in their respective courses. This first conference concentrated on the treatment of psychology in these courses. Three more such conferences were held at Keele, Leicester, and Nottingham, to explore the contributions of other basic subjects, such as sociology and philosophy, and to compare the techniques used in both study and practical training. The talks given at these conferences and some account of the discussion they provoked were published in a series of monographs.[1]

The Committee set up to organise the conferences also arranged smaller working parties whose purpose was to consider practical outcomes and what steps might be taken to foster the development of courses of training in an interprofessional setting. In the field of teacher education, an interprofessional working party has since met from time to time to review developments, and in 1969, it sponsored a further national conference, at Bulmershe College of Education.[2]

There are signs of a growing awareness of the need to bring the helping professions into a much closer association with the educational system. Dr M. E. M. Herford, writing in *Education*[3] makes a plea for a comprehensive counselling service for young people which would integrate the work of the schools, the health service, the youth employment service, youth clubs, and the probation service.

> The service for youth must be approached comprehensively. The Schools must be the base for action and exploration outside; they must be linked to the youth service in clubs and other centres. Creative use of leisure is part of education. The probation service, relatively isolated on the fringe, must become part of the counselling, preventive service for youth. There should, again, be suitable joint appointments as well as whole-time posts between schools, youth service, probation service. These would be mutually stimulating and provide a vigorous career structure, and cross-fertilizing influence. None of these services can any longer be considered as a private departmental concern. Each has a community function and is a community responsibility; they are organically interdependent and must be planned and organised comprehensively. Departmental planning can only isolate and destroy vitality.

Given this recognition of the need for integration, it seems obvious that the integration should operate at the level of both initial training for the professions concerned and at the level of post-certificate and post-graduate education. When the inter-professional conferences and working parties mentioned above brought together workers from the different fields, a good deal of the discussion revolved round what might be called interprofessional idiosyncrasies—the results of historical accident in the development of the respective training systems. As we are all products of these, it is difficult to discount the effects and adopt a viewpoint which ignores local colour and vested interest and tries to ask fundamental questions. We can say that the conference, and more particularly the working party discussions, did make good progress, once the inevitable initial professional defensiveness was overcome.

What has emerged so far has been a surprisingly large area of common ground, on the one hand; on the other, certain differences have been seen to be not accidental and arbitrary, but fundamental. Common courses of education will have to provide for both similarities and differences. Comment on this can appropriately fall under two headings, content and process: for in the preparation of people for all these professions, it is generally agreed there are subjects, organised fields of study which are especially relevant to the profession in question; there are also specific skills to be acquired.

With regard to content, one difference between teaching and the rest quickly emerged: in preparation for teaching there is both a professional and a curricular content to be acquired. The former obviously may have an area of overlap with the professional content needed by the social worker, but the latter does not have a curriculum of subjects to be familiar with, through which in the teachers' case much of the relationship between teacher and child is mediated. Granted, curricular studies would have no counterpart in the social workers' education; but what did emerge from the discussion was that the study of a special subject or subjects 'for its own sake' by the student, as is now customary in courses of teacher education, might well be equally valid in the other courses of professional education and for the same reasons, i.e. it is part of the workers' equipment as a cultured, civilised human being.

The overlap in the area of professional studies is obvious enough, and once again recent developments in teacher education have brought the professional needs closer together. In the social work field it is a question of bringing together relevant contributions from a number of basic disciplines or forms of thought: psychology and sociology are obviously relevant and most people want to include some philosophic study dealing with values, ethical issues, and so on. This contributory approach to the study of what is described by Professor Paul Hirst as 'practical-theory', is now being advocated as the best formulation of the nature of education as a subject of study[3]; furthermore many of the topics chosen for study would obviously be common ground in the education for the different professions: the educative function of the family and the relation between home and school would be one of these common topics. It is further suggested that the advantage of having these common topics explored by groups with different professional biases would be considerable. Even in the areas of study where the professional interests would diverge, as in the study of the historical development of educational systems and institutions on the one hand and in the study of social administration on the other, there would be gain from the relating of these studies in mixed discussion groups. It is now being recognised, for example, in the field of education, that the history of education has been too narrowly conceived and will gain from a closer relating of this subject to the development of other institutions within the context of the welfare state.

Turning now from content to process, the working parties have in particular explored the possibility of common ground in practical work training, the acquisition of the special skills needed by teachers and social workers. Theoretically this involves the assumption of some common ground between education and therapy, as is indeed envisaged by Dr Herford. This can be seen as arising from the fact that both education and therapy involve bringing about changes in a pupil or client which will enable him or her to fulfil needs and cope with problems more adequately. In both cases something has to be learned—knowledge, skill, attitudes—which is relevant to the need. The difference can perhaps most profitably be thought of in terms of education and re-education, since the social worker is more likely to be specifically involved in repairing defects of knowledge, changing unsatisfactory attitudes, relearning of social skills and so on. But clearly also many teachers need skills in remedial work, and have to cope with the effects of unsatisfactory home background and defective relationships between child and parent.

Another aspect of practical work which is being explored is that of the skills needed by the supervisor in the process of training the student teacher or social worker. The term 'supervision' is used in both contexts, but the discussion brought out very clearly that it described somewhat different practices. For example, the school practice supervisor normally operates by sitting in as non-participant observer on a lesson given by the student. The student has prepared the lesson and the lesson notes are available for comparison with the actual lesson. After the lesson the student has the benefit of the supervisor's criticism. There is a large element of judgment and assessment in this process, and it assumes a capacity in the student to identify with the supervisor's 'non-participant' point of view.

In the case of social work supervision, as it happens, it is often not possible for a supervisor to be present at the interview between social worker and client; it would be recognised as radically altering the situation for a third person to be present. Furthermore, it is more clearly recognised in this social work context that for the student to benefit fully, the supervisor must start where he or she, the student, is, with the account of the interview produced by the student after the event. The supervisor's function is to help the student to explore in retrospect all the implications of the situation, to see more than he was able to see at the time, to develop further insights. It is suggested that teacher training would gain from making use of this other kind of supervision.[4] Certainly the traditional school practice procedures need reconsideration both from the point of view of determining what the specific role of the college supervisor is and to meet the demand from within the profession for more school-based training. It is suggested here that the respective roles have been rather more clearly defined and worked out in the field of social work training, and that teacher education would benefit from a greater awareness of this.

There are, of course, as many practical problems in achieving greater cooperation in training as there are in more closely integrating the professions as a whole. Different ministries and departments are involved, both locally and nationally. Different salary scales operate; changing jobs, or operating in two at once, is fraught with difficulties. Each profession has its own built-in habits of mind and established practice. Present exigencies, particularly in the field of teacher education, where an acute shortage exists, mean that it is difficult to get approval for the development of the multi-professional colleges envisaged in the Robbins Report. We must hope that in the long run solutions to the practical problems will be found, and that a broadly based and flexible system of interprofessional education will replace the present patchwork systems. Meanwhile it is important that experiments of the kind mentioned above should be instituted whenever it is practicable so that new ideas can be tried out in practice and the results assessed.

REFERENCES

1. *Sociological Review Monographs*
   Nos. 1 and 2. *The Problems arising from the Teaching of Personality Development*, Keele, 1958, 1959.
   No. 3. *Moral Issues in the Training of Teachers and Social Workers*, Keele, 1960.
   No. 4. *The Teaching of Sociology to Students of Education and Social Workers*, Keele, 1961.
2. A review of interprofessional developments up to that time is summarised by M. Craft in 'Developments in interprofessional training', *Higher Education Journal*, Vol. 17, No. 3 (1969), pp. 11–14.
3. *Education*, Vol. 126, No. 3263, 6 August 1965, pp. 277–8.
4. For a full discussion of this see J. W. Tibble, ed. *The Study of Education*, Routledge & Kegan Paul, 1966.
5. An account of an experiment in the use of this kind of supervision in teacher education appears in *Education for Teaching*, November 1965.

20

Family, School, and Society

William Taylor

This concluding paper reviews some of the theoretical and practical deliberations of this volume, and sets them in the context of wider educational and sociological considerations.

If one thing is clear from the variety of contributions by teachers, social workers, welfare officers, and university educationists to this volume, it is that there is a very general acceptance of the desirability of forging links between home and school, of clearing away barriers to communication and sources of misunderstanding between teachers and parents regarding the education of their children. At the practical level it is perhaps obvious enough that the child who is being held back in his school work by inadequate care at home or by bad housing conditions should be helped, by some combination of educational and social guidance and practical assistance, to overcome the handicaps to educability to which he is exposed. There seem to be few questions in our minds about the value of attaching teacher/social workers to schools where they are required, of trying to secure the cooperation of apathetic and uninterested parents in providing their children with the best possible chance to take advantage of the schooling that they are being offered. The need for improved provision of this kind is so obvious, and the supply of suitably trained people so inadequate, that there is a danger that the broader issues which underlie attempts to link schools and homes more closely may be neglected I want to suggest that our efforts will be better directed and more likely to be successful if we try, for example, to define more clearly what we mean by opportunity before we try to furnish more of it, to recognise the social discontinuities that exist between the roles of families and schools, parents and teachers, to relate the home–school link to wider aspects of the social structure, and to take into account the historical background to the relationship between the parent and the teacher in our society.

It seems to me that the whole business of home–school relationships cannot be discussed realistically if our context is the over-simplified one of providing more educational opportunity for the individual child, of satisfying certain needs which the individual child is believed to possess, of removing handicaps to the educability of the individual child. We are concerned here with one of the most fundamental relationships in society, that between the primary socialising agency of the family and the inducting agency of the school, a relationship that provides a background against which many of the battles between private and public interest are fought out, a context within which occupational roles are assumed and social character built up. The fundamental questions that need to be asked about home–school relationships are neither sociological, or psychological, or biological; they are political and moral, in the sense that they are concerned with the means by which the individual is inducted into the wider society, the extent to which the family is entitled to sequester certain social advantages that are not universally available—either because they are scarce resources or because they are not recognised as advantages at all—with the respective rights and obligations of the individual and the family on the one side, and the school and the society on the other. And whilst it is obvious enough that in many respects the interests of individual and family, teacher, school, and state coincide, it is equally obvious that there are many ways in which there may occur conflict between what each assumes to be the best course of action, and that these conflicts have to be resolved by the decisions of judges and juries, administrators and teachers, social workers and educational welfare officers, who must all possess certain criteria by means of which decisions are evaluated, must uphold certain principles which are applied to the resolution of particular problems and difficulties.

Many considerations of home and school relationships give too little attention to this matter of criteria, being based on a facile assumption that the interests of parent and teacher in the development of the child are the same—or can be made to be so through efficient liaison and communication—and that all that stands in the way of complete cooperation in a common endeavour is the existence of certain misunderstandings of purpose and mutual lack of information. I have written elsewhere of the possible value of some degree of misunderstanding in facilitating the relationship of individuals and groups,[1] and I think that we should be very cautious in assuming that freeing the channels of communication will of necessity make it easier for parents and teachers to work together, especially if by more intimate contact the discrepancies in the value orientations and aspirations of the two roles are exposed more clearly than at present. It is possible, of course, that what we are after is not just better communication and understanding but some degree of redefinition of the rights and duties of the role-incumbents; and this brings us back to the problem of discovering criteria by means of which these rights and duties can be defined and rendered operationally viable.

Nowhere is this problem of criteria greater than with respect to the provision of educational opportunity. In the words of Benn and Peters:

> The man who presses for 'equality of opportunity' is urging that certain factors, like wealth, which have hitherto determined the extent of an individual's opportunities, should be neutralised. But he may very well be urging at the same time discrimination according to other criteria. Because in the mouth of the egalitarian 'equality' is a term of approval, he is bound to distinguish between differences in treatment that are reasonable, and therefore compatible with equality and those that are not, and are thus 'inequalities'. His procedure is to criticise established criteria, and to elaborate new and more reasonable ones; and there is nothing wrong with it. But the statement of his objects in terms of 'equality', when his aim is to substitute reasonable for objectionable distinctions, is frequently misleading, not least to himself. His position is not greatly clarified by saying that he seeks not 'equality of treatment' but 'equality

of opportunity'; neither phrase means very much unless we know the nature of the criteria under attack.[2]

Now it is of some importance that the criteria we employ when discussing opportunity have altered a good deal in recent years, and in ways that do little to aid the clarification of our ideas and practices. Tawney and the Trades Union Congress knew what it was that they wanted when they urged the claims of 'secondary education for all' during the first two decades of this century; the extent to which children who could have benefited from continued education were being denied this was plain enough to see. During the 'thirties, Lindsay, Gray, and Moshinsky, and others gave criticism of this state of affairs statistical support by showing that there were large numbers of children of good ability who were not catered for by existing provision. Setting out to examine the problem of 'how far the education ladder is effective; whether in fact it is, as it has been described, a greasy pole; and what are the main difficulties that beset the path of the child, the parent, the teacher and the local education authority', Lindsay found that

> proved ability to the extent of at least 40 per cent of the nation's children is at present being denied expression, and the full extent of unproved ability is not yet known, only because a sufficiently comprehensive test has not yet been applied, and that of a very conservative estimate of 20 per cent who may be described as below average ability, social environment, in many cases remediable, is the main contributory cause.[3]

The 'thirties hardly provided the sort of political and economic background for reforms designed to improve this situation: the problem became one of finding enough jobs for the educated, and the spectre of the political dangers of an underemployed intelligentsia was frequently invoked. But the war again highlighted the wastage of talent that, despite the existence of the special place and scholarship system, had characterised educational provision during the first four decades of the century; the 1943 White Paper and the 1944 Education Act attempted to remedy this wastage by providing a wider range of opportunities in secondary and higher education, and in removing some of the financial handicaps to a longer period of education for those from homes of humble means. The criteria employed to discriminate amongst those who could benefit from such extended education and those who could not were based largely on the work that psychologists had done during the interwar period on the classification and measurement of abilities, and reflected the recommendations of the consultative committees regarding the wider use of objective and standardised tests as a means of reducing the effect of such educationally 'irrelevant' factors as home background, wealth, and the occupational level of the parents. Such criteria were in their essence simple: age, ability, and aptitude. These provided the basis from which the earlier criteria of inherited social advantage could be attacked; they had the great advantage of being regarded as largely hereditary themselves. From the economic and strategic point of view it was irrelevant whether intelligence and attainment owed most to heredity or to environment; what mattered was to identify those with superior capacities early, give them an appropriate education and make them available to do the work of a technologically advancing society. But from the moral standpoint of the egalitarian the assumptions regarding the hereditary basis of ability were important, particularly since it appeared that the distribution of such ability was not the same as the distribution of existing social advantage. For the teacher, the I.Q. had the great merit of being readily measurable, independent of the quality of teaching provided, and supportive of the forms of school organisation that reflected the existing provision of school buildings and divisions within the teaching profession itself. We have still to estimate the effects of a generation of teaching a particular type of differential psychology in training colleges on teachers' attitudes to children's abilities, of the influence of statements that implied that the educator must accept the constancy of the I.Q., and the fact that he was powerless to alter it.

Perhaps the archetypal Mr Rivers of Brian Jackson's Honey Bell School represents the pure form of the teacher who has absorbed, and, within his own terms, successfully applied, teaching of this kind.[4] There were, of course, plenty of cases where I.Q. and performance were discrepant, and where children performed a good deal better or worse than their measured scores indicated.

To deal with these a complex vocabulary of terms such as 'late developers', 'premature burn-outs', and, at a lower level, 'smart Alecs', was developed in lecture theatre and staff room, and it was recognised—just as Lindsay had recognised in 1926—that the home background of the pupil could affect the extent to which he might attain or fall below his scholastic and intellectual potentiality. But such cases were still discussed in the context of a set of assumptions about ability that regarded it as something qualitatively distinct from, if perhaps quantitatively affected by, differences in home background and cultural level. There still existed a criterion in terms of which the existence of opportunities could be measured, deficiencies exposed, barriers to educability recognised and removed. And while this criterion existed, it helped to mediate the relationship between school and home, providing an external standard to which teachers could refer, a standard of judgment that was, albeit grudgingly, accepted by many parents as 'fair', even when it worked against their own first preferences. Whereas wealth and social advantage were unreasonable bases for discrimination in educational provision, ability, so defined, was not—as long as it could be assumed to have a substantial hereditary component and was susceptible to accurate prognostic measurement.

Within the last few years we have seen the crumbling of many of the assumptions that provided the rationale for the educational arrangements to which I have referred. We have begun to speak, as Sir Edward Boyle did in his celebrated foreword to the Newsom Report, of the need to provide all children with the opportunity of acquiring intelligence,[5] not simply of manifesting it. We have become much more aware of the role of the social determinants of educability, of the relationship of early socialisation, language development and school performance,[6] the way in which achievement motivation is fostered in the child, and the effect of all these and many other factors on aptitudes for scholastic and academic work. We have lost a great deal of our faith in the prognostic value of objective tests, interviews and other selective devices; sometimes, indeed, we have gone too far in repudiating what are still valuable diagnostic and assessment devices. The effect of all this has been to leave us without any generally agreed set of criteria in terms of which the provision of educational opportunity may be discussed. Whilst recognising that children will still differ in their performances and in their response to schooling, and that the advantages of a cultivated background and parental 'support' (itself a rather ambiguous term, as Swift has indicated[7]) will count for a great deal, we are unsure as to the way in which home, school, peer group, and hereditary endowment interact together to produce performances of different kinds and at different levels. Along with a growing awareness of the variegated patterns of home influence on attainment there is the beginning of a systematic sociology of educational institutions, a realisation that what Waller called 'the separate culture of the school'[8] is itself an important factor in the child's progress, and that organisational goals and limits can leave their mark on the individual's attitudes and aspirations.

It is against this background that the current concern with secondary reorganisation and the interest that we have been showing in the link between home and school needs to be viewed. It is frequently suggested that the social arguments for the abolition of the tripartite system have been allowed to outweigh the educational considerations involved, with the implication that the latter are less favourable to the comprehensive school. But, as I have already suggested, the basic considerations are neither social nor educational, but moral and political. If we no longer possess a criterion that will legitimise early selection, allocation, and the subsequent differentiation attendant upon them, then it becomes morally imperative to shift the basis of the allocation procedures from performance in intelligence and attainment tests and response to primary schooling to a more flexible procedure operating within secondary and post-secondary education, where the range of choices available is such as to make it easier for child, parent, and teacher to match interests, attainments, and a suitable type of course. There is, of course, still a selective factor operating within the system, and home background continues to exercise its influence, an influence regarded less as a supplement to or an obstruction of a good level of performance than as a dynamic element in this performance itself. But although there must still, in many cases, be a denial of the social claims of the family, and many parents who had hopes for a professional career for their offspring will have to rest content with more mundane occupations, at least the process of denying these claims will be less traumatic, supported by a gradual build-up of evidence and conviction, and involving no institutional segregation in a separate and poorly esteemed type of school. What Burton Clark calls the 'cooling out' process can be brought into play.

> ... whereby systematic discrepancy between aspiration and avenue is covered over and stresses for the individual and the system is minimised. The provision of readily available alternatives in itself is an important device for alleviating the stress consequent on failure and so preventing anomic and deviant behaviour. The general result of cooling out processes is that society can continue to encourage maximum effort without major disturbance from unfulfilled promises and expectations.[9]

The current dissolution of a morally legitimate criterion for the allocation of educational opportunity confronts us with the virtual inevitability of an open door policy in secondary, and, to a lesser extent, higher education. Such a policy, like so many measures in other fields of social welfare, weights the scales in favour of the families who are best placed to take advantage of the easier access that it affords, and underlines the need for broader measures of social reform, in housing, child care, income policy, and so on, if the balance is to be redressed and the operation of fortuitous social influences on educability minimised. It is here that the teacher/social worker, and the other community agencies that we have been discussing, become important, contributing to the process of educational guidance that reconciles the social claims of the family, the particular dispositions of the individual child, and the requirements of society and the occupational milieu. But such workers and such agencies cannot of themselves do much to lessen the structural handicaps that at present inhibit opportunity and, *pace* Barbara Wootton,[10] we should avoid creating the impression that the facilitating and ameliorating functions that they perform are any substitute for more thoroughgoing reform.

The need for careful analysis of the basis factors inherent in the home–school relationship does not end with a definition of what we mean by educational opportunity. There are other, and perhaps more fundamental, issues. Historically, I think that it would be true to say that the school has often served to separate the child from the home, sometimes with the partial cooperation, or at least the acquiescense, of the parents, sometimes without. During the nineteenth century the Public schools were able to increase in number and prestige largely because of the demands of the new middle class for a type of education that would provide the attributes of cultivation that the first generation members of this class did not possess. These were boarding schools, and reflected the Victoria conviction that the family did not constitute the best environment for the growing child. Within the publicly provided system of education, the state and church schools served the function of civilising a brutalised proletariat; in country areas schools became the chief instruments of rural depopulation, giving pupils the literacy and the wider perspectives that would enable them to leave the kinship group and seek their future in the town. More recently, as we have seen, the school has become the chief agent of social mobility, and if it has given parents new opportunities to feel satisfaction and fulfilment in the success of their off-spring, it has also served to separate the child from the family and to offer the possibility of failure and social disesteem.

Psychologically, as well as socially and historically, the school has served to divide children and parents. As parsons has pointed out, the primary school class emancipates the child from the basic emotional ties he has with his own family, encourages, the internalisation of social values and norms other than those current in the family house, and begins the process of selection and allocation relative to the adult role system that will be continued and given greater emphasis in later stages of schooling.[11] Given these tasks, the orientation of teachers must be different from that of parents, who are concerned with the whole child in a way that is different from the teacher's concern, not simply because the parent has two or three children to deal with while the teacher has forty, but because there are certain differences in role-disposition built into the parental and teaching functions. The parental role emphasises acceptance of the child, warts and all, irrespective of standards of performance or of levels of attainment—the provision of short-term incentives such as the eleven-plus bicycle, and the willingness of some parents to accept the teacher's evaluation of their child and to make it their own, may distort but do not fundamentally change the essentially ascriptive, subjective basis of the parent–child relationship.

For the teacher the situation is different. However much her training may have emphasised the need to give individual attention to the whole child, and however much she may be disposed to follow this prescription, her role imposes upon her a more objective, achievement oriented approach, where performance will be evaluated and the claims of the family and the child adjudicated in accordance with the type of criterion considered earlier in this chapter. This question of criteria is a crucial one; it may be illustrated by reference to the situation that might exist if a fire were to break out in the classroom whilst the teacher was talking with the parent of one of the children in the room. If there was only time to save one child, the parent would have no difficulty in deciding who should be saved—her own. But if the decision was the teacher's, presumably there would not be a single survivor, because, in this situation, the teacher has no *relevant* criterion by which to select one child rather than another. At one level, the family and the school, the latter representative of community values, committed to the principles of social justice, the former properly and selfishly concerned primarily with the welfare of its own members, stand in clear opposition to one another. Better communication between parent and teacher, more teacher/social workers and an attempt to remove the grosser handicaps to educability will not eliminate this opposition, which is a basic characteristic of a society in which occupational access is formally open, kinship relationships beyond the nuclear family are attenuated, but the family is still regarded as the basic unit of association, with full rights over the socialisation and training of its children. The dilemma of the socialist cabinet minister who sends his children to Eton is, vicariously at least, the dilemma of us all.

In previous chapters details have been given of some of the research that is exposing the continuing inadequacies of a system formally dedicated to the fullest possible provision of educational opportunity, and of the efforts that are being made to secure greater understanding between teachers, pupils, and parents, between home and school. There is much more that could be done, and the admirable work of the teacher/social workers and educational welfare officers could usefully be expanded and given additional support. What I have tried to do in this chapter is not to belittle the importance of the sort of provision that has been discussed in this volume, but simply to point out the need for us to keep very clearly before us the fact that work of this kind can only be performed within the context of a complex set of traditions, value assumptions, and attitudes regarding the relationship of the family and society, the individual and the state. A proper recognition of the difficulty and intractability of the task of reconciling differences in the structured role performances of the individuals and groups concerned, and an awareness that important moral and political assumptions underlie these performances, need not and should not prevent us from pressing ahead with actions designed to alleviate immediate problems and deal with existing deficiencies. But such a recognition may be helpful in our tolerance of the failure that will inevitably attend some of our efforts, and remind us of the fact that a technique that does not have its roots in an adequate theory is, in the long run, unlikely to be either helpful or enduring.

REFERENCES

1. 'Learning to live with neighbours', in *How and Why do we Learn*, ed. by W. R. Niblett, Faber, 1965.
2. R. Benn, and R. S. Peters, *Social Principles and the Democratic State*, Allen & Unwin, 1959, p. 120.
3. A. D. Lindsay, *Social Progress and Educational Waste*, Routledge, 1926, p. 7.
4. B. Jackson, *Streaming—an Education System in Miniature*, Routledge & Kegan Paul, 1964.
5. Central Advisory Council for Education, *Half Our Future*, (Newsom Report), H.M.S.O., 1963.
6. See, for example, the work of Basil Bernstein.

7. D. F. Swift, 'Who passes the eleven-plus?', *New Society*, 5 March 1964.
8. W. Waller, *The Sociology of Teaching*, Wiley, 1932.
9. B. R. Clark, 'The "cooling-out" function in higher education', in *Education, Economy and Society*, ed. by Floud, Halsey, and Anderson, Free Press, 1961. See also H. Schelsky, 'Family, and School in Modern Society', *ibid.*
10. B. Wootton, *Social Science and Social Pathology*, Allen & Unwin, 1959.
11. T. Parsons, 'The school class as a social system: some of its functions in American society', *Harvard Educational Review* Autumn 1959.

Index